That Will Never Work

That Will Never Work

The Birth of Netflix and the Amazing Life of an Idea

MARC RANDOLPH

Little, Brown and Company
New York Boston London

Little, Brown and Company
Hachette Book Group
1290 Avenue of the Americas, New York, NY 10104
littlebrown.com

First Edition: September 2019

Little, Brown and Company is a division of Hachette Book Group, Inc. The Little, Brown name and logo are trademarks of Hachette Book Group, Inc.

The publisher is not responsible for websites (or their content) that are not owned by the publisher.

The Hachette Speakers Bureau provides a wide range of authors for speaking events. To find out more, go to hachettespeakersbureau.com or call (866) 376-6591.

ISBN 978-0-316-53020-0 (hc) / 978-0-316-46066-8 (int'l pb)
LCCN 2019943360

10 9 8 7 6 5 4 3 2 1

LSC-C

Book design by Marie Mundaca

Printed in the United States of America

For Lorraine — the one who thought it would never work. Although you didn't believe in the idea, I knew that you always believed in me.
I love you.

Contents

Contents

Author's Note

This book is a memoir, not a documentary. It's based on my rec-
ollection of events that happened twenty years ago, so most of the
conversations in this story have been reconstructed. What mattered to
me, as I wrote, was rendering the personalities of Netflix's founding
team as vividly and as accurately as possible. I wanted to show them as
they were, to capture the mood of the time. Most importantly, I wanted
to illustrate what we at Netflix were up against — and what it felt like
to somehow, despite all the odds against us, succeed.

That Will Never Work

1.

Against Epiphanies

(January 1997: fifteen months before launch)

I'M LATE, AS USUAL. It's only a three-minute drive to the parking lot where I meet Reed Hastings to carpool to work, but when your son throws up on you at breakfast, and you can't find your keys, and it's raining, and you realize at the last minute that you don't have enough gas in your car to get you over the Santa Cruz Mountains into Sunnyvale — good luck with making a 7:00 a.m. meet-up time.

Reed runs a company called Pure Atria that makes software development tools — and that recently acquired a startup I helped found, Integrity QA. After Reed bought our company, he kept me on as his VP of corporate marketing. We take turns driving.

We usually get to the office on time, but the *way* we get there changes, depending on who's driving. When it's Reed's turn, we leave on time, in an immaculate Toyota Avalon. We drive the speed limit. Sometimes there's a driver, a kid from Stanford who has been instructed to navigate the twisting, mountainous turns of Highway 17 with care and precision. "Drive like there's a full cup of coffee on the dashboard," I've heard Reed tell him. And the poor kid does.

Me? I drive a beat-up Volvo with two car seats in the back. A kind description of my driving would be *impatient*. But maybe *aggressive* is

3

more accurate. I take turns fast. And when I get excited about something, I go even faster.

On this day, it's my turn to drive. As I pull into the parking lot, Reed's already waiting, huddled beneath an umbrella, leaning on his car. He looks annoyed.

"You're late," he says, shaking off his umbrella as he slips into my car, picking a crumpled Diet Coke can and two packages of diapers off the front seat and tossing them into the back. "Traffic's going to be terrible with all the rain."

It is. There's a wreck at Laurel Curve, a stalled semi at the Summit. And then the usual Silicon Valley traffic, coders and executives in long lines on the highway, like ants returning to an anthill.

"Okay," I say. "But I've got a new one. Customized baseball bats. Totally personalized and unique. Users fill out their information online, then we use a computer-controlled milling machine to craft a bat to their exact specs: length, handle thickness, size of the barrel. All one-of-a-kind. Or not. If you want an exact re-creation of Hank Aaron's bat, we could do that, too."

Reed's face goes blank. It's an expression I know well. To an outside observer, it would look like he's just staring out the dirty windshield at the redwoods whizzing by, or the Subaru going a *little* too slowly in front of us. But I know what's behind that look: a rapid-fire evaluation of pros and cons, a high-speed cost-benefit analysis, a near-instantaneous predictive model about possible risks and scalability.

Five seconds go by, then ten, then fifteen. After about thirty seconds he turns to me and says, "That will never work."

We've been doing this for a few weeks. Reed has been working overtime finalizing a huge merger that will put us both out of a job, and once the dust settles from that, I'm planning to start my own company. Every day in the car, I pitch ideas to Reed. I'm trying to convince him to come on board as an advisor or investor, and

I can tell he's intrigued. He's not shy about giving me feedback. He knows a good thing when he sees it. He also knows a bad thing when he hears it.

And my morning-drive ideas? They're mostly bad ideas.

Reed swats this one away just like he did the others. It's impractical. It's unoriginal. It will never work.

"Also, baseball's popularity is waning with younger people," he says, as we roll to a stop behind a sand truck. The sand is on its way to San Jose, where it will eventually be turned into concrete for roads and buildings in booming Silicon Valley. "Don't want to be tied to a declining user base from the start."

"You're wrong," I say, and I tell him why. I've done my research, too. I know the numbers for sporting goods sales. I've looked into baseball bat production — how much the raw materials cost, how expensive it is to buy and operate the milling machine. And, okay, I might have a personal connection to this idea: my oldest son just finished his rookie Little League season.

For every one of my points, Reed has an answer. He's analytical, rational, and doesn't waste time with niceties. I don't, either. Our voices are raised, but we're not angry. It's an argument, but it's a productive one. Each of us understands the other. Each of us knows that the other is going to offer stiff, uncompromising resistance.

"Your attachment to this idea isn't strictly rational," he says, and I almost laugh. Behind his back, I've heard people compare Reed to Spock. I don't think they mean it as a compliment, but they should. In *Star Trek*, Spock is almost always right. And Reed is, too. If he thinks something won't work, it probably won't.

The first time I met Reed, we were taking a cross-country plane trip from San Francisco to Boston. Reed had just acquired my company, but we'd never spent any meaningful time alone together. I'd been sitting at the gate, waiting to board, reading through a binder of materials on memory leak detectors and software version management, when someone tapped my shoulder. It was Reed. "Where are you sitting?" he'd asked, frowning at my paper ticket.

When I told him, he took my ticket, marched to the counter, and upgraded me to first class.

That was nice, I thought. *I'll get a chance to read, relax a little, maybe even get a little sleep.*

But that was my first lesson about Reed. When the flight attendant came, he'd waved away the free mimosas, turned his body ninety degrees, and locked eyes with me. Then, for the next five and a half hours, he'd given an exhaustive overview of the state of our business, barely pausing to take a sip of sparkling water. I'd hardly gotten a word in edgewise, but I didn't care. It was one of the most brilliant business analyses I'd ever heard — like being hooked up to a supercomputer.

We're not in first class anymore. We're in a Volvo that could use a wash. But I still find Reed's mind fascinating and his demeanor refreshing. I'm grateful for his advice, for the consulting I'm getting for free on these rides "over the hill" into Silicon Valley and back. By total luck, I've ended up in the same company — and the same town — with someone who understands my vision and can provide invaluable help, not to mention savings on gas. But it's still frustrating to hear that an idea I've spent a week researching is totally unfeasible. A part of me is starting to wonder if all of my business ideas are built on a foundation as unsteady and shifty as the sand loaded into the truck ahead of us.

That truck, by the way, is still in the left lane, moving slowly, holding everybody up. I'm frustrated. I flash my lights. The truck driver looks at me in the rearview mirror, doesn't even react. I mutter a few irrational obscenities.

"You need to relax," Reed says, gesturing to the traffic ahead of us. He's already told me — twice — that my habit of constantly changing lanes is, in the end, counterproductive and inefficient. My driving makes him insane — and a little carsick. "We'll get there when we get there."

"I'm gonna pull my hair out," I say, "and I don't have much left." I run my hand through the remnants of my curls, and then it happens: I have one of those all-too-rare epiphany moments. It seems like everything happens at once: The sun comes out of the clouds, and it stops drizzling. The sand truck wheezes to life and merges into the proper lane, and traffic starts to move. It feels like I can see for miles, down into the clogged heart of San Jose: houses, office buildings, treetops waving in the breeze. We pick up speed, and the redwoods fall away behind us, and in the distance I see Mount Hamilton, its crest sparkling with fresh snow. And then it comes to me. The idea that will finally work.

"Personalized shampoo by mail," I say.

Silicon Valley loves a good origin story. The idea that changed everything, the middle-of-the-night lightbulb moment, the *what if we could do this differently?* conversation.

Origin stories often hinge on epiphanies. The stories told to skeptical investors, wary board members, inquisitive reporters, and — eventually — the public usually highlight a specific moment: the moment it all became clear. Brian Chesky and Joe Gebbia can't afford their San Francisco rent, then realize that they can blow up an air mattress and charge people to sleep on it — that's Airbnb. Travis Kalanick spends $800 on a private driver on New Year's Eve and thinks there has to be a cheaper way — that's Uber.

There's a popular story about Netflix that says the idea came to Reed after he'd rung up a $40 late fee on *Apollo 13* at Blockbuster. He thought, *What if there were no late fees?* And BOOM! The idea for Netflix was born.

That story is beautiful. It's useful. It is, as we say in marketing, *emotionally* true.

But as you'll see in this book, it's not the whole story. Yes, there was an overdue copy of *Apollo 13* involved, but the idea for Netflix had nothing to do with late fees — in fact, at the beginning, we even charged them. More importantly, the idea for Netflix didn't appear in a moment of divine inspiration — it didn't come to us in a flash, perfect and useful and obviously right.

Epiphanies are rare. And when they appear in origin stories, they're often oversimplified or just plain false. We like these tales because they align with a romantic idea about inspiration and genius. We want our Isaac Newtons to be sitting under the apple tree when the apple falls. We want Archimedes in his bathtub.

But the truth is usually more complicated than that.

The truth is that for every good idea, there are a thousand bad ones. And sometimes it can be hard to tell the difference.

Customized sporting goods. Personalized surfboards. Dog food individually formulated for your dog. These were all ideas I pitched to Reed. Ideas I spent hours working on. Ideas I thought were *better* than the idea that eventually — after months of research, hundreds of hours of discussion, and marathon meetings in a family restaurant — became Netflix.

I had no idea what would work and what wouldn't. In 1997, all I knew was that I wanted to start my own company, and that I wanted it to involve selling things on the internet. That was it.

It seems absurd that one of the largest media companies in the world could come from those two desires. But it did.

This is a story about how we went from personalized shampoo to Netflix. But it's also a story about the amazing life of an idea: from dream to concept to shared reality. And about how the things we learned on that journey — which took us from two guys throwing ideas around in a car, to a dozen people at computers in a former bank, to hundreds of employees watching our company's letters scroll across a stock ticker — changed our lives.

One of my goals in telling this story is to puncture some of the myths that attach themselves to narratives like ours. But it's equally important to me to show how and why some of the things we did at the beginning — often unwittingly — *worked.* It's been over twenty years since those first car rides with Reed, and in that time, I've come to realize that there are things we discovered that, applied broadly, can influence a project's success. Not exactly laws, not even principles, but hard-won truths.

Truths like: Distrust epiphanies.

The best ideas rarely come on a mountaintop in a flash of lightning. They don't even come to you on the *side* of a mountain, when you're stuck in traffic behind a sand truck. They make themselves apparent more slowly, gradually, over weeks and months. And in fact, when you finally have one, you might not realize it for a long time.

2.

"That Will *Never* Work"

(spring 1997: one year before launch)

As a kid, one of my strongest memories is of my father building minia-ture steam-powered trains. They weren't the tiny electric models you buy as a kit, the pieces all built to fit together, matched to a track that you just have to plug in. No, these were for the real fanatics: fully functional miniature trains, their steel wheels powered by steam. Every component — wheels, pistons, cylinders, boilers, cranks, rods, ladders, even the miniature shovels the miniature engineer would use to shovel miniature pieces of coal — had to be built by hand. About the only pieces you didn't build yourself were the screws that held everything together.

That was fine with my father. He was a nuclear engineer who had found that his skill set was much more lucrative as a financial advisor to major firms who were investing in nuclear power and weapons de-velopment. His work allowed my family to live in comfort out in the New York City suburbs, but he missed the lab. He missed the instru-ments, the calculations, the sense of pride in building something. After a long day on Wall Street, he'd come home, take off his tie, and change into one-piece work overalls, the kind that real train engineers wore. (He collected engineer uniforms from around the world.) Then he'd head to the basement. It was time to build.

I grew up in a pretty normal, upper-middle-class household. The fathers of Chappaqua took the train into the city for work; the mothers took care of the kids in beautiful houses that were a little too big; the kids got into trouble while their parents went to school board meetings and cocktail parties.

When the youngest of us finally began school, my mother started her own real estate firm. Our house was built on a hill flanked by apple orchards, with a big pond in the back. I spent much of my childhood outside, roaming through the acres of woods that surrounded our house. But I also spent a fair amount of time indoors, reading in my parents' well-stocked library. Two large portraits of Sigmund Freud hung there. In one of them, he was alone; in the other, he was posed next to his wife, Martha Bernays. These were surrounded by a half-dozen smaller photographs and renderings, framed and signed correspondence, and shelves filled with his books: *Civilization and Its Discontents, Beyond the Pleasure Principle, The Interpretation of Dreams.*

It was the sixties. Freudian analysis wasn't exactly uncommon. But we didn't have a miniature Freud museum in the library because anybody in the house was spending time on a therapist's couch. It was because he was family. He was Uncle Siggy.

It's a little more complicated than that. Freud was in fact my father's great-uncle, making him my great-grand-uncle.

Still, no matter how convoluted the chain of connection, my parents were proud of the family association with Freud. He was a success, a giant of twentieth-century thought, as important an intellectual figure as had existed in their lifetime. It was like being related to Einstein: proof that the family had excelled on both sides of the Atlantic.

My family also had a connection to another important twentieth-century figure: Edward Bernays. Bernays was my grandmother's brother, and Uncle Siggy's nephew. If you've ever taken any course in advertising, if you've taken a course in mass media in the American twentieth century — heck, if you've even watched *Mad Men* or seen a cigarette ad — then you're familiar with his work. Bernays is, in many ways, the father of modern public relations, the person who really figured out how to apply new discoveries in psychology and psychoanalysis to marketing. He's the reason we eat bacon and eggs for breakfast. He's also the reason we celebrate Thomas Edison (and not Joseph Swan) as the inventor of the lightbulb. He's the guy who, after helping popularize bananas for United Fruit, turned around and waged a propaganda campaign alongside the CIA to stage a coup in Guatemala.

So, not always the most laudable stuff. But even though a lot of what Uncle Edward did wasn't all that admirable, it did stick in my head that I could do what my father did, every night in our basement — use the tools he'd been given to create something. I was an indifferent student in high school; I majored in geology in college. But if I ever wanted to look at my destiny on a piece of paper, all I had to do was look at my birth certificate. *Marc Bernays Randolph.* Marketing was my middle name.

My father's trains were beautiful. They took him years to build. When he was finished with one, he'd give it a coat of paint, and then another, and then another. Then he'd call me down to the basement, hook the train's boiler up to an air compressor, and perch the train on tiny blocks above his workbench. As the air moved cleanly through the valves, we'd watch the back-and-forth movement of the pistons, the smooth revolution of the drive wheels. We would admire the hand-built systems of rods and connectors that smoothly transferred power to the wheels. My father would even use compressed air to sound the miniature whistle.

I loved that high-pitched noise. To me, it was like a formal announcement of another completed effort, another beautifully made thing. But my father was often melancholy when he heard it. According to him, a *real* train whistle, powered by steam — not air from a compressor — was a more emotional sound, one that he could only hear in his imagination. There was no track in the basement for his trains. The vast majority of them never saw real movement — just air compressor tests. After I went back upstairs and he turned the air compressor off, he'd lovingly remove the train from the workbench, place it on a shelf, and start a new one.

Over time, I realized that for my dad, it wasn't finishing the train that he liked. It was the years of labor: the days at the lathe, the thousands of hours at the drill press and milling machine. I don't have many memories of watching those trains run. What I remember are all the times he excitedly called me down to the basement to show me a piece he'd just built — a piece that, when connected with fifty others, might amount to a single axle.

"A piece of advice," he told me once, peering through the magnifying glass over his left eye. "If you really want to build an estate, own your own business. Control your own life."

I was in high school at the time. Most of my energy was directed at girls, rock climbing, and convincing the guy at the liquor store that I was old enough to buy beer. I wasn't quite sure what an estate was, but I thought I caught his drift. Sure, sure, I thought, why not.

But twenty years later, in the early nineties? I thought I finally knew what he meant. I'd spent years working in marketing for other people, at large corporations and small startups alike. I was a co-founder of *MacUser* magazine, as well as MacWarehouse and MicroWarehouse, two of the first mail-order sources for computer products. I'd spent years at Borland International, one of the software giants of the eighties. At all of these places, I'd been focused on direct marketing: sending letters and catalogs directly to individual consumers and studying the way they responded. I'd enjoyed it, and I was good at it. I had a knack for connecting products to customers. I knew what people wanted — or if I didn't, I knew how to figure it out. I knew how to reach them.

But I'd always been working, in some sense, for someone else. At Borland, I'd been part of a huge corporation. And even as a co-founder at *MacUser* and MacWarehouse, I'd helped develop an idea that was only partly my own. As rewarding as those jobs were, part of me had always wondered what it would be like to build a company from the ground up, completely solo — if it would be more fulfilling if the problems I solved were *my* problems. That, after all, was what my father was telling me, hammer in hand. That's why he descended like Vulcan to his workbench under our house in Chappaqua. He wanted to set up his own problems, and then knock them down.

By 1997, so did I. I was a year shy of forty. I had a wonderful wife, three kids, enough money to buy a house that was a little too big for us on a hillside overlooking Santa Cruz.

I also had, somewhat unexpectedly, quite a bit of time on my hands.

Barely six months after acquiring our company and giving me the green light to build out the marketing department I'd inherited, Reed had agreed to the corporate merger that would make all of us — me, Reed, and the two people I'd *just* brought in to work with me — redundant. For the next four months or so, while the feds went over the paperwork, we had to come to work every day. We were still getting paid, but we had nothing — and I mean nothing — to do.

It was tremendously boring. The Pure Atria offices were nothing like the laid-back startup offices of today. No nap pods, no pinball machines in the lobby. Think: cubicles. Think: fake office plants. Think: a watercooler gurgling at regular intervals.

Reed was busy finalizing the merger and had already started making plans to go back to school. As his tenure as CEO was coming to an end, he was feeling a little burned-out. He wanted to change the world, but he was increasingly convinced that he couldn't do so as a tech CEO. "If you really want to change the world," he said, "you don't need millions of dollars. You need *billions*." Barring that, he thought the way to effect change was through education. He was increasingly passionate about education reform, and he thought that no one would take him seriously unless he had an advanced degree in the field. He had his eye on Stanford. He had no desire to start a new company…but he also indicated that he wanted to keep his toe in the water, as an investor or an advisor, or both.

At first, I filled my limbo merger time with athletic pursuits. Along with a big group of fellow East Coast transplants homesick for ice rinks and pucks, I conned a few Californians into comically lopsided parking-lot hockey games. We'd while away a few hours in the shadows of the office park, body-checking each other into parked cars and batting a scuffed-up tennis ball through homemade PVC-pipe goals.

I also spent some time at the driving range, and those first few weeks brought me a revelation: I'll never be good at golf. I'd always thought that if I spent enough time on it, I could practice my way into a decent golf game, and for weeks I tested that hypothesis. I'd take an hour-and-a-half lunch, then stop by the range on my way back to the offices.

But no matter how many balls I hit, I never got any better.

I think a part of me knew, even then, that a perfect swing wouldn't cure what ailed me. What I needed wasn't a sweaty hockey game or a birdie at DeLaveaga. What I needed was the feeling of being deeply engaged with a project. What I needed was purpose.

Hence the ideas for a new company. Hence *personalized shampoo by mail.*

I kept a little notebook of ideas in my backpack and carried it with me everywhere I went: driving, mountain biking, you name it. It fit into the pocket of hiking shorts really nicely. I'd even take it surfing — leaving it in my backpack on shore, of course. There's a reason why rejected idea #114 is "personalized surfboards, machine-shaped to your exact size, weight, strength, and surfing style." They say the best ideas are born of necessity, and nothing's more necessary than a properly shaped board when you're scrambling for waves at Pleasure Point.

I'm an idea guy. Give me hours of empty time in a Silicon Valley office with a fast internet connection and multiple whiteboards, and you're going to need to buy more dry-erase markers. I probably would have come up with business plans just to get out of embarrassing myself at the driving range.

But I also felt a sense of responsibility for the people I'd already brought over to work with me, who had left perfectly good jobs and were now sitting on their hands. Christina Kish, whom I'd worked with at a company called Visioneer, which made desktop scanners, had gotten one workweek in before the merger. Te Smith, my friend from Borland, had gotten laid off her first day.

I wanted to make their decision to follow me worth it. I wanted to provide them with a place to land when we were all out of a job. And, selfishly, I didn't want to lose them. When you find people as capable, smart, and easy to work with as Christina and Te, you need to keep them around.

So I started looping them in on my ideas for a new company. They were perfect sounding boards. I'm a great idea guy, but I'm horrible at follow-through. I'm not good at details. But Christina and Te are.

Christina was a project manager. A little buttoned-up, with her dark hair pulled back into a simple ponytail, she had years of experience turning visionary ideas into tangible products. Along with a sharp eye for detail, she had a real genius for scheduling, and a ruthless ability to get things done on deadline — even if she had to kill someone to make it happen. She was well versed in the art of translating a visionary idea out of the realm of *possibility* and into reality.

Te was a specialist in PR and communications. She knew everyone, and everyone knew her. She not only knew how to write an attention-grabbing press release, she knew who was important to know in the press — and what to say to get them to return her call. She was the mistress of the press tour, choreographing them like state dinners. She was schooled in dress codes and even the most obscure protocol. She *always* knew which fork to use. For her, publicity was a kind of stage, and she was the queen of it, a diva. Like Madonna, she required only one name. To everyone — from a disheveled user group moderator to the most formal business section editor — she was simply Te.

The two women couldn't be more different. Christina is intense and somewhat self-contained. Te is an eccentric, a wild dresser with an explosion of wavy hair and a Boston accent that has endured through decades of life in California. Christina wore sneakers to work and ran marathons. Te taught me what Manolo Blahniks were and had an alter ego named Tipsy Bubbles, who came out after a couple glasses of champagne.

But both women were — and continue to be — sharp, detail-oriented, and no-nonsense.

And once I'd sniffed out that Reed would be amenable to funding a new company if I could come up with a good enough idea, I went to Christina and Te for help. We started spending hours at the whiteboards in Pure Atria. We made good use of the company's high-speed internet (a rarity in those days — and even in Silicon Valley, it wasn't *that* fast) to do background research in hundreds of diverse fields, looking for the perfect opening. Long before an idea made its way to Reed's car, it had been examined and vetted by Christina and Te.

Those whiteboard sessions made me feel better than any parking-lot goal or long drive on the range ever could. Even if every idea I brought to the whiteboard was bad, even if Christina and Te's research made it clear just how implausible some of my middle-of-the-night revelations were, I knew that eventually we'd land on something good. Like my father in the basement, there was pleasure in the work. We were designing something. Someday, we might get to build it.

* * *

"Okay," I said, sighing on another Tuesday morning, this time in Reed's immaculate Toyota. "That one's toast, I guess."

Reed nodded as we accelerated smoothly up to 55 mph. Exactly the speed limit. No more, no less.

We'd been discussing idea #95 in my notebook: food custom-blended specifically for your pet. The idea was good, but it was too expensive. And Reed had pointed out that it was a liability nightmare.

"What if someone's dog dies?" he'd asked. "We're out a customer."

"And they're out a dog," I said, thinking of my own Lab, who had chewed a hole in the fence that morning.

"Sure, sure," Reed replied absentmindedly. "But the point is that customizing a unique product for every customer is just too difficult. It never gets easier. The effort to make a dozen is exactly twelve times the effort it takes to make one. You'll never get ahead."

"But we have to sell *something*."

"Sure. But you want something that will scale," he said. "You want something where the effort it takes to sell a dozen is *identical* to the effort it takes to sell just one. And while you're at it, try and find something that's more than just a onetime sale, so that once you've found a customer, you'll be able to sell to them over and over again."

I thought of all of my most recent ideas: personalized surfboards, dog food, and baseball bats. All of them were made one-of-a-kind. And aside from dog food, these were things you bought only occasionally (surfboards and bats). Dog food you bought a few times a month.

"What's something you use relatively often? Something the same person uses over and over again?"

Reed thought for a moment, his head tilted slightly back. The Stanford student in the driver's seat turned slightly and said, "Toothpaste."

Reed frowned. "It takes a month to use a tube of toothpaste. Not frequent enough."

"Shampoo," I said.

"No," Reed said. "No more shampoo."

I thought for a second, but my brain felt slow that morning. I was two cups of coffee into my day, but I was still tired from the night before. My three-year-old had woken up in the middle of the night with a bad dream, and the only thing that had coaxed her back to sleep — dried the tears and closed the eyes — was a well-worn copy of *Aladdin*, wedged deep into the entertainment console in our living room. I'd ended up watching most of it, even after she'd fallen back to sleep.

"Videotapes?"

Reed looked at me. "Don't remind me," he said, shaking his head. "I just got nicked forty bucks by Blockbuster on a movie I returned late. But…" He let his voice tail off as he turned to stare again out the window, his face blank. Then his eyes arched upward and he nodded.

"Maybe," he said.

That morning, Christina and Te and I met in my office, as usual. When I told Christina how the drive with Reed had gone, she walked up to the whiteboard and slowly erased the thicket of lists, projections, and calculations we'd scrawled across it in the past few days.

"So long, Fido," said Te.

"We need a product that already exists in the world," I said. "But that we can help people access online. Bezos did it with books. You don't have to write books to sell them."

It was true. Amazon had just gone public, proving to everyone that services that were once considered strictly limited to physical stores could now be done online — and could be done even better. E-commerce was the next wave. We all knew it. That's why people were starting online shops for pretty much anything that could fit in a box — diapers, shoes, you name it.

And it's why I was spending my mornings with Reed, batting ideas back and forth until they shattered into dust.

"I was thinking VHS tapes," I said to Christina. "They're kind of small. People don't necessarily want to own them after they've watched them once or twice. Video stores do pretty well. We could let people rent online, then ship tapes directly to them."

Christina frowned. "So we'd pay to ship things two ways: there and back. You can't expect people to pay for the shipping."

I nodded. "Sure."

"That's gonna be expensive," Christina said, jotting down some figures in a tiny notebook. "First you have to buy the tapes, then you have to pay to ship them — *twice*. Plus whatever you'd mail them in, plus storage for all the tapes that you've bought..."

"Not to mention," Te chimed in, "who wants to wait a week to watch *Sleepless in Seattle*?"

"I'll wait forever," I said.

"My point is that when you want a movie, you want it *now*," Te said.

"Yeah, but have you *been* in a Blockbuster lately?" Christina muttered, still staring at the neat, orderly rows of writing in her notebook. "Terrible. Disorganized, apathetic. Kind of low inventory, too."

I picked up my hockey stick from the corner of the office and started absentmindedly batting a tennis ball against a file cabinet. Te had moved back to the whiteboard and written VHS ONLINE STORE at the top in blue marker.

Once again, we were off to the races.

That night, I went home and looked at our video collection. It was smaller than I'd imagined. *Aladdin, The Lion King, Beauty and the Beast,* all in their Disney slipcases. Now that I was thinking about mailing them, they looked gigantic.

At dinner, my wife, Lorraine, wiped spaghetti sauce off our three-year-old daughter, Morgan's, face with one hand and spoon-fed applesauce to Hunter, our youngest, with the other. I tried to teach my older son, Logan, how to twirl his spaghetti on a fork, using his spoon. I tried to explain my new idea to Lorraine. Neither attempt went particularly well.

I made an effort to come home for dinner every day, and my work had a way of following me home. Lorraine didn't mind, up to a point. And she was usually a very good barometer about whether or not something sounded feasible. When it came to new ideas, I tended to get a little enthusiastic.

This time, Lorraine listened to me with a skeptical expression. It had been almost twenty years since I'd first seen her in Vail, Colorado, the friend of my ski-patrol buddy's roommate. She'd come to ski with her boyfriend, and . . . well, let's just say that once I entered the picture, things didn't work out between them. I loved her then for the same reasons that I love her now: her keen mind, her down-to-earth common sense. She reins me in.

Watching Logan maneuver a forkful of pasta toward his open mouth, I mustered the last of the day's enthusiasm to sell Lorraine on my brilliant idea. "Think about how much you hate dragging these three to Blockbuster," I said, pointing to Morgan's sauce-streaked face and Hunter's grinning, toothless mouth. "A nightmare. And this could solve it."

Lorraine pursed her lips and dangled her fork over her largely untouched plate of food. I knew that when we got up, she'd have to eat it quickly, standing up near the sink, while I started the lengthy process of corralling the three kids into their baths and then to bed.

"First of all, you have sauce all over your shirt," she said.

I looked down. It was true. Not a great shirt — a white T-shirt advertising BORLAND BUG HUNT '87 only passes for high fashion within forty miles of Scotts Valley. And the sauce stain wasn't helping. I dabbed at it with one of the wet wipes we kept near the table anytime the children were eating.

"Second of all," she said, smiling broadly. "That will *never* work."

Lorraine's reasons were much the same as the ones Christina and Te gave me at the end of that week. The tapes were too bulky to ship.

There was no way to guarantee that users would ship them back. There was a high likelihood they'd get damaged in transit.

But more than anything, it was expensive. It's easy to forget how much VHS tapes used to cost. There's a reason the only tapes we had in our house were kids' movies — back in the nineties, the only studio that was pricing VHS tapes to sell was Disney. And even then, they were only doing it for movies that had been out for years. For Disney, *Bambi* was pretty much always a new release — because new customers who had never seen it were born every day.

Not looking for a kids' movie? Tough luck. You were looking at $75 to $80 a tape. There was no way we could afford to assemble a VHS library big enough to tempt users away from the video stores.

Christina spent days looking into Blockbuster's and Hollywood Video's business models, and what she found wasn't encouraging.

"Even the brick-and-mortars have a hard time," she said. "To make any money, you have to turn a tape twenty times in a month. You need a steady stream of customers. That means you really have to stock what people want — new releases, ideally. Crowds don't line up at Blockbuster every Friday night for Jean-Luc Godard. People want *Die Hard.* That's why there's a whole wall of them."

"Okay. We could also focus on new releases," I said. "Two can play that game."

Christina shook her head. "Not really. Say we buy a tape for eighty bucks and rent it for four. After postage, packaging, and handling, we're clearing maybe a dollar per rental."

"So we have to rent something eighty times just to break even," Te said.

"Right," Christina said. "The video stores can rent the same new release twenty-five times in a month, because they don't have to wait for the postal service. They can just have a twenty-four-hour rental period. Plus they're not paying for packaging or shipping, so they're clearing more money on each rental, too."

"So we limit a rental period to two days," I said.

"Still takes *at least* three days to ship," Christina said, looking down at her notebook. "*Best*-case scenario — and it's not likely — you get the movie back after a week. You could rent the same tape four times a month. If you're lucky."

"So by the time you could rent a new release enough times to make some money off it, it wouldn't be a new release anymore," Te said.

"Exactly," Christina said.

"And you're still competing with Blockbuster," Te said. "There's one within ten or fifteen minutes of almost every potential renter in America."

"What about rural areas?" I said. But my heart wasn't in it. I knew they were right — unless tapes got cheaper, or the post office got faster, renting movies through the mail would be almost impossible.

"Back to the drawing board," I said, eraser in hand.

3.

Please, Mr. Postman

(early summer 1997: ten months before launch)

FOR THE NEXT few weeks, I batted ideas around with Christina and Te, argued about those ideas with Reed, and watched them slowly turn to ash on the floorboard of my Volvo, somewhere between Scotts Valley and Sunnyvale. I started to get discouraged.

I don't remember how we first learned about DVDs. Christina might have uncovered the then-nascent technology during her market research. My co-founder at Integrity QA, Steve Kahn, was a home theater tech geek and might have mentioned them at the Pure Atria offices. I might have read about them in the newspaper — they were in test markets in San Francisco and six other cities in 1997.

But I suspect I learned about them from Reed. He actually *read* all the free tech journals that got mailed to Pure Atria — journals that, in my case, only accumulated in a dusty pile in the corner of my office. And sometime after the online video rental idea crashed and burned, he'd complained to me about another exorbitant late fee he'd incurred at a video store. Movies were on his mind — and movies by mail had been one of the few ideas I'd had that had caught his eye.

One thing's for certain: I didn't see a DVD on a shelf.

Prior to 1997, DVDs were only available in Japan. And even if you found one, there was no way to play it — no DVD players were for sale in the States. It was easier, far easier, to find a laser disc than a DVD.

Even on March 1, 1997, when the first DVD players went on sale in U.S. test markets, there were no DVDs available for purchase outside of Japan. It took until March 19 for any titles to be released in the United States, and the few that were available weren't exactly hot new releases. *The Tropical Rainforest. Animation Greats. Africa: The Serengeti.* The first mass release of titles — thirty-two in total — came a week later from Warner Bros.

The history of the format is a fascinating one, and it's too long for this book. But essentially, everyone — movie studios, the video player manufacturers, the big video chains, the computer companies — wanted to avoid a repeat of the VHS/Betamax wars, in which two competing technologies battled it out in the marketplace, confusing customers and setting back the adoption of the VCR for years. And nobody — aside from cinephiles and collectors — really liked the expensive, large laser discs that had come out a few years before, either. There were various competing technologies in development in the mid-nineties, and all of them were compact disc–sized.

Take note of that: *compact disc–sized.* That was what caught my eye. A CD was much smaller than a VHS tape. And much lighter. In fact, it occurred to me that it was probably small and light enough to fit into a standard business envelope, requiring nothing more than a 32-cent stamp to mail. Quite a difference from the heavy cardboard box — and expensive UPS shipping rates — a VHS would have required.

Christina did some digging and found out that the studios and manufacturers were planning on pricing the DVD as a collectible item — $15 to $25 per disc. That's a far cry from what had happened in the eighties, when studios responded to the newly ubiquitous video store by raising the prices on tapes. Once the studios realized that the video rental stores were making all the money (by buying one VHS cassette and then renting it out hundreds of times — a right established by the Supreme Court as the "first sale" doctrine), they had decided that the only way to respond was to price the VHS high enough that they essentially captured their "fair share" of all that rental income. They knew that by raising the price like this they were saying good-bye to consumer purchases, but it was worth it because most people didn't *want* to own a movie.

The studios had learned from that mistake, and they wanted DVDs to be like CDs: collectible consumer products. If DVDs were priced low enough, they reasoned, customers would forget about renting and instead buy movies, the same way they bought albums on CD. The studios envisioned customers with shelves of movies in their family rooms — avoiding the rental middleman altogether.

Cheaper inventory, cheaper shipping — it was looking like movies by mail could work, if (and this was a big if) DVD became a popular format. With other huge categories — books, music, pet food — slowly being taken online, the movie rental category (which brought in $8 billion a year!) was a tempting target. Betting on DVDs was a risk, but it might also be our way to finally crack that category. With the whole world consumed by VHS rental, we might be able to make DVD rental by mail work — and have the video rental by mail category to ourselves for a while.

VHS by mail was dead. But DVDs by mail could work.

Now if only I could find one.

I have a longtime fantasy of working as a postman. After a few years in California, it had become a running joke with Lorraine and me. Anytime I got fed up with office politics, or worried about the perpetual boom-bust cycle of startups, funding, and bubbles, the two of us would sit on our deck with a glass of wine and imagine our alternate life somewhere else. I'd work as a mail carrier in a tiny town in northwest Montana, she'd homeschool the kids, and we'd cook dinner together at 5:00 when I had finished my route. No more crises. No more all-nighters. No more weekends in the office. No more travel. No more getting up at three in the morning to write down all the thoughts that had woken me up from a sound sleep.

Part of the fantasy was a wistful yearning for a slower, simpler life — for getting off the treadmill. There was something tempting about a job that you could leave behind at the end of the day. And for Lorraine, I'm sure the fantasy of the simple life was equally vivid. For years she had tolerated my tendency to drift off midsentence if a work thought pushed its way in. She had gotten used to waiting out the two- or three-second lag time between when she said something and I finally was able to drag my focus away from what I was working on to respond.

The simple life was tempting economically as well. Silicon Valley is not only one of the most expensive housing markets in the country — *everything* is pricey here. Even though we had saved a fair amount of money from some of my earlier ventures — and were earning a living wage — there was a feeling that we were running as fast as we could just to stay in place. On the porch, Lorraine and I would lapse into long fantasies and their attendant economic realities: *With the money we had saved, and the money we would make selling our current house, we could afford a palace in Montana. I could almost be retired at forty. And with even a part-time postal job, we would be doing great...*

But like all wistful yearning, our vision for a new life in the woods was probably best left unfulfilled. If I actually lived in, say, Condon, Montana, and only had my daily mail route to keep me busy, I'd probably quickly learn just why postal workers...go postal.

The truth is, I like headaches. I like a problem in front of me every day, something to chew on. Something to solve.

That summer, I was doing a lot of chewing at Lulu Carpenter's, a cafe at the top of Pacific Avenue in downtown Santa Cruz. Reed and

I would meet there for breakfast once or twice a week, before driving into work. From one of the sidewalk tables where Reed and I usually sat, with our backs to the cafe's huge open windows, we would look directly across the street at the Santa Cruz post office, looming over Pacific Avenue like a church.

The Santa Cruz post office is a grand, many-columned building. It's an appealing, distinctly old-fashioned place — granite and sandstone exterior, glossy tiled floors, a hallway of post office boxes, their brass handles somewhat tarnished. I wasn't sending many letters by 1997 — I was in tech, and email was king — but watching the stream of people parading in and out the doors of the post office made me want to start a correspondence with someone. It made me think back to my first jobs as a junk mail king, when I used to mail thousands — no, hundreds of thousands — of letters a week.

It made me want to mail things again.

"Look," I said, eyeing the delicate leaf etched in foam on the surface of my cappuccino. I was thirty minutes into the "DVDs by mail" pitch that Christina and Te had helped me formulate. "Let's just try it. Mail a CD to your place. If it breaks, it breaks, and we know that this idea could never work. If it gets there, you got something to listen to on Tuesday night."

Reed's eyes bored into me. It was eight o'clock on a Monday morning, and not only had he probably already been awake since four, he'd also already had a double shot of espresso. Now he was halfway down a cup of regular coffee. He'd already reminded me several times that neither of us had ever actually *seen* a DVD.

Me? I was excited as a bird. I'd been up early as well, surfing at the Lane as the sun came up. But even hours later, sipping coffee on dry land, I could see this latest idea ahead of me, just starting to differentiate itself from the horizon, rising in the distance as an indistinct swell. It was still too early to see if it was going to be rideable or not — but regardless, it was best to maneuver into position anyway.

Reed sensed that I was fidgety. "Alright, alright," he said. "Finish your scone."

We walked down the street to Logos, the used record store on Pacific, and waited out front until they opened for business. They didn't carry DVDs yet, of course. But we thought a CD would be close enough. I bought a used Patsy Cline Greatest Hits compilation — if this didn't work out, at least it was a disc someone might want to listen to. Within minutes, Reed was cracking the CD out of its clamshell while I ducked into Paper Vision, an office supply store, to look for an envelope. It seemed stupid to buy a whole box of envelopes just to mail one thing, so I bought a greeting card — two puppies in a wicker basket, barking HAPPY BIRTHDAY. It came with its own pink envelope. Reed printed his address on it in the post office, while I fed coins into the vending machine to buy a 32-cent stamp.

In went the CD. On went the stamp. I licked the seal of the envelope, kissed it for luck, and dropped it in the slot under the worn brass sign saying LOCAL MAIL ONLY.

Speaking of luck: Many months later, well into the Netflix experiment, I went on a tour of the Santa Cruz post office. By then, the company was a go. We hadn't launched yet, but we were far beyond the early days of just throwing ideas out the window of a Toyota Avalon on Highway 17. We were close enough to actually launching that I decided I needed to see exactly how our DVDs would move through a post office, so we could tweak the design of our mailers.

I felt like a little kid as I passed the stained baskets on the back side of the mail slots, the loading docks, the delivery office. The Santa Cruz postmaster himself traced the path that, he explained, was exactly the same one our pink envelope had taken nine months earlier: from stamp to slot to sort to bag to the delivery truck that would ultimately take it to Reed's mailbox. I was expecting a highly automated system running at high speed under great pressure, something capable of destroying even the sturdiest of our prototypes. Or if it wasn't happening here, I thought that the letters would be sent to a larger facility in nearby San Jose, to be sorted and mangled there, before coming back to Santa Cruz for delivery. But what I found was something more human, more analog. Hand-sorted for immediate dispersal, local mail was given directly to the drivers. It was a surprisingly fast and gentle process.

"Is this how it's done everywhere?" I asked.

The postmaster laughed in my face. "Definitely not," he said. "This is local mail. All the other mail for out-of-town gets trucked over to San Jose and they sort it there."

"So, what you're telling me is that if I mailed a naked CD inside an envelope and addressed it to anywhere else, it would have gotten scratched, cracked, or broken?"

"Most likely," he said.

Lucky us, I thought.

It's called a false positive — also known as being lucky. If we'd used any other post office — or if Reed had lived in Los Gatos or Saratoga — our CD might have been destroyed. Hell, if we had mailed it to my house in Scotts Valley instead of his place in Santa Cruz, the thing wouldn't have made it. And I wouldn't be writing this book. Or maybe I would be, but it would be about shampoo.

Instead, the very next morning, less than twenty-four hours after our pink envelope vanished into the slot, I met Reed in a parking lot in Scotts Valley and he pulled out our envelope. Inside it was an undamaged CD.

"It came," he said.

"Thank God," I said.

So long, customizable surfboards. Good-bye, personalized baseball bats.

When that CD arrived safely, I think Reed and I both knew we'd found our idea. All of Christina's and Te's objections — the turnaround time, the convenience factor — were still valid. But if it only cost 32 cents to mail a DVD, and we could buy them for twenty bucks apiece, we both knew we had a shot.

One of the real factors separating DVDs and VHS, Christina and Te and I found out, was the size of the library. Even in places where DVDs *were* available in the United States, there weren't that many titles. By mid-1997, there were still only about 125 titles to choose from. There were *tens of thousands* of movies on VHS.

"So the thinking is," Christina said when I showed her the CD, "we get in early? Beat the video stores to the punch, and then have more inventory?"

I nodded. "It's more like 'have *any* inventory.' Nobody has a DVD player yet, so it's going to be a while before the video stores even start carrying DVDs. We've probably got a long window of being the only game in town."

"Might make up for lag time," Te said. "If people can't find a DVD in a store anyway, they won't mind waiting as much."

Christina's brow was furrowed, but I could see that she was starting to agree.

"Okay," she said. "Has anyone actually watched one of these?"

We had our idea. Now we just had to figure out how to pay for it.

When you start a company, what you're really doing is getting other people to latch on to an *idea*. You have to convince your future employees, investors, business partners, and board members that your idea is worth spending money, reputation, and time on. Nowadays, you do that by validating your product ahead of time. You build a website or a prototype, you create the product, you measure traffic or early sales — all so that when you go to potential investors, palm outstretched, you have numbers to prove that what you're trying to do isn't just a good idea, but already exists and *works*.

For instance: A few years ago, when my son graduated from college, he moved out to San Francisco with a buddy of his, intent on starting a new company. In less time than it took to drive from our place in Scotts Valley to San Francisco, he had built a website on Squarespace, set up a credit account on Stripe, bought some banner ads using AdSense, and set up some cloud-based analytics on Optimizely to measure the results. All within a single weekend.

(One of the ideas they tested? *Shampoo by mail.* What can I say, the apple doesn't fall far from the tree.)

But back in 1997, you could raise $2 million with a PowerPoint. In fact, you *had* to. There are a lot of reasons for that, but the most fundamental had to do with time. In 1997 there was no Squarespace. No Stripe, no AdSense. No Optimizely. No cloud. If you wanted to build a website, you had to have engineers and programmers build it for you. You had to have servers to serve the pages. You had to figure out a way to accept credit cards. You had to do your own analytics. Forget a weekend. Try six months.

And you needed money for that. Money to hire people, to rent space, to buy equipment...money to *survive* until you could prove your idea had merit, and until you could raise your first serious funding.

It was kind of a catch-22: You couldn't prove to your investors that your idea would work unless they gave you money to prove that your idea could work.

You had to sell them on your *idea*.

But before you could accept that first dollar and sell your very first share of stock, you had to put a dollar sign on it. This is called valuation. You come up with a number: What your idea is worth.

In common parlance, it's typically a good thing when someone says, *Hey, there's a million-dollar idea!*

But in Silicon Valley, that's not very much.

To wit: Netflix is currently worth around $150 billion. Back in 1997, though, Reed and I decided that the intellectual property — the idea for DVD by mail, plus the fact that he and I were the ones working on it — was worth $3 million. That wasn't a ton — but it seemed like enough. Enough to take seriously, but not so much that no one would want to risk money on it.

We figured that it would take $2 million to get the company off the ground: $1 million to get the site launched, and another $1 million to run it while raising our next round of funding. We'd need an angel investor. Luckily, both of us knew one: Reed.

Reed wanted to be our angel investor because, even though he was leaving Silicon Valley for the education world, he wanted a way to stay connected to it. Funding us was his way of keeping his toe in the water. It would allow him to remain a part of the startup culture that he loved so much. Starting and running small companies had given his life order, meaning, and joy, and I think he may have been scared of losing that as he transitioned into the education field. As an angel investor in our company, he'd have a kind of safety net, a tether back to a world he understood and knew how to navigate. It was fear of missing out, pure and simple.

I decided not to put any money in. For one thing, I'd just had my third child — my son Hunter. And, unlike Reed, I'd be donating a *lot* of time to the project.

My risk was my time. His was his money.

But by not putting any money in at the outset, I'd effectively changed my ownership percentage. To understand why, you need to know a little bit about how startup companies raise money. There's math involved, but bear with me.

As I mentioned earlier, Reed and I had assumed that the value of Netflix (which at that point was just two guys and an idea) was $3 million. So to keep the math easy, I decided that to start, there would be six million shares of Netflix stock, each worth fifty cents, and each representing a small fraction of ownership in the company. On day one, there were only two owners of the company — Reed and I — and we split it down the middle. Each of us received three million shares — or 50 percent of Netflix. Now, if nothing had happened since then, and I still owned 50 percent of Netflix, my world would be a little different. As I mentioned, Netflix is now worth about $150 *billion*. Owning half of *that* would be a nice piece of change.

But then comes something called "dilution."

Remember, at this point it's just two guys and an idea. We need to build a website. Hire people. Rent an office. Buy whiteboard markers. (I *really* like whiteboard markers). So we need money. Reed was willing to give it to us, but he had to receive something of value in return. So what happens is that we sell him stock. We don't sell him shares that we already have, we *create* new shares and sell him those. And since we've already said that each share is worth fifty cents, in exchange for Reed's $2 million, we sell him four million shares.

So now everyone's happy. We now have a company that is worth $5 million, and its assets include the idea (which we valued at $3 million) and the $2 million of cash. But now the ownership has shifted. I still own my three million shares, but now there are *ten* million total shares, so my percentage of ownership has changed from 50 percent to 30 percent. At the same time, Reed's ownership has increased. He now owns seven million shares: the three million of his original shares for the idea, *plus* the four million shares he received in exchange for his investment.

So he's gone from owning 50 percent of the company to 70 percent. We're now 70/30 partners.

This didn't bother me at all. Dilution is a normal part of the startup world. True, my share had decreased from 50 percent to 30 percent — but I'd much rather own 30 percent of a company that has money to pursue its goals than 50 percent of a company with no cash on hand.

Could I have tried to split the investment with Reed, in order to have stayed 50/50 partners? Sure. That's called "going pro rata" and it happens all the time. But my pockets weren't as deep as Reed's, I had more familial responsibilities, and, unlike him, I'd be spending almost every waking hour of the next few years on our idea. Plus, I thought that putting significant amounts of my own money into the project would limit my capacity for other types of risk-taking. If I stood to lose a million dollars — and not just my job — I'm not sure I ever would have been able to take some of the imaginative leaps that were so crucial in the early going.

In Silicon Valley, tech talent is the scarcest resource, and an unknown fledgling company can have a hard time attracting top employees. But Reed — thanks to the Pure Atria deal — had clout. Within a few days he'd put us in touch with one of the key players in what would become early Netflix's eccentric, largely foreign-national ops team: Eric Meyer, a muppetlike Frenchman with a frenetic manner who would eventually become our chief technology officer. Eric had worked with Reed earlier in his career but now held a senior position at KPMG. I knew it would take some convincing to get a talented (and highly paid) software developer like Eric to join our ragtag bunch. So I started as soon as I got his number.

In the meantime, I needed to come up with something approaching a business plan. Notice that I used the word "approaching." I never intended to get there. Most business plans — with their exhaustive go-to-market strategies, detailed projections of revenue and expenses, and optimistic forecasts of market share — are a complete waste of time. They become obsolete the minute the business starts and you realize how wildly off the mark you were with all your expectations.

The truth is that no business plan survives a collision with a real customer. So the trick is to take your idea and set it on a collision course with reality as soon as possible.

But we still had to figure out where to start, and for that I leaned on

Christina. We spent hours at the whiteboard in my office, trying to visualize what an online video store would actually look like. Christina drew every page of the proposed website by hand, sketching out meticulously how every piece of content — the DVD title images, the synopses, the ordering information — would fit. I started looking for office space — or at least for conference rooms where we could meet, once I had a team together. The Best Western down the street from my house in Scotts Valley was my top contender. You could rent the conference room there for $250 a week.

All of this might seem like it happened fast. And it did — in a matter of weeks, we'd gone from a list of nebulous ideas to a semicoherent plan for moving forward. But here's the thing about Silicon Valley in the late nineties: *everything* was fast.

It hadn't been *slow* in the eighties — not exactly. But progress had occurred on a more incremental scale. It was an engineering driven culture, so it all moved at the speed with which things could be built. At Borland International, where I worked in the eighties, the very architecture of the corporate campus — engineers on the top floor, in the window offices, and everyone else on the floors below them — enforced a sense of hierarchy: engineers were on top, and everyone else worked for them. Along with that hierarchy was a certain staidness. Change happened logically, according to plan.

By the mid-nineties, things had changed. Jeff Bezos's success at Amazon had shown us that it wasn't just more powerful hardware or more innovative software that would lead to future progress — it was the internet itself. You could leverage it to sell things. It was the future.

The internet was not predictable. Its innovations were not centralized on a corporate campus. It was a whole new world.

Here's how tangibly — and quickly — things had changed. In 1995, when I was wrapping up my time at Borland, you could actually buy a published book that listed every website in existence. Since there were only about 25,000 sites, that book was less than one hundred pages long. But by March of 1997, when Reed and I were making our brainstorming commutes over the Santa Cruz Mountains, there were about 300,000 websites. By the end of that year, there were a million — and the number of users had grown to a hundred times that number. We weren't the only ones trying to figure out new ways to monetize the internet. There were thousands of people like us looking for the right angle, the right product, the right way to take advantage of a brand-new medium.

I've heard people call the mid- to late-nineties in Silicon Valley "the era of irrational exuberance." And I agree about the exuberance part. Who wouldn't be exuberant about the advent of one of the most revolutionary, game-changing technologies in the history of our species?

But irrational? Not quite. The excitement we felt at the dawn of the internet era was *completely* rational. We were on the edge of an open green field — unplowed, unplanted. Talk to enough entrepreneurs and engineers about the mid-to-late nineties, and what they'll describe to you sounds like something straight out of the journals of Lewis and Clark. We all felt like pioneers on the eve of a great expedition. There was enough land for everyone.

4.

Getting the Band Together

(July 1997: nine months before launch)

A WEEK AFTER WE mailed the CD, I found myself at the head of an eight-top at the Cupertino Hobee's, halfway through a massive BLT. Half-eaten burgers and crinkle-cut fries littered the table, pushed aside to make room for binders, notebooks, and coffee cups. We were really doing it.

For the uninitiated, Hobee's isn't exactly fine dining. It's basically a diner: tables molded to the wall, laminated menus with pictures of food on them and no stains, because they go into the dishwasher at the end of every shift. A cup of coffee costs two dollars and it's endlessly refillable.

We didn't choose Hobee's because the food was good. And we weren't meeting at Hobee's in an effort to keep our idea secret. In fact, secrecy was the least of our concerns. I'd realized by then that telling people about my idea was a *good* thing. The more people I told my idea to, the more I received good feedback, and the more I learned about previous failed efforts. Telling people helped me refine the idea — and it usually made people want to join the party.

So why Hobee's? Location, location, location. We used a compass to draw equal-size circles around Christina's house in Foster City and my house in Scotts Valley. When you intersected those two circles, Stevens

Creek Boulevard in Cupertino was in the exact center. No more than a thirty-minute drive for anyone.

Who was anyone? Christina, Te, and I, of course. Eric Meyer, our provisional CTO, looking at his overly foamy cappuccino with Gallic disdain. Boris and Vita Droutman, a married Ukrainian couple with heavy accents and, Eric assured us, a genius for coding. And Reed, on the rare occasions he could get away from the Pure Atria offices.

We had to meet at Hobee's because we were in a weird, in-between place: moving toward being a real company, but without any kind of office. Or the money to rent one. Christina, Te, and I were still employed at Pure Atria, and it wouldn't do to have people coming in and out of our offices there all day, working for a different company. So we stole time after-hours, or during lunch breaks, heading to Hobee's for two-hour meetings to discuss our company-to-be: what we were going to do, how we were going to do it, and when we could start.

Christina and Te did hours of market research, and over their Cobb salads would present it to us. "In the past week, I've gone to fifteen video stores, and here's what I learned," Te would say, before Christina pulled out her preliminary drawings of what she thought the site might look like. Boris and Vita would huddle with Eric, talking about tech specifics in a language so advanced I really understood only every other word. I was usually doing about three things at once. While my body was at the table, attending to these conversations, my brain was often elsewhere, trying to figure out how to convince a new person to join our team, or what we should call ourselves, or where we'd land, once we had our funding finalized. We couldn't stay at Hobee's forever.

I also needed a CFO, and I had my eye on a guy I knew from Borland named Duane Mensinger. He fit the profile exactly: professional, with a work history that included close to a decade at Price Waterhouse. In casual California, where shorts and flip-flops were the norm, he was never seen in anything except a button-down shirt. But the very qualities that attracted me to Duane — he was careful, organized, and risk-averse — were the ones that kept him from committing to becoming part of our merry little group of outsiders. While he repeatedly and ever so politely told me no, he kept his iron in the fire, agreeing to help us build our financial models and acting as a kind of "rent-a-CFO."

I had the opposite problem with a man named Jim Cook — who ended up as one of the most important members of the Netflix team. He was a friend of Christina's, a burly guy who had worked in finance for years at Intuit and always had a shit-eating grin on his face. I liked that about him — it's good to have optimism in the startup world. The problem, however, was that he desperately wanted to be the CFO. He certainly looked the part. Jim dressed like a banker: pressed pants, crisply ironed dress shirts, every last one of them light blue. He was organized, detail-oriented, and efficient — and unlike Duane, he was accustomed to startup risk-taking. Like the rest of us, he actually enjoyed it. I thought that made him perfect to run operations — to figure out just how we were going to buy, store, and ship DVDs.

But he didn't agree. It took me a few meetings before I realized that his big grin was more than just optimism — it was a negotiating tactic. My strategy, when I'm not getting what I want in a negotiation, is to sigh and display my weary sadness, to make the other party feel like a child who has disappointed his parents. You know the drill: *I'm not mad, I'm just disappointed.* Jim's was to just broadcast a huge creepy grin at me. It was unnerving.

But it didn't work. Jim would sign on as our director of finance and operations in October. In the end, I realized that he was more interested in the finance *title* than he was in the actual job. I'm usually wary of title inflation — although it's something that seems like it costs you nothing to give, it actually is far more expensive than it seems, since it causes a cascading series of overpromotions. For just this reason, I had already decided that no one would get a VP title — at least at first. Instead, they would all be directors, and their titles would reflect what they actually *did*, not what they wanted to do. But in Jim's case, a little rule-breaking was unavoidable. He was too valuable to lose over a job title, so I reluctantly agreed to add the finance piece, while impressing upon him that with Duane on board — albeit in a temporary way — the real place we needed him at the start would be in operations. CFO would come. He would just have to be patient.

In the meantime, I had to find a place for Jim — and all the rest of us — to work. We needed an office. I had strong feelings about being a Santa Cruz company — of bucking the prevailing norms of Silicon Valley and not moving to a cookie-cutter office park in Sunnyvale or San Jose. Santa Cruz spoke to me. It's a beach town, a surf town. A whiff of the sixties still clings to it. There are probably more Volkswagen vans than there are people. Its prevailing ethos, as a city, is the opposite of Silicon Valley's "growth at all costs" model. People in Santa Cruz are typically against development. They've opposed widening the roads. They don't want it to grow.

Growth is God, over the Santa Cruz mountains. But in Santa Cruz, it's vulgar.

I wanted some of Santa Cruz's laid-back ethos for my company. I didn't want to attract just the same group of ambitious young tech workers from over the hill. I wanted freethinkers, people who were slightly outside the box. I wanted things to be different.

I wanted life balance — for me and for my co-workers. I wanted Santa Cruz's access to trails and waves and a more relaxed way of life, and I didn't want to have to spend two hours every day commuting to Palo Alto. If I was going to start my own company, I wanted it to seamlessly integrate with my life. I wanted my kids to be able to come by the office for lunch, and I wanted to be able to drive home for dinner with them without spending hours inching along in a conga line of cars.

I was looking at office space in Santa Cruz. But until we had money in hand, we were stuck with the Scotts Valley Best Western.

That Best Western is still there, by the way. I drove by last week, hoping to sit at the conference room table where we'd ended up spending weeks of time before we had a real office. I wanted to check my memory — how big was the conference table? What color was the worn carpeting? I parked my car and walked around outside the building, trying to be discreet. But when I peered through the window at the first office space Netflix had ever had, I didn't see a long table, or ergonomic chairs, or the ever-present scratched-up water pitchers surrounded by plastic cups. I saw a room full of things none of us would have had any use for: a sad treadmill, a collection of mismatched dumbbells, a dirty yoga mat unfurled in the corner.

Time is cruel, and there are no monuments in tech.

I was spending a lot of time eating lunch that summer. In addition to Hobee's, I was driving up to Woodside a few times a month, in an ongoing attempt to woo a video store owner named Mitch Lowe.

I'd first met Mitch in Las Vegas, at the annual conference for the Video Software Dealers Association (VSDA, for short). I'd gone in June on a hunch, with no real plan other than to conduct the most general kind of research. It had seemed prudent, given that we were looking to start an e-commerce business focused on video rental, to acquire something more than a vague idea of what it meant to rent videos. In the back of my mind, I was hoping that someone might sell some kind of software for running rental stores that we might be able to convert to working online.

I'd had to use a little subterfuge. The VSDA was a "trade show," which means that ostensibly it was only open to members of the trade, not the general public. So, a month or so before I left for Vegas, when I went to register, I decided that I was now the general manager of "Randolph Video of Scotts Valley, California." I answered the questionnaire as best I could:

Employees?: 7.

Annual revenue?

That was a hard one — I had no idea how much a video store did in business. Let's see, how about $750,000?

And then a few weeks later, my badge showed up in the mail.

I don't know what I expected from the VSDA show. Probably some booths, some roundtable talks, the normal dry business convention I recognized from my years in direct marketing. I think I had the idea that the whole thing would be presided over by stereotypical video store employees. If you're old enough to remember video stores, you know the type: early twenties, big glasses, permanent sneer.

What I found was entirely different. VSDA was *insane*. There were thousands of people there, swarming around hundreds of elaborate, ridiculously appointed booths. Models wandered the convention center, handing out studio swag. Celebrities posed for photos. Bright colors festooned every banner, and spotlights lit up the room. Movie soundtracks blared from gigantic speakers, so loud the floor was shaking. It was like some unholy mix of Disney World, a Hollywood movie premiere, and the Indiana State Fair.

I stood in front of a green screen, then had my smiling face inserted into a poster for *Mission: Impossible*. I posed for a picture with Wallace and Gromit. I stood in wonder beneath the thirty-foot Barney standing sentinel at the entrance to the exhibit hall, and watched him open and close his mouth in greeting.

I felt like I was on hallucinogens.

For hours, I wandered from booth to booth, essentially trying to figure out how the video store business worked. Who were the major players? Who made money? And how? My strategy was to play the rube — to Columbo my way to an understanding. But I wasn't getting very far.

By the end of the day, I'd made my way past the huge booths to what, at these kinds of conventions, is called the "pipe-and-drape" section — so called because each booth is separated from the next by a waist-high framework of metal pipes, draped with curtains to hide the ugliness. This was the home of the lesser-trafficked, lower-real-estate booths. Gone were the fancy electronic displays. There was no sign of John Cusack or Denise Richards. No commemorative mugs or 3-D glasses greeted me. Instead, middle-aged guys sat behind card tables, chatting placidly about return rates and inventory.

Here were the people I wanted to see. The software guys.

I ended up at a booth near the back, talking to a nondescript man in his mid-thirties with a mustache. He had a kind expression, a sweet manner, and a hand-lettered name tag that simply said "Mitch." I laid my Columbo act on thick.

"At my store, my seven employees and I have been using pad and pencil to keep track of rentals," I said. "What does this type of software actually *do*?"

His smile suggested that he might be on to me, but he didn't let on. As we talked, I learned that Mitch ran a small chain of video stores called Video Droid. He had ten locations and managed thousands of titles in each one of them. I was interested in the way he talked about the practical challenges of maintaining an inventory of both new and classic films, but what really fascinated me was his deep knowledge of movies and his even deeper connection with his renters. He paid attention to what they liked, what they asked for, and what they wanted. He was a movie buff, and he wanted to help his customers find the kinds of movies they'd love. That meant giving them not only what they thought they wanted but what they didn't even know they wanted.

Mitch was a walking, talking IMDb. He watched movies all day at the store, then went home and watched a movie while he was eating dinner, then stayed up late watching even more movies. Unlike the stereotypical video store employee — snobbish and elitist, proud of his vast knowledge — Mitch was gregarious and friendly, eager to share his passion. Over his decades in the business he had talked to thousands of people about what they watched, what they liked and disliked, what else they had seen. It was this deep internal database of movie knowledge and human insight that enabled him to predict exactly the right movie for a person's mood, interests, and tastes.

He was a movie sommelier.

He also wasn't falling for my Columbo routine. About ten minutes into our conversation, he smiled at me — seemingly guileless, but with a glint in his eye — and said, "What are you really up to?"

I hemmed and hawed, and then I told him the outlines of my idea for videos by mail. He seemed mildly interested. We exchanged numbers, and I left the booth thinking I might have found a low-profile minor player to bounce ideas off of. *What a nice guy*, I thought.

Later that day, looking for a map of the convention center, I opened the VSDA program. On the inside cover was a half-page, full-color photograph of the man from the pipe-and-drape section. Beneath it was printed his name. *Mitch Lowe: VSDA Chairman.*

After VSDA, Mitch and I kept in touch. He lived in Marin, so we mostly met by phone, but I kept him abreast of what we were up to, asking him questions if I thought his answers would be helpful. I met him a few times in Woodside for coffee. By the time we were starting to raise money, I was actively recruiting him, and I started buying him lunch at Buck's.

Buck's is one of the temples of Silicon Valley. So many companies have been birthed there — conceived, funded, or otherwise organized — that the owners should probably start demanding a cut. The food is very good, elevated comfort-food diner fare, but the atmosphere is what you go for. Probably the most notable piece of décor — and the place is packed to the gills with stuff — is a motorless car suspended from the ceiling. Remember Soap Box Derby? Home-built wooden cars that you roll down a hill to race, in Boy Scouts? Well, consider this Silicon Valley's version.

Every year, there was a motorless car race on Sand Hill Road in Palo Alto, with multimillion-dollar VC firms fighting for bragging rights. Instead of wooden cars, these were spaceships on wheels. Their sponsors had sought out cutting-edge, hi-tech, carbon-fiber composite materials. They had used their connections to get time in the Lockheed Martin wind tunnels. They had procured bearings that cost thousands of dollars apiece. Even the wheels were lighter, stronger, and more expensive than what you would find on a drag racer.

And in Buck's, one of these ridiculous contraptions — it had lost at Sand Hill but had once held the downhill motorless speed record — was hanging from the ceiling over you as you ate, a constant reminder that anything was possible with enough effort, enough ingenuity, and enough money.

Every booth at Buck's bears the residue of venture financing. The napkins there have felt the imprints of thousands of pens, sketching out improbable ideas that just might work. In a way, it's the VSDA of Silicon Valley — a crazy, slightly hallucinogenic place that seems engineered to confound outsiders. That's exactly why I took Mitch there.

I was gathering intelligence at those lunches. I'd float possible solutions to problems Christina and Te and I had discussed, and just by hearing Mitch shoot them down, I'd learn something. He had the perfect combination of content knowledge and industry knowledge — he loved movies as much as he loved the logistics of renting them.

Mitch wasn't — and even now, he isn't — a Silicon Valley guy. He was a down-to-earth business owner with incredibly progressive ideas. In fact, the very name of his video store chain, Video Droid, was a reference to his very early wager that eventually, movies could be distributed from kiosks. (George Lucas at one point came after Mitch, serving him with a cease-and-desist order, claiming he held the rights to the word *droid*. That lasted about as long as it took Mitch to demonstrate that his use of the word predated *Star Wars* by many years.)

His look and manner screamed "normal guy." But the more I talked to him, the more hints I got that there was something much more interesting behind the façade. He let slip once that he'd once worked as a smuggler of clothing in and out of the Eastern Bloc under communism. He shyly admitted that his mother had a porn Oscar. Not as a performer, but as a friend to the industry. Mitch's family house in Muir Woods had been used as a set for dozens of adult movies in the seventies and eighties.

Eventually, I openly offered him a job. But he politely demurred. He loved running his family's company. He loved the video business. He wasn't exactly itching to leave Marin.

And yet...he kept agreeing to meet me at Buck's. And it wasn't because of the bison meatloaf — as good as it was. He was intrigued. He kept giving me advice and guidance. And I kept buying us lunch. I ate so many Reubens that spring and summer wooing Mitch Lowe that I think I gained what I came to call the "Founder's Fifteen." I just kept loosening my belt, hoping the calories would pay off.

5.

Show Me the Money

(fall 1997: eight months before launch)

SPEND ENOUGH TIME AROUND Silicon Valley, and you'll start to hear a funny acronym: OPM. Particularly if you're hanging around with battle-scarred entrepreneurs with a couple of startups under their belts, OPM will pepper conversations about early-stage companies. Sometimes it's used in the context of sage advice: *"You want to know the most important principle of starting a company? It's OPM."* Sometimes you'll hear it as a cautionary warning: *"I know you're confident, but please stick to OPM."* Sometimes it's just a mantra, repeated as part of a kind of yogic practice in the conference rooms of office parks across the land: "OPM, OPM, OPM."

What's OPM, you might ask? Just a bit of startup slang.

Other People's Money.

When entrepreneurs implore you to remember OPM, what they're saying is: When it comes to financing your dream, use *only* other people's money. Entrepreneurship is risky, and you want to ensure that the only skin you have in the game is...well, your actual skin. You'll be dedicating your life to your idea. Let others dedicate the contents of their wallets.

By dedicating my time — not my money — to our DVDs by mail concept, I was following my own OPM advice. Reed wasn't. He'd agreed, as we've seen, to put up $2 million of his own capital as seed money. But after a few weeks, he reconsidered the amount. He didn't have cold feet, exactly. But he didn't want to be the only backer.

"I like the idea, but I'm worried we might be in an echo chamber," he said.

"You're worried about us getting stuck up our own asses," I said.

Reed nodded. "You do have a tendency to get high on your own bullshit."

"It's not bullshit if you believe it," I said.

That's true, by the way. For most of my career, I've gotten flack before for my boundless faith in whatever it is I'm selling. Even before Netflix, I'd convinced more than a few people to take pay cuts to work for me, to leave steady work to hop aboard a startup with a slim chance of survival. But in every case, I wasn't just spewing hot air. Whether it was the latest generation of spreadsheets or DVDs by mail, I genuinely believed in what I was selling.

I had absolute faith in what Reed and I were doing. But I saw his point. Asking other people for money forced us to allow other voices into the room — to listen to people outside the Pure Atria offices or Reed's Avalon. It forced us to validate the idea.

That's another benefit of using OPM: before you pour your life into starting a company, it's not a bad idea to get just a little bit of reassurance that you're not completely out of your mind. Convincing someone to part with their money tends to separate those who are blindly supportive ("I love that idea!") from those who are supporting you with their eyes wide open. I often counsel young entrepreneurs to start by asking people what they think, but then *immediately* follow up the inevitable "I love it" reply with the ask: *"Can I count on you to invest a few thousand dollars?"* The backpedaling is so fast and furious that it makes Lance Armstrong look like my grandmother.

Plus, it's never too early to be in contact with future investors you might need later, when you're raising your next round of funding. The "seed" in seed funding usually refers to the business, newly planted and hoping to grow. But it also refers to investors, who are getting in on the ground floor.

In the end, Reed reduced his original $2 million pledge to $1.9 million. We would reach out to others for the remaining $100,000.

I should start by saying that asking for money is hard. Really hard. But it's nothing compared to what it feels like to beg for spare change on the sidewalks of Hartford, Connecticut.

When I was in college, I spent two months each summer leading thirty-day backcountry expeditions for the National Outdoor Leadership School (NOLS), a wilderness program that uses the wilderness to teach leadership skills. As a young adult I spent months in the mountains with NOLS, as have my own children, and I've remained involved with the school to this day. The program teaches self-reliance, teamwork, and wilderness skills, and has taken me everywhere from the rivers of northern Alaska to the glaciers that ring the peaks of Patagonia. I owe it a lot. It taught me discipline and self-reliance, and imbued in me a healthy respect for the natural world. It taught me knots, navigation, and how to catch a trout with my bare hands.

Almost everything I ever learned about being a leader, I learned with a backpack on.

In those college summers, I'd usually spend the third month recuperating at home and visiting family. But the summer after my junior year, I picked up some work at an outfit whose official name was the Wilderness School. Unofficially? They called it "hoods in the woods." Not politically correct, and, as it turned out — not factually correct, either. While the kids were in fact adjudicated youth, most of the ones I met that summer were bright, curious, and well behaved. But a catchy name sticks.

My friend, a documentary filmmaker, was making a short film about the program, and he needed somebody to carry around his food, supplies, extra film, spare batteries, a boom mike, and a twenty-pound Nagra tape recorder. (This was 1979 — way before camcorders.)

I was technically a sound guy for a documentary film. But really? I was a mule.

Still, after that month in the woods, something resonated. I signed up to work the following summer for the Wilderness School as an instructor.

The Wilderness School took inner-city kids from disadvantaged areas in Hartford, New Haven, and Stamford and introduced them to wilderness exploration. Many of the kids in the program had never been outside their city — had barely stepped off a sidewalk. The program had them canoeing rivers, climbing cliffs, and hiking the trails of the Catskill Mountains. It taught basic outdoor skills — how to start a fire, how to build a shelter, how to purify drinking water — as a way to teach leadership and teamwork. But the real objective was to put the kids in situations that seemed impossible, and prove to them, over and over, that they were capable of much more than they imagined.

Working for the Wilderness School taught me a lot about humility. Like most of the other leaders and instructors, I grew up in a leafy suburb, a child of privilege. On the surface, we didn't have much in common with the kids we'd be leading into the woods. Most of us had grown up well fed, with secure housing and plenty of money. Many of these kids had endured homelessness, unstable housing, and hunger.

Taking a kid who had never left Hartford — who had grown up in poverty, who had already endured more deprivation than I would ever know — and dropping him into the woods outside Cornwall or Goshen was a huge change, to say the least. To help us better understand what a shock this kind of experience could be, the Wilderness School gave us a number of different training experiences, each designed to be similarly disorienting for us. All of them took place in the cities — Hartford, Stamford, New Haven — where our students were from. All of them were engineered to make us as uncomfortable as our charges.

The most impactful of these exercises? Blindfolding us, driving us to a random intersection in Hartford, confiscating our wallets and watches, and telling us that we'd be picked up in three days. No food, no water, no prearranged place to sleep. Just a phone number written on our arm, in case we decided to give up. It went without saying that all of us would rather freeze to death under an overpass than admit defeat and call it.

I was dropped off at the corner of Charter Oak and Taylor at 5:00 p.m. on a Tuesday. At first it didn't seem that different from a regular afternoon in any city. I'd eaten a late lunch, so I wasn't worried about hunger. My map-reading skills came in handy, and I was quickly able to locate the Connecticut River. I knew how to survive in green spaces. When night came, I improvised a shelter with a trash bag and some fallen tree branches. The night was warm, and when I couldn't sleep, I walked down to the river and talked myself into a few beers with a group of teenagers partying down there. I didn't particularly want to stay up until sunrise with them, drinking the night away — but I knew that beer had enough calories to stave off hunger. And it would pass the time.

When I woke up the next morning I was starving. I hoofed it into town, drawn by the unmistakable odor of fried food, and wandered into a downtown food court. I circled the tables like a vulture, trying to work up the courage to ask someone to buy me a breakfast — or at the very least give me one of their bagels. But then I had a different idea. Why bother to ask? Instead, I watched businessmen scarf down Egg McMuffins and bagels, waiting for them to leave so I could discreetly slide into their seat. I didn't fish anything out of the trash, but I was not above scavenging a plate of half-eaten hash browns. I was like one of the pigeons crowding the plaza, alert to every sign of movement. I was also very aware of the way people looked at me — or pointedly *didn't* look at me — as I went in for other people's scraps.

I had never been looked at like that before.

By dinner on that second day, my stomach had curled into itself from hunger. Half-eaten pizza just wasn't going to make it. I needed to cut out the middleman, get myself a few dollars, and buy myself something. I needed money. People had it. And all I had to do was walk up to them and ask. I caught a glimpse of myself in a bank window, saw my reasonably clean, preppy, East Coast clothes, my still relatively clean-shaven face, and asked myself: *How hard could it be?*

Answer: very hard.

One of the ways people measure a marketing or sales assignment is by analyzing the difficulty of the ask. What are you asking for, and what are you promising in return? Years later, when I was first entering the marketing profession, I looked to bottled water as one of the great triumphs of salesmanship: marketing in its purest form. *Give me your money, and I'll give you . . . water. Something that is almost free, and that is available almost everywhere. Something that covers 75 percent of the earth's surface.*

But that's nothing, compared to begging for spare change. Panhandling is salesmanship at its purest. It's the totally naked ask: money for nothing.

We're conditioned not to ask for things — and when we do ask for them, we've learned that we have to offer something in return. But asking for money and offering nothing back — no service, no product, not even a song — is truly terrifying. It's like looking into an abyss.

That day in Hartford, I thought a bare, outstretched hand was too stark. So I picked a plastic cup out of the trash and stationed myself on a pedestrian-friendly street downtown, slightly off the beaten path. I was a hundred miles from home, but I didn't want to take the chance of running into anybody I knew — friends, friends of friends, friends' parents. In my mind I rehearsed my line: *Spare any change?* I considered a longer story — I was stuck after hitchhiking, I'd been robbed on the bus, I had lost my wallet. The only thing that was out of bounds was the truth: I was participating in a strange urban test for my summer employment leading underprivileged youth through the Connecticut countryside.

The first person to pass was a brusque, tall lawyer type in a suit. I chickened out before he was within three feet. Couldn't even make eye contact. The same thing happened with a construction worker shrugging his way out of his work vest on his way to the bus stop, then a nurse in her scrubs, hurrying to the pharmacy across the street. Every time, I'd resolve to make eye contact and ask for money — and then my body would recoil. Little by little, my shoulders slumped, my head started to hang.

I had climbed mountains. Rafted rivers. Run triathlons. But this was the hardest thing I had ever tried to do.

And then I finally did it. A friendly-looking woman, about my mother's age, turned the corner and walked toward me. She was moving fast enough to be going somewhere, but slow enough to look like she was enjoying herself. I mustered up the courage to look her in the eye and ask, my voice barely a whisper, "Do you have any spare change?"

"No," she said, her face turning to stone as she walked right past me.

But I had broken the ice. Over the next four hours, I made a dollar and seventy-five cents, enough for a hot dog back at the food court. I got gradually better at asking. I learned to keep it short. To make eye contact. To slump, but not too much. To use a voice loud enough to be heard, but not loud enough to seem demanding or scary.

But the breakthrough for me was simply telling people the truth. *"Can you spare some change? I'm really hungry."* There was something about speaking from the heart that cut right through. It got people's attention and broke down their cynicism and defenses.

The key was getting over the shame of asking — of showing the most basic, essential need to a stranger. It's more difficult than it sounds.

It made me feel sleazy to ask. It made me feel low when people said no. But by far the most difficult thing to bear was the invisibility. Mustering up all your courage and desperation, then debasing yourself in front of a stranger, only to be *totally ignored* — that was worst of all.

Believe me, after *that*, asking an investor for $25,000 was *nothing*.

One of our first targets for funding was a guy named Alexandre Balkanski. He is one of a long line of colorful Frenchmen in my life. There was Philippe Kahn, my old boss at Borland International, who showed up to my job interview shirtless, wearing a pair of Umbro running shorts. There was Alain Rossmann, the CEO of Unwired Planet, who had once completely flipped out on me when I turned down his job offer. (I mean, come on. Was there anything more ridiculous than having an internet browser on your phone?) And there was Eric Meyer, of course, who was joining my nascent company as the CTO.

Then there was Alexandre, a major player in DVD and video technology. His company, C-Cube Microsystems, made deo compression software, for converting analog video and image material into digital bytes that could be easily stored or transported. In Alexandre we thought we had the perfect person: someone who would understand what we were doing and why it would work, and whose deep knowledge of the field could give us valuable insight into how to position our service.

Reed and I drove out to his company HQ in Milpitas. Acknowledging the importance of the meeting, I had dressed up a little, trading my hiking shorts for clean jeans and my ever-present T-shirt for a polo. Reed was wearing what was, for him, a fancy outfit: dark jeans and a white button-down. By now I wasn't nervous — Reed and I were veterans at this kind of thing, and we knew that we had something that was worth buying. But when the receptionist showed us to a couple of chairs in the foyer and no one came out for five, then ten, then fifteen minutes, I think both of us started to sweat a little.

He's really icing us, I thought.

Then the door opened, and a tall, fit-looking guy stepped out. He was wearing a blazer and slacks and expensive-looking leather slippers.

"Hello," he said, in a vaguely European accent.

Uh-oh, I thought. *Is he French?*

When you pitch a business idea to someone, you never expect to make it all the way through your presentation. It's like presenting a case to the Supreme Court: within a few moments of making your first point, the questions will invariably start. If they don't, you're probably in trouble. Nine times out of ten, they're not quiet because they're politely listening — they're quiet because they're totally uninterested. Or worse: they're thinking your arguments are so weak and pathetic that they don't even warrant an argument.

So we were prepared for interruptions, for questions, for probing analyses of our business idea. What we weren't prepared for was Alexandre, who, halfway through our pitch — *DVDs by mail! The largest inventory in the world! First to the space!* — shook his head, knocked his knuckles on the glass table between us, and said, in an accent that I still couldn't place:

This is sheet.

(Transliteration mine.)

Shit? Really? We had almost $2 million on the line, a team of excited people, and a genuine opportunity to be the next Amazon. I looked at Reed, who was staring at Alexandre with an expression that was impossible to read, if you didn't know him. I knew him, though. He was worried.

Alexandre told us DVDs were a flash in the pan. "No one is adopting this tech long-term," he said. "The big jump was from analog to digital. Once movies are in a digital form, it won't make sense to move the bits around on pieces of plastic. That's terribly inefficient and slow.

It's just a matter of time before people are going to be downloading their movies. Or streaming them. At some point, probably soon, you're going to be stuck with a warehouse full of useless DVDs."

"I'm not so sure about that," I said. "I think it could be a while before that happens. We've got at least five years."

Alexandre shook his head. "Sooner," he said. "Why should I invest in a company that won't be around five years from now?"

The thing is? He was right about nearly all of it. DVDs *were* a middle step between analog VHS tapes and downloads or streaming. He knew better than anyone that the technology to make DVDs themselves obsolete was just around the corner. It was his field, after all. And a cursory glance at Netflix's current business will bear out his theory that eventually, viewers would access almost all of their movies directly through the internet.

But he had the timeline all wrong. What he didn't understand was Hollywood. We knew that the studios were betting big on the DVD format and, more importantly, were betting on DVD *ownership*. They didn't want a repeat of the eighties, when video stores had established themselves as middlemen to consumers, renting the same video out dozens of times. Movie studios didn't want to have to jack up the prices of movies just to earn their share of the home viewing market; they wanted to get their films directly into consumers' homes, and DVD — a new technology that they could price competitively — represented an opportunity to hit the Reset button.

As for online downloading? Sixty-five-year-old studio execs weren't exactly the most tech-savvy people around. They were terrified of what had happened to the music industry. Napster had inaugurated the age of illegal file sharing, and although DVDs had been developed with more robust piracy prevention mechanisms than CDs, movie studios were still wary of allowing customers to access movies as easily shareable digital files.

Alexandre also underestimated the "last-mile" problem. In most of the country, downloading a movie was still functionally impossible, or at least impractical. High-speed internet was only intermittently available, and frankly, it wasn't that fast yet. Plus, the internet terminated at the computer — not the television. Even if you *could* download a movie in less than a few days, there was no way of getting it from your computer to your television — and most people didn't want to plop down in their office chair and cue up *Total Recall* on their Compaq Presario.

Alexandre's whole life had led up to the moment when movies and television would be able to be streamed over the internet. C-Cube, in many ways, was the enabler of what made all this possible. But like most pioneers, Alexandre was too early.

In the meantime, we had a business model that worked in a DVD world. We could afford to wait. Every piece of brand equity that we were building — all those customer relationships, all of our movie-matching expertise — would still be relevant and useful when the world shifted.

Or so we told Alexandre. But he batted away every counterargument with a dismissive wave of his well-manicured hand. And if you're arguing with a potential investor, it's already over. We left that office deflated, surprised, and a little nervous. On the trip back to Sunnyvale, I drove fast, as I usually do, taking corners at speed all the way home. Reed didn't say a word.

In Silicon Valley, no one ever really tells you no. After a pitch, you'll typically hear a sentence that begins with "This is great, but…" You get so used to it that if you hear a sentence starting with "This is great," you mentally start gathering your papers and feeling for your keys.

This is great, but I'd love to see more traction before committing.

This is great, but why don't we talk again when you have ten thousand subscribers?

This is great, but that's not an investment premise we're focusing on right now.

Alexandre didn't tell us, *This is great*. He told us, *This is shit*.
And that scared the hell out of us.

It was time for an even harder ask: I would be pitching Steve Kahn. While normally I would be looking forward to pitching someone I knew so well, in this case it was complicated and awkward. Because Reed was pushing me to go back on a deal.

Steve had been my first boss at Borland, and in many ways he was — and still is — a mentor. He's a buttoned-down guy who was constantly having to do damage control for me. He once told me that when he'd see me knocking on his office door, he typically had one of two thoughts: *Who'd he piss off this time?* Or *What crazy thing did he dream up now?* I'm sure he was asking himself one of these questions on the day I walked down to his basement office at Pure Atria to ask him to lunch.

Even before we had definitively decided we were moving forward with the idea that would one day become Netflix, I knew I wanted Steve on my board of directors. For one thing, all boards need at least a third person to break ties.

For another, Steve was a voracious video technophile. He'd taken his spoils from our sale of Integrity QA and used it to ignite a home video theater system arms race with Bob Warfield, our fellow Integrity QA co-founder. Theirs was an ongoing, take-no-prisoners competition. Surround sound, stadium seating, noise-canceling wall hangings, leather recliners, state-of-the-art projection systems....If you could hook it up to a home theater, Steve and Bob already had it — or they soon would. There was about a forty-five-day window when any piece of video technology was state-of-the-art, and Steve and Bob were always fighting to be the proud owner of that window.

But the most important reason I wanted Steve on the board? He was a friend. Not only would he be helpful, honest, and thoughtful. It would be great to have one person who truly had my back.

Asking him to join the board had been easy. I was essentially asking for a favor that required nothing but a little bit of his time in return. When I took him out to lunch — an all-you-can-eat Indian buffet located in a strip mall near the office — he had listened patiently as I laid out the idea for him, my tikka masala sitting untouched in front of me. It hadn't taken long for him to say "Sure," but I could tell by the way he said it that it really hadn't made a difference what the idea was.

Now, Reed thought I needed to ask him for more than just his time. If he was going to be on the board, Reed explained, he had to have some skin in the game.

But asking him for $25,000 — solely for the privilege of being on our board — was going to be hard. I dreaded it. I put it off for days. It felt like a bait-and-switch — the favor I'd asked that had cost him nothing now had a price tag attached.

We went to the same Indian restaurant — I thought it might be good luck. I was nervous. Steve barely had a chance to pick his menu up when I blurted it out. *Could you put twenty-five thousand dollars in?*

I'll never forget the look on Steve's face. He exhaled, pursed his lips, and laid down his menu, and a generally weary expression slowly spread over his face. Even in that moment, hovering over a basket of garlic naan, slowly ripping a paper napkin to shreds underneath the table, I recognized it. It's the face of being in an impossible bind. The face of "there's no right answer."

If Steve said no, that he *wouldn't* put $25,000 toward the business, he would look cheap. Like he didn't truly believe in the idea (even though he probably didn't). But if he said yes, he'd be out $25,000, money he hadn't expected to spend — and on top of that, we'd both know that he would be doing it not because he loved the idea or thought it would work but because I'd asked him to. Because he had seen in my face and heard in my voice the same thing that had gotten me over the hump on the streets of Hartford. That I was truly hungry.

When he said yes, both of us knew it had nothing to do with the idea. Steve told me later that he said to himself, "Well, that's $25,000 I'll never see again."

I was most nervous about asking my mother.

Plenty of people ask their parents for money during the seed stage of startups. In fact, back then nobody even called it a "seed round." People called it the "friends and family round."

Still, there's something slightly pathetic about being almost forty years old, married, with three kids and multiple successful companies to your name...and calling your parents asking for cash. You're right back to being eight years old, tugging on your mommy's leg, asking for fifty cents for a candy bar at the grocery store.

Still, I did it.

I asked my mother because asking my father was out of the question. He was stern and unyielding about money. His parents had lost everything in the Depression, and as a result he was extremely risk-averse with his finances. He kept his books in old-school ledger accounts, everything from income to investments to monthly utility bills. (When he died, I went through his papers, and every gas bill from 1955 to 2000 was entered in his precise engineer's hand.) On Wall Street, he'd seen people lose everything. The way he thought about business had more to do with large companies and banks — things had to be solid, profit-driven, real — than it did with venture capital and startups that didn't make money for a couple of years, if ever. If I'd pitched him on the initial idea for Netflix, he would have gotten out his magnifying glass and picked the idea apart.

My mother, though scrupulous with money, enjoyed a splurge now and then. Plus, she was an entrepreneur herself. When I was in high school, she had started her own real estate firm, it had prospered, and now she had money of her own. In fact, she'd put both me and my siblings through college with it.

She was on the East Coast, so I couldn't ask her in person. I dreaded that phone conversation. Sales is theater: every pitch, every call, every interaction in which you, the businessperson, are trying to convince someone else — the customer, the client, the potential investor, you name it — is a little performance, in which each side plays a role. But a son calling his mother to ask for money? That isn't just theater. It's Kabuki theater. Everything is ritual and prescribed.

Both of us knew that she would eventually say yes — she was my mother, the money wasn't *completely* unreasonable, and she had always supported me and my career. She had confidence in me. In fact, one of the reasons I was asking was that I knew she'd invest. What's more, I knew that *she* knew that I knew.

We both understood that her thought process would go something like this:

> A) *I have no idea what he's talking about.*
> B) *Wait a minute, what?*
> C) *Oh, for crying out loud.*
> D) *I guess I'll do it. I'm his mother, after all.*

In other words, I knew that I would play the somewhat indulged son. She'd play the skeptical but generous mother. Both of us would be acting out age-old roles, cemented by decades of family dynamics. And that was alright for both of us.

How's that for making Uncle Siggy proud?

I don't remember much about that awful phone call. I wasn't as practiced in the "art of the ask" then as I am now. I'm sure I let slip some truly heinous salesmanship clichés: *I'm calling today to give you the "opportunity" to invest in my company,* etc. If I'd been at home back in Chappaqua, I probably would have retired with her to the library to discuss the investment over brandy.

Even now, I cringe thinking of that phone call.

I'm sure my mom asked polite, curious questions. I'm sure I gave polite, enthusiastic answers. The only thing I really remember — and I thought this was the epitome of grace, when she said it — was that she knew that her investment would bear fruit in the long term. "I'm sure in fifteen years I can use this money to buy an apartment in the city," she said, laughing.

She wanted to prove to me that the money she was investing wasn't just a gift — that it was a real investment, even though *she* knew and *I* knew that the reasons she was investing had nothing to do with my pros and cons and my projections, and everything to do with the fact that she was my mother and I was her son.

I almost wished she had said no. Because now I had to actually do it.

6.

How It Feels to Deposit a Check for Almost $2 Million

(fall/winter 1997: half a year until launch)

AFTER WEEKS OF HOUNDING him (for whatever reason, Reed seemed reluctant to actually sign and date the check), your first investor finally hands you the check that will let you rent an office, hire employees, and buy a few folding tables.

It's more than that, of course. The check represents the ability to start. It's the difference between an idea in your head and a company in the world. It's the difference between nothing and something.

It's everything. It's also quite a bit of money.

You scrutinize the check, looking again and again at the dollar amount. You make sure there are enough commas. That the date is correct. That the signature resembles the one you know.

A part of you wants to drive all the way down to Santa Cruz, to the bank with the recessed lighting, the gleaming tile, the golden safe door half-open behind the counter, gleaming from the darkness like a yacht's steering wheel. To change your shirt into something with a collar, maybe wear a tie — to dress up for the occasion.

One point nine million dollars is a lot of money. You feel nervous handling it, like you've robbed it off someone else. Better to go to the closest bank you can find. Who cares if it's in a strip mall in Los Gatos? You need to get this thing out of your hands, fast.

You begin to feel like a fugitive.

In line at the bank, you touch the check with your sweaty hands, again and again, until it's damp in your pocket. To anyone else it might look like you're getting away with something.

You've handled money before, of course. And you've worked for companies that threw around amounts considerably larger than this.

But you've never held it in your hands.

The line moves slowly, but eventually you reach the teller. You think: this will make her day.

You think: I bet she'll be impressed. I bet she'll discreetly signal to the manager, and he'll usher me into a back office, where there will be antique furniture and a Persian carpet. He'll pour me some champagne and make polite conversation while an underling handles all the details.

One million nine hundred thousand and 00/100 dollars.

You hand it over and there's nothing. No glimmer of recognition, no hint of surprise on the teller's face. Business as usual.

"You want any cash back?" she asks.

With Reed's money in the bank — and with the Pure Atria merger a done deal — we could finally move out of the Best Western. But we didn't have to move far: I found a place just across the street, in a nondescript office park in Scotts Valley. The lease seemed exorbitantly expensive to me. It was also multiyear, which introduced a note of optimism into the proceedings that I hoped wasn't entirely foolish.

It was a far cry from the glittering corporate campus I'd known at Borland — or the gleaming blond-wood-and-succulents open-plan monstrosities currently in vogue, which all seem to include fireman poles and beanbag chairs. Our office park was completely anonymous. It looked like the kind of place where a dentist might have his office, or a tax attorney. In fact, there were a few psychiatrists there, and an optometrist. Mostly, though, the office park had been taken over by small startups, which entered and exited leases in a revolving door of boom and bust.

There was a flower bed out front next to the flagpole, and in it were planted perpetually fresh flowers and plants. Nothing really grew there, or was tended to, exactly. Instead, adult, in-bloom flowers were planted into the soil, and when they died they were dug up and replaced with a new round of in-bloom tulips or pansies or daffodils. Cost was no object, as long as the flowers were in bloom. Passing a gardener with a wagon of fully bloomed tulips to be hastily inserted into the earth, it was hard not to see the garden as a particularly perverse metaphor for the life cycle of a startup. *Plant, bloom, die...* and be replaced.

Our office was a big, open room with a hideous green carpet. It had once housed a small bank, and in fact the walk-in safe was still accessible, its door left unlocked. There were a few offices on a long wall, a conference room, and an office in the corner with views of the parking lot and the Wendy's across the street. As the CEO, I claimed it. And then had nothing to put in it.

This was not a luxurious space. We spent less than a thousand dollars furnishing it. There were no Aeron chairs, no Ping-Pong tables, no refrigerator full of LaCroix. There were six or seven folding tables, the cheap ones that caterers use. There was a mismatched set of dining room chairs I'd scavenged from my storage unit. If you wanted more than that, you had to bring it from home. I distinctly remember several employees dragging beach chairs into the space, the seats and legs still covered in sand. The first time Lorraine came to the offices, she pointed at our conference table and asked, "Are those our old dining room chairs?"

Instead of furniture, we spent money on technology. We bought dozens of Dells online and had them shipped to the office. We bought our own servers — in 1997, there was no shared cloud — and installed them in the corner. We bought miles of cable, and wired the office after-hours, ourselves. Extension cords and ethernet cables twisted through the office like orange and black snakes. Wires hung down from the ceiling like vines.

I don't remember our move-in day. We might have ordered some pizzas and made a few Costco runs. But more likely, people just trickled in, bringing with them whatever they needed to do their work. If you stood in the first Netflix office sometime in the fall of 1997, you would have seen a room that resembled some unholy cross between a computer geek's basement and a politician's on-the-road campaign war center. And that's just the way we liked it.

Our office sent a clear message: *This isn't about us, it's about the customers.* The reasons for working there weren't exotic perks or free food. It was the camaraderie and the challenge, the opportunity to spend your time solving hard, interesting problems with smart people.

You didn't work for us because you wanted a beautiful office. You worked for us because you wanted the chance to do something meaningful.

At the same time that we were moving into our offices in Scotts Valley, I was contemplating — and ultimately preparing for — a move of my own.

For the first few months of the Netflix experiment, I was living a five-minute walk away, in a tiny rental house. Lorraine and I had moved there in 1995, after years of living up in the mountains. Tired of the thirty-minute drive into Santa Cruz — and my hour-and-a-half trek over the hill to work each day — we'd sold our house in the mountains and moved into a small rental in Scotts Valley, putting away money for the future.

I enjoyed walking to and from work. Being so close to home made it easy for me to leave at dinnertime, rush home to be with my family for a few hours, and then return to the office to finish up the day's work. But it wasn't a sustainable solution for the future. I wanted a yard that was larger than a postage stamp, and Lorraine wanted a big house to raise our kids in. There were three of them, and in our tiny rental, it always seemed like they were running into each other. They didn't have much space to play outside, either, and we were so close to the highway that the noise of cars kept us up at night.

But our attempts to find a new home hadn't been going anywhere. There were no places in our price range anywhere close to Santa Cruz, and when we looked over the hill, toward San Jose, what we saw was even less encouraging. Realtors, hearing what we had to spend, showed us places that were almost comical in their inadequacy. One place had grass growing on the roof — and it wasn't on purpose. Another came with a flock of goats.

Then, in October, a three-story house on fifty acres in the hills outside Scotts Valley came on the market. It had once been a vineyard, and in the early twentieth century it had been a country resort. The owners were octogenarians who couldn't maintain the property anymore. The first time we took a tour, dragging the kids along with us, we fell in love. It was perfect for us: a big house on a lot of land.

It was also just shy of a million dollars.

That night, somewhat panicked, I called my mother for advice. She was a real estate agent and knew my family almost as well as I did.

"We really want this house," I said. "But it's a lot of money, more than I've ever spent. And I'm just starting this new company. Do I really need the added risk? What should we offer?"

"If you want it, don't try for a bargain and risk losing it," she told me. "The anxiety of paying that much won't last. But the enjoyment of living there will last forever. Go all in."

So we did.

Did I have buyer's remorse? Of course I did. Even the night after the papers were finalized, when Lorraine and I were sitting on the deck with a few of our friends, drinking a bottle of wine and watching our kids chase each other in the lengthening shadows cast by the redwoods that towered over our new lawn — even then, when we were ostensibly celebrating our great fortune, I was thinking: *Is this the biggest mistake of my life?*

What if the company failed? What if I lost my job? What if DVDs-by-mail never took off?

"Remember our post-college days?" Lorraine said that first night, after our guests had driven away. "Our splurges?"

When Lorraine and I were first married, we were about ten thousand dollars in debt. At the time, I was working my first job in direct-mail marketing and making about thirty thousand dollars a year. Lorraine's income was about the same; she was making cold calls as an entry-level stockbroker. We set a goal to get out of debt in a year, and for the next twelve months we kept a meticulous notebook, counting every single expenditure, no matter how minor. Toothpaste: $1.50. Donut at the train station: 75 cents.

Once a week, we allowed ourselves two big splurges: a square pizza from the Athens Pizza joint down the street, and a case of bar bottle Schlitz. When we'd drunk the beer, we took the bottles back for the rebate.

"We did it once, we can do it again," I agreed.

By nature, I'm not a cheap man — in fact, much of my behavior in business is a kind of rejection of my own father's meticulous carefulness when it came to money. The expenditure notebook was an aberration, a reaction to a particular problem. Normally, when there's money, I spend it. Not wastefully or stupidly — but in the boom-bust cycle of Silicon Valley economics, I've always believed that you should spend the money you're given. Spend it wisely, but spend it.

Although I had quite a bit of startup success early on, I was never a big equity holder — so although I did okay, there weren't huge rewards. My first actual windfall came when I joined Borland, just a few months after my thirtieth birthday. My timing was good: the products took off, and so did our stock. I was wealthy... but only on paper, since all I really owned were stock options. One night at a bar in Hong Kong, I was bellied up next to Doug Antone, Borland's senior VP of sales. We were talking about how well the stock had done, and when I shared that I hadn't realized any of that, he almost spit out his drink.

"What are you waiting for?" he asked. "As soon as any of *my* stock vests, I sell it. There is plenty more upside if the stock keeps going up. But if it goes down, you'll be glad you took something off the table."

From that day on, not only did I adopt that philosophy, but I became one of its biggest advocates. I always told my employees to sell when they could. One of my favorite expressions actually came from Lorraine's old boss from her entry-level stockbroker days: "Bulls make money. Bears make money. Pigs get slaughtered."

(That boss was later indicted for insider trading. He might have done better to have actually followed his own advice.)

Despite my professed ambivalence toward money, anytime I paused that first fall at Netflix, anxiety about my finances set in. The only cure, it seemed, was work. I didn't worry about Netflix's future when I was deeply engaged in ensuring it. And I didn't despair about our new house when I was working on it. I spent every Saturday and Sunday for months fixing the place up before we moved in: ripping out vines, clearing out brush with a tractor, removing dead trees that the previous owners had left where they had fallen ten, twenty, even thirty years prior.

I had a vision of bountiful grapes and fruit trees. After an East Coast childhood of canned fruit salad and pears in heavy syrup, I wanted nothing more than to walk out in my backyard, pluck a piece of fruit right from the tree, and eat it standing on land that I owned. But to do that, I needed to do some planting. I needed to clear a space, plant a sapling, and week by week, month by month, nurture the tender thing that grew there under my care.

My daily routine in the fall and winter of 1997, in the months before we moved, was everything I'd ever hoped it would be. I'd wake up and help Lorraine get the kids ready for school, and then I'd hop in my car for the three-minute drive to the office. If the weather was nice and I wasn't in a hurry, I'd walk there. All day I'd find myself working on an idea I'd come up with, in the pleasant company of a team of people I'd hand-picked for their obvious talents. We were deep in the planning trenches. For someone with ADHD and — I've long suspected — a mild case of OCD, there are few more pleasant places to be.

Every day at work, I had my pick of hundreds — no, *thousands* — of problems to work on. And since I was in charge of and surrounded by brilliant people, I could focus on what interested me. That's one of the great pleasures of being at the helm of a startup in the planning stages. The company is small enough that everyone in it has to wear multiple hats, but big enough that you never have to wear one that doesn't fit properly.

Here are just a few of the issues that faced us that fall:

1. SETTING UP AN OFFICE

You never have to think about it when you're working at a large public company like Borland or Pure Atria, or even when you're an employee at an established startup. But I was learning that when you're in charge, it ultimately falls on you to ensure that the most basic elements of office life — telephones, printers, staples for the stapler — are there for your workers. We needed to buy phones. We needed to buy computers. We needed to wire the office so that all of our gadgets actually worked. And even if we spent roughly five minutes total thinking about décor, somebody still had to buy the folding card tables and set them up in something approximating a straight line.

Not only that, I had to make decisions about things I'd never considered. Did we want the office cleaned weekly or biweekly? How do you organize keys? Which bank should we use? Should I hire an outside firm for HR?

In a way, all of these decisions were a kind of microcosm of the problems facing us as innovators in the late nineties. When you're building a business from the ground up, you start from scratch — from zilch, from nada. And you have to figure out how to make it work. The same was true for a tech startup in 1997, especially one that focused on using the emergent power of the internet to sell a *brand-new* piece of technology. DVDs were barely in the world, high-speed internet was in its infancy, and there were no premade templates for online sites. If you wanted to do something, you had to build it yourself — from scratch.

2. BUILDING A TEAM

Now that we were an actual company, we needed to fill out our roster a bit. We had a core of seven people — Christina, Te, Eric, Boris, Vita, Jim, and I — but there were a lot of holes. We needed someone who could connect us with DVD users. We needed someone who could connect us with studios and distributors. And we needed back-end coding and tech talent — the shortest resource in Silicon Valley. We would always need that.

By late fall, I'd somehow convinced Mitch Lowe to join our ragtag bunch. He says, jokingly now, that the reason he finally decided to drive an hour and a half each way to work for us was so that he could finish more of the presidential biographies he was working his way through on tape. He was going chronologically, starting with Washington, and after several years he was only up to John Tyler. (He's *really* into presidential history.)

But I think the real reason Mitch joined us was because he'd gotten a little bored with his stores and was starting to realize that his movie kiosk experiments were still a few too many years ahead of their time. The software company he had been pitching when I met him at VSDA, Nervous Systems, Inc., was still a few years away from viability as well.

With Mitch we had an invaluable resource: someone who understood the rental business perfectly, had a deep Rolodex of studio execs and distributors, and knew how to reach customers with the movies they'd want. He brought a wealth of experience and knowledge. I knew as soon as I convinced him that he'd be one of the most important hires I ever made.

His wife, though, still thought it would never work.

To help us connect further with customers, Te brought in Corey Bridges to work on customer acquisition — or, more specifically, on something we jokingly called Black Ops. A onetime English major at Berkeley, he was a brilliant writer with a gift for creating characters. He'd realized, early on, that the only way to find DVD owners was in the fringe communities of the internet: user groups, bulletin boards, web forums, and all the other digital watering holes where enthusiasts met up. Corey's plan was to infiltrate these communities. He wouldn't announce himself as a Netflix employee. Posing as a home theater enthusiast or cinephile, he would join the conversation in communities geared to DVD fanatics and movie buffs, befriend the major players, and slowly, over time, alert the most respected commenters, moderators, and website owners about this great new site called Netflix. We were months from launch, but he was planting seeds that would pay off...big-time.

As for tech talent? Through Eric's contacts, we hired a talented engineer from Pure Atria named Suresh Kumar, as well as a brilliant but eccentric German named Kho Braun. Eric, Boris, and Vita all said Kho was a genius. He usually rolled into the office around three or four in the afternoon and stayed till the wee hours of the morning. Sometimes, if I got to work especially early, I'd see him at his desk at six in the morning, surrounded by dried-out tea bags and half-eaten muesli bars. He was the one to wire the office, completing the whole task himself overnight. He was industrious, creative, and mostly silent. For the entire time we worked together, I'm not sure I heard him say more than twenty words.

3. BUILDING THE BASICS

I firmly believe that a healthy startup culture arises from the values and choices made by the startup's founders. Culture is a reflection of who you are and what you do — it doesn't come from carefully worded mission statements and committee meetings.

You can talk until you're blue in the face about how your employees are your greatest asset, or about how you want to ensure that your office is a great place to work, but eventually you have to start taking the small steps to put your words into practice.

So once the check had been deposited, I had to make some decisions. How much would we pay people? Would employees get benefits? How about dental?

Answers:

> *Not all that much.*
> *Absolutely.*
> *Nope.*

Everybody in the early days took a pay cut to work for us. That wasn't because we were cheap. It was because we didn't know exactly how long we needed to make our money last — and because we'd need a lot of it to build up our stock of number four on this list.

In those days, I kept a jar of silver dollars on my desk, which I got in rolls of forty from the bank, and at every weekly meeting, I'd hand one out as a "bonus" to the employee who'd made that week's largest contribution to the company's success. "Don't spend it all in one place," I'd say.

Still, if I was going to ask everyone to sacrifice on behalf of our future success, I wanted them to participate once that success (hopefully!) arrived. While our salaries at that point were well below what might be available elsewhere, each of those early employees received a large stake in the business in the form of stock options. They wouldn't be making a lot up front — but we were betting on ourselves that the eventual payoff would be huge.

4. BUILDING AN INVENTORY

Our goal was to have the most complete collection of DVDs in the world. It made good marketing copy — and it would separate us from our brick-and-mortar competitors, who were still living in a world where only a handful of their customers owned a DVD player. It barely made sense for them to carry DVDs at all, never mind one copy of every DVD ever released.

Not only was that *our* goal, but we planned on having multiple copies of popular titles. That way, when renters wanted to watch something, we would never leave them hanging.

But how did we decide how many DVDs of, say, *The Mighty Ducks 2* to order? Eventually, of course, we developed complex algorithms to accurately match supply with anticipated demand. But back then, we were just guessing. Or more accurately Mitch Lowe was guessing, using his decades of consumer knowledge to come up with an ideal lending library. (As it would turn out, he was rarely wrong. He knew a blockbuster when he saw one — and he could smell a turkey like it was in the oven in the next room.)

He could also help connect us with distributors. In 1997, DVD distributors were a motley bunch, spread across dozens of states. They were small niche companies, and sometimes it took days to get somebody on the phone. It could take weeks to get a shipment — and half the time it wouldn't have everything you ordered in it. In our quest to build a library of every DVD in existence, we often spent weeks looking for a single copy of a single hard-to-find title. Even though there were only a few hundred movies available on the format, it took us months to build a sizable library.

And then what? We had to find somewhere to put it.

This was Jim Cook's territory. Remember that bank vault? He converted it into a storage facility, and for months experimented with different ways to store, locate, and ship what we hoped would eventually be thousands of discs a day.

Shelving? Bins organized alphabetically? Jim's task those early months was daunting. When I walked back to the vault in the early months, it looked like a cinephile hoarder's basement. But eventually it began to resemble nothing more than a video store — titles organized alphabetically and by genre, with hot new releases segregated into their own section.

5. BUILDING A MAILER

One of the biggest problems we had to solve before launch was the mailer. My initial test with Reed had been a simple greeting card envelope, but we couldn't send thousands of DVDs across the country as naked discs inside flimsy envelopes. We needed a real mailer, one that would protect the disc on an unpredictable journey through the interstate postal system. It also had to be sturdy enough that it could be used *again*, when the customer sent the disc back. We had to make it easy to use. Intuitive to figure out. And it had to be small and light enough to qualify as first-class mail. The moment our mailer veered into fourth-class-mail territory, our costs went up and delivery speeds went down. And neither of those outcomes would be sustainable.

We experimented wildly: cardboard, cardstock, craft paper, Tyvek, plastic. We tried squares and rectangles of all sizes. We inserted tabs. We tried foam pads. Thousands of designs ended up on the cutting-room floor after Christina, Jim, or I deemed them unworkable. There were days I went into the office and couldn't tell if the table near the back was filled with Netflix mailer materials or the detritus from one of my son's preschool cut-and-paste projects.

Getting the mailer perfect was key — it was the first physical point of contact we'd have with our users. If our discs arrived broken, or late, or dinged, or scratched — or if a user couldn't figure out how to mail discs back to us using our packaging — then we were doomed. It was a massively important project, and one that I was heavily involved with in the early days. I stayed late tinkering with prototypes, sketched out ideas on napkins during meals. Sometimes, at night, I dreamed about mailers.

6. BUILDING A WEBSITE

This one is probably the hardest to imagine. The advent of the cloud and the proliferation of website-building tools — Squarespace and the like — have made it easy for anyone with a MacBook and an internet connection to buy a domain, upload some photos and text, and throw a website together. But in 1997, at the dawn of the e-commerce age, the idea of a website was still only a few years old. And if you wanted to use the internet to *sell* something, then you had to build it all yourself.

You had to buy not only server space but…the servers themselves. You had to do more than buy a template for an online store — you had to *write* the code for one.

That meant thousands of hours of design, coding, testing, and fine-tuning. What did we want the website to look like? How did we want a user to navigate it? How would it look when you searched for a film? How would films be organized on the site? What kind of content did we need displayed for each film?

Once a customer had chosen a movie, what would they see? How would they input their information? What would happen if they made a mistake when entering their state's abbreviation or their credit card information?

It is no exaggeration to say that the questions were nearly infinite. And to answer them, we had to coordinate two vastly different camps: the designers (mostly me and Christina) and the engineers who actually had to build the thing. Engineers are, by necessity, literal-minded. They will do *exactly* what you instruct them to do. So Christina very quickly learned that she could leave nothing to chance. She began drawing the site by hand, painstakingly replicating exactly what we wanted for each and every page, along with dozens of notes in the margins about how each piece would interact with the next. Then she'd hand it over to Eric, and his team would build it. We'd look at what they'd built and make further suggestions, which they'd incorporate.

Back and forth, back and forth, back and forth.

We did this for months.

Getting the picture? We had a lot to do.

But there was real pleasure in it: in the planning, in the problems, in the puzzles we had to solve. I had so many tasks set in front of me, so many little pieces I had to prep and build, that there wasn't much time for anxiety about the future. It all disappeared when I was in those offices. I forgot about the half-finished bedrooms in the new house I could barely afford. I forgot about Logan's private school tuition bills. I forgot about Alexandre Balkanski frowning and telling me, *"This is sheet."*

I felt like my father, working on one of his trains. I found satisfaction in lining up all the tasks, investigating all the problems, and then working to solve them. I was in the basement, building something, knowing that someday in the near future I'd have to invite everyone else in to have a look.

7.

We Were Almost CinemaCenter

(six months until launch)

ONE OF THE THINGS I'm asked about most often is the Netflix culture. How did we establish it? What kind of presentations did we make to new employees? How did we figure out the way we wanted to work together, interact with one another, speak to each other?

Now, of course, Netflix's culture is famous. There's a much-downloaded PowerPoint presentation given to all new employees.

But the truth is, it wasn't the product of meetings or careful planning or roundtable discussions. It arose organically, through a shared set of values among a team of people who had been through their fair share of offices — startups, major corporations, and everywhere in between. Netflix, for all of us, was an opportunity to work at the kind of place we'd always dreamed about. It was a chance to do things truly our way.

Culture isn't what you *say*. It's what you *do*.

I'd recruited almost everybody in that office. I knew how they worked. I knew that Christina loved to impose order on chaos — and that she'd thrive if given a lot of chaos to handle. I knew that Te's creativity would flourish if she was given free rein to try out her most out-there ideas. I knew that Jim Cook would solve almost any problem put in front of him — but you had to give him room to work.

I knew that I, and everyone else on that initial team, would thrive if given a lot of work to do and a lot of space to do it. That was really all our culture amounted to. Handpick a dozen brilliant, creative people, give them a set of delicious problems to solve, then give them space to solve them.

Netflix would eventually codify this as Freedom and Responsibility. But that was years later. At the time, it was just how we did things. We didn't have set hours for work. You could come in when you wanted, leave when you wanted. You were being judged by what you could accomplish. As long as you were solving problems and getting things done, I didn't care where you were, how hard you worked, or how long you stayed.

My philosophy was informed by years of wilderness expeditions with NOLS. I've been taking backpacking trips in the mountains since I was fourteen. It keeps me sane. I love the smell of the mountain air, the stillness of the outdoors, the sense of peace that comes from reducing life to its barest essentials.

But more than anything, what I love about backpacking trips are the people I take with me. When you're out in the woods, you're separate from the rest of human society. And as a result, you have the opportunity to form a new culture, with its own rules and laws and traditions. You really get to know people when you're sleeping on the ground, eating simple food you prepare yourself, and smelling like you haven't showered in a week (since usually you haven't). Some of my greatest friendships have been forged in the wilderness. And the bonds with my family have been strengthened immeasurably by our time together on a river, climbing a peak, or surfing a remote reef break.

What happens on a backpacking trip also turns out to be a perfect model for what happens in a startup. Startups are small, they're often lean, and they've separated themselves from the dominant mode of thinking within their space. They're made up of like-minded people who are on a journey, who share a common goal.

And they often end up totally lost in the woods.

What I learned, in those early months at pre-launch Netflix, was that working at a startup is like going on a backcountry trip where there are no trails. Say you were on such a trip, and knew that your next campsite was eight miles ahead, on the other side of a steep ridge. Say you had a specialized team — a couple of people carrying pack rafts, a couple more people with all the food and equipment, as well as some incredibly quick trail runners with light packs who could act as scouts.

One possible route goes straight up and over the ridge to the campsite; one is less arduous but longer, and involves several water crossings; and one is a measured, stately hike up a series of gradual switchbacks. Which do you choose for the group?

The answer is none of them.

If there's no one trail, why are you trying to force everyone to go the same way?

The scouts with no packs should take the steep route, get there quickly, and scope out the best place to camp, with good access to water, flat spots for the tents, and good protection from the elements. The guys with the pack rafts should use the water along the route to float to camp, arriving a little later but more rested. The pack mules should take the slower but least taxing route.

Your job as a leader is to let them figure that out. You've presumably chosen this group for such an arduous off-trail trip because you trust their judgment, and because they understand their job. So as a leader, the best way to ensure that everyone arrives at the campsite is to tell them where to go, not how to get there. Give them clear coordinates and let them figure it out.

It's the same at a startup. Real innovation comes not from top-down pronouncements and narrowly defined tasks. It comes from hiring innovators focused on the big picture who can orient themselves within a problem and solve it without having their hand held the whole time. We call it being loosely coupled but tightly aligned.

From the beginning, I resolved to treat everyone who worked at Netflix as an adult. At Borland, I'd seen what happened when companies decided *not* to do that.

When I worked at Borland, the company was at its decadent eighties height. Set on a dozen beautifully landscaped acres, the campus boasted a koi pond in the lobby, a redwood grove, walking paths, a theater, a full restaurant, a health club with racquetball courts, weight rooms, fitness studios, and an Olympic-size pool. And of course, as befits a company where nothing was too good for its employees, there was a hot tub.

But even a Jacuzzi wasn't enough to ensure that everyone was happy. Not long after moving onto the new campus, I was returning from lunch with Patty McCord, at the time one of Borland's human resources managers, when we noticed a group of engineers soaking in the company hot tub. Stopping to say hello, we couldn't help but overhear that they were bitching about the company. That's right: sitting in the company hot tub, complaining about their situation. What's wrong with this picture?

It was a funny moment, but as Patty and I headed back to work, we couldn't help but wonder: If we were supplying our employees with fine dining, a fitness center, and an Olympic-size pool and they were still complaining, what are the factors that really drive employee satisfaction? Or more importantly, what does it take to get other people to sign on to help you with your dream — and be happy doing it? What we found was surprising. And surprisingly simple.

People want to be treated like adults. They want to have a mission they believe in, a problem to solve, and space to solve it. They want to be surrounded by other adults whose abilities they respect.

Years later, Patty would end up revolutionizing the field of HR at Netflix, and much of her philosophy can be traced back to the realization we both had that day at Borland: People don't want hot tubs — not really. They don't want free snacks or Ping-Pong tables or kombucha on tap.

What they *really* want is freedom and responsibility. They want to be loosely coupled but tightly aligned.

Following one problem through its various guises and iterations should give you a good idea about how we functioned pre-launch. This particular problem brought us into contact with another young company, one with its own unique culture — a culture that couldn't have been more different from ours.

When we started acquiring DVDs, there were only 300 or so titles available. By the time we launched, in April of 1998, there were 800. The relatively low number of DVDs in existence was, in some ways, a boon for us — it meant that we could feasibly acquire a couple copies of each one and accurately claim that we carried every DVD that had ever been released.

But the relatively small DVD library was also a liability. Many of the titles available weren't exactly blockbuster material. Sure, some of the studios were producing DVDs people might have actually wanted in 1997 — *The Birdcage*, *The Mask*, *Se7en*. But the vast majority were decidedly less upmarket. It was a total grab bag: *National Velvet* next to *Free Willy*, *Elmo Saves Christmas* next to *Sports Bloopers Encyclopedia*. There were low-budget documentaries about trains, NASA, and World War II. There were dozens of nature films, and "magazines" with short video articles. Bollywood was big. So were karaoke videos, and concert films of orchestras and marching bands.

Basically, the selection was all over the place. No one really knew if DVD was going to take off, and how it would work if it did. Would DVDs be a format used mostly for movies? Were they a good technology for listening to music? Would people want to use DVD five-channel sound to watch two-hour live performances by the USC marching band in their home theaters?

So manufacturers and studios were kind of just experimenting. The library was a mix of somewhat newish releases, established classics, forgotten oldies, and discs that seemed designed to show off home theater equipment. If you looked at the library, you'd think that the audience for DVDs was mostly nerds, college sports fanatics, and anime fans.

The distribution was similarly idiosyncratic. VHS was still king, so many distributors weren't even carrying DVDs. And I don't blame them. Why would anyone buy a library of things for which there was not any demand? As a result, DVDs became the province of the fringe distributors. These distributors were flaky. They didn't return phone calls. In our quest to acquire at least two copies of every DVD, we'd spend days tracking down a title, only to play phone tag for a week.

Through all of this process, Mitch Lowe was invaluable. He knew how to deal with distributors, even the small, elusive ones. He knew how to make them call us back. He was charming, persistent, and happy to call in the many favors he'd earned after his years as VSDA chairman.

One of the most valuable skills he had was knowing *exactly* how many copies to buy. In those early days, there was no algorithm, no equation — just Mitch. He knew when to buy three copies and when to buy thirty. Two copies of every DVD was our minimum, but we bought many more for titles that Mitch thought would be in demand — far more than a video store would have for a comparable VHS title.

The question of inventory was one that we thought would give us an edge over the video stores. There was a finite amount of space in a brick-and-mortar video store, so part of their job was learning how to deal with the inevitable shortages. Mitch and others in the business — most notably Blockbuster — called this *managed dissatisfaction.* What do you do when a customer comes into the store looking for a copy of *Die Hard 2,* but all of the copies are checked out? You try to rent them something else that they might like just as much. You try to make them happy enough so that they'll come back. But even then, customers leave with a bad taste in their mouth.

Since we weren't tied to a physical location, we thought we could avoid managed dissatisfaction entirely. The closest thing to instant gratification that we could give our customers was always having the title they wanted in stock. So while a video store would have bought 5 or 6 copies, we bought 50 or 60. When L.A. *Confidential* was released, we bought 500. It was expensive, but we had four things going for us.

First, $2 million in the bank. Let's see Ye Olde Video Closet at the northeast corner of Boring and Main compete with *that*!

Second, the cost of all those extra discs wasn't expensive inventory, it was *inexpensive* advertising. It was like those old Mastercard commercials. A disc: $20. A reputation for having every DVD and always being in stock: *priceless.*

Third, we were counting on the DVD market continuing to grow. What seemed like ten times too many copies today might very well be just what we needed when the market was ten times as big.

And lastly? Well, if we really screwed up, we could always sell our extra DVDs.

While Jim tried to figure out a way to squeeze all those DVDs into the bank vault, Christina and I wrestled with a different problem: How would our customers find a DVD? What search terms could they use? How would we group movies on our site? What information would they use to make their selection?

When you rent DVDs, you have to have information about them. Think about the back of a DVD case: there's a synopsis, a list of the cast, the director, and the producers, a few well-chosen (and often misleading) quotes from leading critics praising the movie you're about to watch. In a video store, that stuff is all in place long before the movie hits the shelves. Sure, places like Blockbuster or Video Droid had searchable in-store databases for actors, directors, genres, and the like. But most of the information a customer wanted was right in front of them — all a potential renter had to do was walk in, see the picture of Tom Cruise on the cover of *Mission: Impossible,* and flip the VHS case over.

We had a harder road. In *our* store, there was no case to flip over. What we were offering renters wasn't just an alphabetically ordered trove of movies, separated by genre. We wanted the ability to filter: for director, for actor, for genre. We wanted renters to be able to follow their interests in a precise way. Did they like movies in which Andie MacDowell appeared? Were they really into the cinematography of Néstor Almendros, who was behind all those beautiful sunsets in *Days of Heaven*? Did they want a horror movie…and not only a horror movie, but a vampire movie…and not only a vampire movie, but a vampire movie with *comedic elements*?

We wanted to be able to offer renters the ability to find exactly what they wanted. That required an immense amount of data — both objective data, like director/actor/producer/date of release, and subjective data, things like genre and mood. We also needed to be able to access data about awards and critical acclaim (or lack thereof). If a renter wanted to watch every Best Picture winner of all time, we wanted her to be able to do so.

How could we go about building such a database? The obvious answer was to hire a few people to comb through the list of DVDs and pull data for all the categories we wanted. There were fewer than a thousand DVDs available, so it was possible.

But we only had twelve employees. We had more than enough to do, so our time was a precious resource. But money? We had a bunch of that. So I started looking for other options. My thinking was that if we could buy it rather than build it, then we should buy it.

Big mistake.

Michael Erlewine is, according to his current Wikipedia page, "an American musician, astrologer, photographer, TV host…and Internet entrepreneur" who founded, in 1991, the All Music Guide (now known as AllMusic). Back in 1998, all I knew was the last part. I'd come across All Music Guide's sister site, All Movie Guide, when I was looking for possible data sources.

I didn't know that Michael had hitchhiked with Bob Dylan, or that he'd been in a blues band with Iggy Pop. I didn't know that he was the author (at the time) of five books on astrology, with titles like *Tibetan Earth Lords: Tibetan Astrology and Geomancy*. I just knew that he had something I wanted: data.

I had something he wanted, too. DVDs.

The goal of All Movie was to compile a detailed catalogue of every film ever made. Erlewine had dozens of employees tracking down, watching, and annotating movies around the clock. Visitors to his website could find the most arcane information about any movie they had ever heard of — and thousands they hadn't.

The problem was that he had no DVDs. An inveterate completist, Erlewine didn't just want detailed information about every movie ever made. He wanted it about every *format* of every movie ever made. For DVDs, he wanted to know what special features were available, which languages were included, the screen ratios, and whether or not there was 5.1 surround sound.

All the information he needed was right there on the DVD case, but distributors weren't really selling to private consumers. So Erlewine's problem was even more profound than ours as we tried to build out our inventory. Because there were so few retail stores that even carried DVDs, acquiring a library of every title would require thousands of hours, hundreds of miles of travel, and a good slug of chance.

We began discussing a deal. We'd give him money — and DVDs — in exchange for his data.

I love negotiation, and I'm pretty good at it. In large part this is because it's easy for me to identify with other people's needs. I'm able to understand what another party in a negotiation wants, what they need — and how they feel about getting it. Because I can quickly identify what the other side wants, I'm able to strategize more efficiently about how we can come to a mutually beneficial solution.

With Erlewine, though, things didn't go so smoothly over the phone. I knew what he wanted, he knew what I wanted, but I had a harder time understanding his reluctance to meet in the middle. Making a deal would help both of us, and our phone calls were cordial — but he kept stalling. He seemed reluctant to come to an agreement, and I couldn't figure out why.

So I flew out to meet him in person. One Tuesday that winter, I got on a plane bound for Grand Rapids, Michigan. When I landed, I rented a Subaru and drove north, to Big Rapids. I was expecting an office park, a corporate HQ, maybe even some good-sized rapids behind the building. But the address Michael gave me belonged to a big house in a residential neighborhood, with not a ripple in sight. Pickup trucks were parked in every driveway. Flanneled men were shoveling snow from their yards. I parked in a circular drive, in front of a three-story colonial that had been modified and joined to several other houses in the immediate vicinity. Covered breezeways connected several of the adjoining houses. I saw people hurrying from building to building, carrying cardboard boxes and, in one instance, a reel-to-reel projector. It looked like a commune, maybe a cult.

I was a world away from our sterile office park in Northern California.

Michael gave me a tour of the premises. At the time he was lean and wiry; undoubtedly from a diet high in kale, yogurt, and granola. He wore an open-neck shirt that showed some kind of necklace. He was direct, soft-spoken, and leaned in when he made a point, listening carefully to what I said in response. I expected at any moment for him to shake his head slowly and murmur, "Ah hah, just what I thought. Taurus with Aries ascendant." But then he could shut off quickly if things weren't going the way he wanted. Conveniently, he seemed guided by an external force, a higher power that was actually in charge.

Negotiating a compromise was not something he could do, since he was, in fact, only the messenger. He would have to check with his boss before deciding.

If the exterior of the All Movie HQ resembled a commune, the interior was like being inside an OCD record collector's head. Every square inch of wall space was covered by floor-to-ceiling shelves filled with LPs, compact discs, and tapes. The rooms had clearly been improvised into working spaces. The first room we poked our head into had three desks, one in each corner. The woman at the desk closest to the door was holding the liner notes to an LP up to a small lamp, a foreign-language dictionary open in front of her. "Norwegian folk music," she said.

In the next room, a man was going through a huge stack of *Daily Variety* from the 1930s.

"What are you looking for?" I asked.

"Filming announcements," he said. "I'm trying to correlate shooting dates."

"He's capturing data on films that never even got made," Michael said proudly.

The tour took nearly an hour. I saw three or four buildings, all filled with these detail-obsessed scriveners. One building, a former garage, was particularly loud. "That's the woodshop," Michael said, opening the door. Saws, pallets, stacks of lumber. And dozens of identical six-foot bookshelves.

They acquired so many books, records, and films that they manufactured their own shelving.

We didn't reach a deal that day or in the weeks that followed. We parried over the silliest details. As soon as I had met one of his demands, he would come up with another one. In one sense, I knew exactly how to appeal to Erlewine. For all his sites' rhetoric about being the world's leading repository of information about music and movies, my visit to

Michigan had taught me something valuable: Erlewine was a hoarder. His *real* motivation wasn't information: It was collecting. He'd cannily found a way to monetize his obsessions, and he needed my DVDs more than he needed my money.

But even with DVDs in hand, I suspected that there was another reason Michael was holding out: He was paranoid about his data. My proposal was that we would use his movie data — release date, cast, and so on — as the bedrock for our own entries. We would append all the DVD-specific information and send that back to him. But Erlewine insisted that *he* be the one to add the DVD data and then send it to us.

I liked the idea of him doing more of the work, but the deal breaker was his insistence that, in the end, he would own *all* of the data. Even though it was our participation that had made this data possible. This was unacceptable to me. We would be building our entire website infrastructure on top of that data, and were he to decide, in a fit of astrologically induced pique, that he didn't like us or our terms, or the way Aries was ascending, he could easily take his crystal ball and go home, leaving us with nothing. We would be royally screwed. And I didn't need to read any tea leaves to make that prediction. An early-stage startup is a delicate ecosystem, in which competing pressures — investor expectations, market realities, and plain-old plausibility — push in from all sides. I didn't need yet another outside force dictating our progress.

I recognized Erlewine's anxiety. It was the same anxiety that many people felt during the internet boom. His services — both All Music and All Movie — had begun as print publications. They'd been analog. The transition to digital made him uneasy. He was sitting on his hoard, and he didn't want anyone to take it away.

Eventually, I started to get exasperated. Under Erlewine's plan, we'd be paying him for the privilege of learning about DVDs we technically owned. But I also knew that he had us over a barrel. We were the ones under a time crunch, and he had the information we wanted. The site was launching in just a few months, and we needed the data he had to even begin to build the database that would power our site.

I stalled. I hemmed and I hawed. Every day, as January flowed into February, Christina and Eric badgered me. We needed the data to be able to build a model of the database. We were writing our own blurbs, adding the movies to "collections," and making other editorial decisions, but all of our content needed to be attached to a root record. Even if we finished the content well before launch date, we knew there were days — if not weeks — of effort to actually connect our content with Erlewine's. We couldn't just plug everything in the day before launch.

There was another problem. Even if we could get a deal, the amount of data he would be sending our way was so massive — especially in 1998 — that it couldn't be done over the internet. We'd receive the data in a pretty analog fashion: reels of magnetic tape. Forget email: this data would have to be shipped to us in a box. That was another reason we needed all the time we could get: once we had the tape in hand, we'd have to "translate" it, teaching our site how to "read" it.

The contract Erlewine had drawn up was completely unacceptable. I hated it. But I had to sign it.

He won.

But the second I signed that contract, I started thinking of ways to get out of it.

I have to hand it to the guy: Michael Erlewine found a way to monetize his obsessive-compulsive hoarding. That company ran according to his principles — it resembled him. Sure, walking through their "offices" was like taking a tour of the inside of an obsessive record collector's skull — but the place had an ethos. It had an identity.

It was not anywhere in the same *ballpark* of how I wanted my company to look, feel, or behave — but it worked for him.

My own approach has always been more measured. I think people are more productive when they're happy, when their lives outside of work aren't totally subsumed by their job. I'm the guy who wanted to put the company in Santa Cruz, remember? I'm the guy who wanted a short commute, and the opportunity to go surfing in the morning before work.

It was a given that once we started working to make Netflix a reality, the hours would be long. All of us knew that, because all of us were Silicon Valley veterans. We'd done the fifty- or sixty- or seventy-hour workweek before. The difference was that this time, we were choosing to do it. We weren't working for someone else's dream. We were working for ourselves.

So yes, I sometimes slept on a couch in the office. And yes, I once saw one of our coders taking a bird bath in the men's restroom. I won't pretend that my diet in the fall of 1997 consisted of much more than takeout eggplant parm (a steal at $6.95) from the Italian place across the street.

But when I needed a morning off, to mountain bike and clear my head, I took it. When Te wanted to chew over PR stunts during a manicure, she booked an appointment.

Nowadays, they call that "self-care." Back then, we just called it common sense. If we were going to try to fundamentally change an entire industry, we needed to have our wits about us.

Even in the trenches of pre-launch Netflix, I kept to a long-standing tradition with Lorraine. On Tuesdays, no matter what, I left the office *promptly* at 5:00 and spent the evening with my wife. We'd hire a babysitter, go for a walk on the beach, and then head to our favorite restaurant, Bittersweet Bistro, for some roasted salmon and a few glasses of wine. Sometimes we'd hit the theater in downtown Santa Cruz and catch a movie.

I needed that time with Lorraine — just the two of us, no kids, no domestic duties. I needed to recharge, to be with my best friend for a few hours and not think about anything else.

I'd instituted date night at Borland, where it wasn't unusual for workers to stay until seven or eight o'clock at night, *regularly*. At first, I didn't mind the long hours — it was just how things worked. But after a few months I feared burnout, and I also worried that I wasn't prioritizing my relationship with my wife. Especially once we had kids, so much of our time together was dominated by family: sports practices, family dinners, getting the children ready for school or sleep. I wanted to make sure that the two of us stayed connected.

Once I'd instituted Tuesday date night, I was fiercely protective of it. Five o'clock was a *hard* deadline. The moment the second hand hit the 12, I was out of there. Last-minute crisis? Too bad. An emergency meeting that could only be held at 4:30? Better make it short. Need to talk to me about something at 4:55? It would have to be on the walk to my car.

At first, this occasioned some conflict. But eventually, after people got the memo — and after I'd remained firm in the face of numerous challenges — my colleagues knew not to schedule anything that would conflict with my deadline. They both respected and worked around it.

In the fall of 1997, as we built our company, it would have been easy for me to break the Tuesday night tradition. There were so many things to do, so many problems to solve. And I had my hand in hundreds of them. My usual routine was to hit the office at around seven in the morning, eat lunch at my desk, and work all afternoon, until six or so. Then I'd drive the five minutes back to my house to be home in time for dinner with my kids. I'd help Lorraine put them to bed, and then, more often than not, I'd head back to the office for a few hours, eventually quitting around ten or eleven.

Then back home, for some winding down and a few hours of sleep. I think I was averaging about five hours a night in those days — often less.

One night when I came home for dinner, my son Logan greeted me at the door and, instead of a hug, said he had a question to ask me.

"Sure, Logan. What's up?"

He studied me for a moment, staring hard at the backpack I was shrugging off my shoulders.

"Is the bacon in there?"

I cocked my head. "What do you mean?"

"Mom said you were bringing some home," he told me.

It took me a second, and then I got it. I couldn't stop laughing for about five minutes.

Lorraine told me later that when the kids asked where I was in those days, she'd say one of two things: that I was bringing home the bacon or climbing the corporate ladder. She only stopped saying it when Logan told some of his friends at school that his dad climbed ladders for a living.

"You're not a housepainter, after all," she said.

Still, a part of me thinks that Logan was right. Those early days, pre-launch, were like climbing a long, endless ladder. There was a problem to deal with at every rung, and each time we solved one, we were one step closer to our goal. We were moving up, and it was thrilling to think of how high we could go.

But no matter how high I'd climbed, or how many steps I saw ahead of me, I always left the office at 5:00 p.m. sharp on Tuesdays. I didn't want to be one of those successful entrepreneurs who are on their second or third startup but also on their second or third spouse. Saving a night for my wife kept both of us sane and in tune with each other.

By November of 1997, we had an office. We had a semifunctional website that we were testing. We had dozens of mailer prototypes. We had the beginning of an inventory. We even had a launch date: March 10, 1998.

What we didn't have was a name.

This is often the case for early-stage startups. Most companies don't keep the same name from ideation to funding to launch. Names are important, and sometimes they take forever to find. Amazon was originally called Cadabra. Twitter started off as Status.

You have to allow for serendipity, for the right name to come along as you develop your service. Sometimes that takes months. But in the meantime, you typically have a beta name, a working title that you use to test your site, set up email accounts, and write on bank documents. And it can't just be *The Untitled Marc Randolph Project.*

Our beta name was Kibble. As in dog food.

Steve Kahn once advised me that when it came time for us to choose our beta name, I should choose something so bad it wouldn't be possible to use it for real. "Six months in," he said, "and you'll be so fried that you'll want to just say, *'Screw it, let's keep the beta name.'* Your sense of what's good and what's bad will be almost entirely depleted. But if you pick something so awful that it's obviously impossible — WeWantToRipYouOff.com, GiveUsAllYourMoney.net — you'll be forced to come up with something new."

That's why, months into our new offices, we were called Kibble.

Our bank statements said Kibble. The website we were testing had the domain name kibble.com. My email address was marc@kibble.com.

Kibble had been my idea. It came from an old advertising and marketing adage: *It doesn't make a difference how good the ads are if the dogs don't eat the dog food.* The idea was that no matter how much sizzle you'd given the steak — no matter how well you'd sold it — nothing mattered if the product was lackluster. It doesn't matter how brilliant your ad campaign for Alpo is if your dog won't eat it.

I'd picked Kibble as a working name because I thought it would remind us to focus on the product. Ultimately, we had to build something people would love. We were going up against some big guns, and we'd never succeed long-term if our service wasn't something people wanted to use — if the dog food we were selling wasn't tasty.

And it didn't hurt that I already owned the domain name. Still do, in fact. Type kibble.com into a web browser and you'll end up on my personal website. Send an email to marc@kibble.com and you'll find yourself in my in-box.

We'd never planned on using Kibble as the name for our service. But Steve was right — as the months went on and the launch date got closer and closer, Kibble was starting to look pretty good.

"Team meeting," I finally said, one Friday afternoon. "We've got to decide on a name."

The entire company — all fifteen of us — filed into my office. Soon after we'd moved into the building, Christina and I had written two columns on the whiteboard. One was filled with words related to the internet. The other was filled with words related to movies. We'd decided that the best name for our company would combine two words: one related to movies, one related to the internet. The best name would combine both terms seamlessly, with a minimum of syllables and letters.

Picking a name is incredibly difficult. For one thing, you need something catchy, something that rolls off the tongue and is easy to remember. One- or two-syllable words are best — and ideally, the emphasis be should on the first syllable. Think of the most popular website names: *Goo*-gle. *Face*-book. These names open with a bang.

Too many syllables, too many letters, and you run the risk of people misspelling your website. Too few letters, and you risk them forgetting the name.

And then there's the issue of what's available. It doesn't matter if you find the perfect name, if someone else already owns the domain or the trademark.

For the past several weeks, I'd invited anyone who had an idea to come add it to the board. I'd already done most of the legwork about availability, trademarks, and the like. Now it was time to make a decision. As the afternoon wore on and the shadows lengthened on the floor, we batted around names, matching up syllables from one column to the other. I've reproduced our final list of names below:

- TakeOne
- TakeTwo
- SceneOne
- SceneTwo
- Flix.com
- Fastforward
- NowShowing
- Directpix
- Videopix
- E-Flix.com
- NetFlix
- CinemaCenter
- WebFlix
- CinemaDirect
- NetPix

There are some real gems here. Directpix.com. NowShowing. E-Flix.com.

We were almost CinemaCenter.

Everyone had a name they liked. Boris and Vita were big fans of my black Lab, Luna, who often visited the offices, and they favored the oblique name Luna.com. It had nothing to do with our service, but it was only four letters long. Jim liked NowShowing. Christina liked Replay.com.

I liked Rent.com. I thought it had, of all the names, the best connection to the idea of renting movies, but I hadn't even added it to the board. Not only did it not say anything about the internet, but somebody else already owned the domain, and it would have cost me $40,000 to buy it. That seemed like a fortune at the time.

All of us — and I mean all of us — initially shied away from Netflix

.com. Sure, it was two syllables. And sure, it satisfied both criteria, movies and internet. But there was a lot of worry in the office about the connotations of "*flix.*"

"It just makes me think of porno," Jim said at our meeting. "Skin flicks."

"Plus, that *x*," Christina added.

"We've got to settle on something," said Te. She'd been almost tearing her hair out. We were just a few months from launch, and she still had to design a logo. "We've got to just decide."

So we did. There was no vote, no momentous ballot-casting. We printed out that spreadsheet and stared at it. Everyone went home to sleep on it. The next day, we all agreed: we were NetFlix.com.

It wasn't perfect. It sounded a little porn-y. But it was the best we could do.

8.

Ready for Launch

(zero hour: April 14, 1998)

SPEAKING OF PORN, A week before the Netflix launch, Steve Kahn invited Reed, Lorraine, and me for dinner.

Wait. It's not what you think.

"You're probably running on fumes at this point," Steve said when he called me. "I just got some new buttkickers I've been dying to test out. We'll have a nice dinner, drink some wine. You can tell me what you're worried about and I'll be reassuring."

"Buttkickers?"

"Huge subwoofers," Steve said. "I put 'em under the floor and attached them to the joists. Makes the whole room vibrate."

It was a Tuesday night, so our usual babysitter could cover for us, and even though the point of date night was to get away from work — to get away from members of the Netflix board like Reed and Steve — by that time, a week pre-launch, it was almost impossible for me to ever fully leave the Netflix offices behind. Even when I wasn't there physically, my mind returned to the offices, looking for solutions to all the little problems we needed to fix before going live.

Steve knew that. He'd known me a long time. He knew I wouldn't be able to truly take a break, so he decided to help any way he could — by at least giving Lorraine a night off.

"Only thing you have to bring is a DVD," he said.

Easy enough. Before I left the office for the day, I swung by the vault, and, without looking, grabbed the top DVD case on the pile of new releases that had just arrived that morning.

I really needed a break. So did Lorraine. "Morgan's been driving me nuts," she said in the car, on the way to Los Altos. "She spent all afternoon stealing lipstick out of my purse and trying to eat it."

This sounded almost unbearably cute to me, but I understood.

Steve lived on the east side of Los Altos, on a street crowded with gigantic new houses. His house wasn't that big, but it was nice. I mean *really* nice. *Architecture Digest* nice. And it displayed (tastefully, of course) all the trappings of wealth that a long, successful career in business afforded.

"I don't think you need to lock the doors," Lorraine said sarcastically as I parked the car. "Not in this neighborhood."

Steve greeted us at the door with glasses of wine, healthy pours of Cabernet (for me) and Chardonnay (for Lorraine). He gave us a tour through impeccably decorated rooms. Two things stand out in my memory: a wall in the study that was covered entirely with bird's-eye maple cabinetry, and a living room filled with modernist furniture that looked straight out of *Beetlejuice*. It was the first time I'd seen more than one Eames chair in the same room.

"The furniture museum is Karen's territory," Steve said when his wife was out of earshot. "I don't know what any of this crap is."

Throughout this tour, I smelled cooking. But Steve and Karen were with us — who was watching the stove? It wasn't until we repaired to the bar for finger food that I saw the white coat of a caterer, disappearing through the swinging doors to the kitchen. This was a first for me: I'd never been to a dinner party with a hired chef.

When Reed and his wife arrived, Steve lifted his empty wineglass. "Cocktails in the garage!" he said, laughing. Within thirty seconds a tray of gin and tonics appeared, carried by a smiling waiter, and Steve took us out to the garage to show off his new Porsche. I'm not really a car guy, but I know when to make appreciative noises. And it wasn't just the Porsche — there was also a full home gym: gleaming, brand-new exercise machines, a treadmill, a stationary bike, all of it atop racquet-club-quality rubber mats. Though he was a decade older than I was, Steve was probably in better shape. Back at Borland, Steve's fortieth birthday resolution had been to run every day on his lunch break, for forty days in a row. And to take me, wheezing, along with him.

Drink in hand, I wondered if all of this — the car, the furniture museum, the caterers in the kitchen — was in my future, too. I thought of my beat-up Volvo, dog toys in the backseat; the house with a leaky roof I couldn't at that moment afford to repair; the stained green carpet of the Netflix offices, which had begun to exude a peculiar stench the closer we got to launch day.

It seemed unlikely. Or at least far, far in the future.

There was still about a half hour before the cooks would be done with dinner. So while Lorraine and Karen poured more glasses of Chardonnay and discussed our kitchen renovations, Steve, Reed, and I repaired to the back deck.

"Bring a suit?" Steve asked.

And that's how I ended up in borrowed Hawaiian swim trunks, bobbing in a saltwater pool, in an impromptu board meeting with two of Netflix's earliest investors.

"There are a ton of things I'd do if we had more time," I said. "For instance, we want to do a thing called The List, which would let you save a list of titles that you want to watch. Mitch has this idea to have a digital clerk who helps you find movies he knows you'll like."

"Makes sense," Steve said, resting his wineglass on the side of the pool. "Every time I go to Hollywood Video I just ask the kid with the nose ring what to rent. The other guy always gives me French New Wave crap."

Reed wasn't really saying anything, but I could tell that he was thinking. About what, who knew. By spring of '98 he'd gotten tired of his classmates at Stanford and had been focusing most of his energy running a different venture: Technology Network. TechNet was a lobbying group that combined Reed's two overriding passions: the tech world and educational reform. It pushed for better protections for tech companies against lawsuits from shareholders, easier visa requirements for foreign tech workers, and improvements to math and science education. Reed was a big believer in charter schools and was using the group to advocate for them, donating money to a growing number of politicians.

Frankly, he had enough to worry about. But I was still relieved when he dunked his head underwater and swam to the other end of the pool. I didn't want his laser focus on any of Netflix's problems. Due to Michael Erlewine, we'd already missed one launch date — it was now April 14 rather than March 10 — and I didn't want Reed to think that we'd have any problem meeting the second one.

As Reed began swimming laps, his six-foot frame gliding through the water like a seal, I told Steve about the version of The List we'd actually been able to construct, under our deadline. Like a lot of our quick fixes, it wasn't built to last. Christina had come up with it: a button a user could push that would flag a movie you were interested in, so that next time you saw it, an icon would appear. The icon? A finger with a red thread wrapped around it.

"The engineers hate it," I told Steve. "They call it the Bloody Finger."

We laughed. And for a moment, the stress of the previous weeks melted away. We had a deadline, sure. We had people counting on us: investors to satisfy, employees to pay, and customers to reach. But when it was all said and done, we were a website that gave people access to DVDs. We weren't changing the world like Reed was. We'd fix the Bloody Finger. But for the moment, it was okay.

After drying off and having dinner — mussels in some kind of sauce, a fish that Steve assured me wasn't really endangered, all washed down by a wine I couldn't pronounce the name of — we headed to Steve's home theater, adjoining the living room. It had been a while since I'd seen it, and he'd made a number of modifications. There were huge leather chairs with massive arms (and cupholders), each separate from each other. Each of them was nicer than anything in my house — and he had twelve of them! He'd installed track lighting in the aisle, just like a real movie theater. The screen was easily eight feet across and took up a full wall, and the projection system hung down from the ceiling. Steve pointed out speakers: tall ones on stands at the front of the room, two massive ones at the back, and a center speaker in the middle of the room that Steve said was just for dialogue. Steve then gestured at one of the seats, second row, slightly left of center. "That seat? That's the money seat," he explained. "Everything is balanced, faded, and toned so that it sounds perfect in that one spot."

Karen started up the popcorn machine just outside the screening room, and I took a look inside the replica candy case that stood by a refrigerator stocked with sodas.

Mounds bars. My favorites.

"So, Marc, you got a movie for us?" Steve asked, once we all had our concessions.

"Sure," I said, fumbling in my backpack until I found it. "I don't know anything about it, but it just came in today. One of this week's featured releases."

Steve saw the cover. "Oh, right, *Boogie Nights*! I remember hearing that was good."

"Worth a shot," I said. I felt good: relaxed, full of wine and seafood and the reassurances of a friend. I sat down in one of the front-row recliners, next to Lorraine. Steve took the money seat, next to Karen. Reed took the row behind them.

The lights went down, the curtain went up, and we watched Dirk Diggler let it all hang out in crystalline, DVD-quality resolution, across an eight-foot screen.

At first I was horrified. Then I laughed until I cried.

"Let's hope your content team knows more about your inventory than you do," Lorraine said.

I had to agree.

That night with Steve Kahn taught me a thing or two about the virtues of preparation. But I've learned most of my lessons on that subject outdoors — particularly, in the mountains.

It's definitely not a place that you can take lightly.

There are river crossings, where a single missed step can plunge you into water that was snowmelt only hours before. If the cold doesn't get you, then it will rush you downstream and stuff you permanently beneath a submerged outcropping or felled tree or, failing that, trap your leg in the rocks and bend you backward, buffeting you up and down until you finally lose the strength to hold your head above water.

There are snowfields. To cross them, you have to step with enough force to forge a solid platform. But it's entirely possible that once you've committed your weight to a step, your platform will give out without warning, leaving you sliding downhill at increasing speed, hoping that you will be able to arrest your slide with your ice ax before you plunge at high speed into the rock-filled moat that forms the boundary between snow and earth.

There are cliffs. To climb them, you must make a pact with the rock, promising to linger on each hold only as long as it takes to move to the next one, the cliff warranting that the tiny edge of rock you have grasped and staked your life on will support your weight. Until it doesn't, and with sudden and unexpected consequences, you're hurtling down, your fall unobstructed until it's broken by the jagged piles at the base of the cliff.

There are dangerous animals like bison, cougars, and grizzlies; poisonous plants, berries, and mushrooms; you risk infections, lacerations, contusions, concussions, and dislocations. There are avalanches, rockslides, mudflows, and icefalls. There are blizzards, downpours, hailstorms, and sudden freezes.

There are countless ways nature can tell you that you are unwanted, alone, and far from medical attention.

But probably the scariest risk in nature's repertoire is lightning. When you're in the mountains, weather moves fast. One moment, the sky is clear and cloudless, and the next it's dark, filled with angry clouds. Is there anything more biblical than a bolt of energy that comes crashing down from the clouds without warning? In an instant, lightning can turn a towering Douglas fir into a blazing birthday candle. And when you're up high, it's certainly no consolation to know that lightning aims for the highest point around — whether that be a tree, rock pile, sailboat mast, ice ax, or head. Lightning doesn't discriminate based on your religion, your educational background, your sexual orientation, how much money you have, or how many pounds you can bench-press. All it knows is that you are out in the open, unaware, and, for at least that particular moment, the fastest and easiest way to move 10 billion watts of potential energy in a single release from turbulent cloud to the ground. If it has to go through your head, down through your organs, and out through the soles of your feet in order to do so...well, then that's just your bad luck.

To maintain your sanity in the mountains, you can't dwell on these things. But the best mountaineers aren't quite sane. I'm no climbing legend or anything, but when I'm at elevation, I'm always asking myself, "What is going to go wrong?" If I have to cross a stream, it's only after I've hiked a few hundred yards downstream to see if there is anything there that might trap me should I lose my footing and be swept down that way. I'm looking for tree limbs on the bank I can grab, areas where the current eddies out into a gentle swirl, so I know what to swim toward. And as I start wading across the stream — or start my way across the log that spans the creek — I'll have loosened the waist belt on my pack. It makes it harder to carry, but infinitely easier to shed should I need to swim.

That's what it's like being in a startup. You spend a lot of time thinking about what might happen. And preparing for it. Sometimes you actually put a backup plan in place, but most of the time you just think through how you will respond — you scout out the rivers for rocks, check out the cliffs for things to grab onto if you fall. Most of the time, the worst doesn't come to pass. But when it does...when the shit *really* hits the fan? Well, you're going to be the guy with the pail and the mop. And wearing a raincoat. And that's the kind of thing that makes the difference between being a success and being the guy who is covered with shit.

Sometimes, as we learned on Netflix launch day, there is no difference. You're both.

On the morning of the Netflix launch, I woke up early — around five. Lorraine mumbled in her sleep as I quietly slid on my slippers and shut the door behind me. The kids would be up in two hours or so, but until then I had the house to myself. In the predawn darkness, I dodged hammers and granite samples in the still unfinished kitchen. It was the last room in the house to be remodeled, and we hadn't gotten very far yet. The décor was straight out of 1971: fluorescent lights, avocado-green cabinets, peeling linoleum over the wood floors.

There was still some coffee in the pot from the previous day, and after heating it up in the microwave, I drank it standing in the kitchen, feeling my mind boot up. I made a new pot, scooping ground coffee into a filter and pouring water into the reservoir of our coffeemaker. It was ostensibly for Lorraine, but I'd probably drink half of it before she got up. I'd need every bit of the caffeine.

In the six months since Reed had written that check, we'd done so much — we'd assembled an inventory, put together a website, built a company with a culture. We'd worked tirelessly to make our dream of an e-commerce site for DVDs a reality.

But up until now, it still had the feeling of an unresolved dream.

The site existed for us — but not for anyone else. The problems we anticipated — and we'd racked our brains anticipating them — were still in the future. We weren't even sure if we'd identified the right problems. The successes, too, were in the unrealized days and months ahead.

There are a great many stages in the life cycle of a startup. But a tectonic shift happens on launch day. Before you go live, you're in the dreamy zone of planning and forecasts: your efforts are provisional. You're making predictions about what can go wrong and what can go right. It's a very creative, heady sort of work. It is essentially optimistic.

The day your site launches, something shifts. Your work now is no longer predictive and anticipatory: it's fundamentally reactive. Those problems you anticipated? You didn't know the half of it. Your planned solutions? They're a drop in the bucket. And there are hundreds — thousands — of issues that you could have never even imagined, and now have to deal with.

That morning, watching the sun rise over the mountains, I was positioning the various teams in my mind, imagining what the day would bring for Jim Cook's crew, for Eric's programmers, for Te and the marketing squad. I ran through the day's plan: the 9:00 a.m. launch, the morning full of press calls, the process of order to shipment.

In other words, I was doing what I'd been doing since the summer of 1997: strategizing. Before you launch, you're making a beautiful battle plan, coordinating the future movements of your troops.

The second you launch, you're in the fog of war.

I got to the office at seven or so in the morning and called our standard daily meeting. Christina, Te, Jim, Eric, and I filed into the conference room to go over the day's schedule.

"We've got press calls starting at nine," Te told me.

For months, Te had been lining up reporters and news outlets who would be interested in writing a story about our startup, hitting her

Rolodex hard so that when our launch day came, people would read about it. All morning I'd be on the phone with these reporters, giving them a pretty canned speech that I'd spent hours trying to make sound natural.

Here's an excerpt:

With this morning's launch of the nation's first internet DVD rental store, every DVD owner — no matter where he lives, no matter how far he lives from a video rental store — is now guaranteed access to every DVD title available — to buy or to rent.

"Who's first?" I asked.

"Steve Perez at the *Santa Cruz Sentinel*," Te said.

Starting with the hometown paper wasn't coincidental. My strategy is always to start with a softball. For your first call, there's nothing like having a friendly voice on the other end of the line.

(And in this case it paid off. Unlike the *San Francisco Chronicle* or Yahoo!, two of the other outlets that covered us, the *Sentinel* gave us prominent coverage, with a photo. Somewhere in my files there's a faded full-page newspaper clip from the day after our launch, featuring a photo of a very late-nineties iteration of me, complete with a pager clipped to my belt, standing next to a Gateway and a mess of cables and wires. The lede?

Still trying to figure out how to program your VCR? Trash it then. Videotapes are as passé as Grandpa's Polaroids.)

"Great," I said, running over my lines in my head. I knew that whatever happened, I'd have to project cheerful calm through the mouthpiece of my telephone. Bombs could go off, the servers could catch on fire, and the site could crash — but I'd just have to close my eyes and keep going.

Netflix makes it incredibly easy to rent a DVD. There's no driving. No searching for parking. No standing in line. We even make it easy to return it. And we're open 7 days a week, 24 hours a day.

We went over, one last time, the process for Jim's team.

"Order comes in," Jim said, "and once we've got credit card authorization, it goes to the printer in the safe. My team finds the disc, slips it into the sleeve, and scans it once to pull it from inventory. Then it's off to Dan. Dan inserts the promo sheet, seals things up, slaps the labels on, and scans it again to show it's shipping. Then into the bin and ready to mail."

Jim was still smiling that stupid grin, but I could tell he was nervous. He'd spent weeks streamlining his process, checking it for flaws and inefficiencies. But there was only so much he could do without the pressure of real orders coming from the site. And one of the big problems was that we had no clue how many orders we'd get on launch day. Five or ten? Twenty or thirty? A hundred?

Corey had been working overdrive on the message boards, pumping Netflix up to tech nerds and cinephiles, and he'd continue to do so throughout the day. But how many orders was that? I wasn't holding my breath for big numbers.

Eric and his team — Boris, Vita, Suresh, and Kho — looked inscrutable. Whether they were nervous or not, I couldn't tell. Most of the stress of the day fell on their shoulders, of course. They'd anticipated all sorts of problems with the site, and they'd formulated any number of solutions to those problems. But they knew that things would go wrong that they hadn't expected, and so the day, for them, was going to unroll in a flurry of Mountain Dew and pizza slices. Eric barked out a few largely incomprehensible reminders to his team, and I took that as an opportunity to look them over. Boris and Vita appeared the same as ever, unflappable and calm. Kho looked like he'd dressed up for the launch: clean black T-shirt, somewhat clean-looking black jeans. His hair looked combed.

Christina was nervous. She'd planned for this day for months. She had hundreds of pages, in dozens of notebooks, detailing the site's operation — how a user would interact with it, what would happen if they made a mistake. Her team had spent many hundreds of hours integrating our own movie content with Michael Erlewine's back-of-the-box data, building informative, interesting entries for all 925 films in our archive. I could see her team through the conference room window, still manually scanning the cover images of the last few DVD boxes to be uploaded onto the site. To them, it was just another day of their usual work. But to Christina, whose understanding of the website's logistics far surpassed anyone else's, it was a stressful day.

"You know," she told me, "this is our fifth launch together?"

It was true. We'd launched a whole series of PaperPort scanners at Visioneer together. And each of us, individually, had dozens of other launches under our belt. But that was then. After all, in software and packaged goods, when the actual launch day arrives, you're already past the point of no return. The product has been finished for weeks — it's come out of the factory, it's made its way into boxes, it's on trucks going out across the country. Launch day is just a press day.

"I feel like this is going to go somewhat differently," I said as we filed toward the bank of computers in the middle of the office workspace.

"I think you're right," Christina said.

We had no idea.

It started well. At 8:45, everyone in the office gathered in front of Eric's computer. The site was going live at 9:00, and we'd already made the rounds of preparations. Was there paper in the printers? Were all the DVDs tucked in their sleeves in the safe? Were all the i's dotted, all the t's crossed?

There were actually two versions of our website. One resided on a server that wasn't online. It was a duplicate version that Eric could use to test out new pages and features. Anything new was posted first to what was called a staging server. Then we would bang on it for a while to make sure that it worked the way we expected it to, and, more importantly, that the new additions played nicely with the rest of the site. Then, once we had some satisfaction that we weren't going to have a disaster on our hands, we would *push* the new version over to what was called a production server, which was hosting the live site.

Up until this morning, the distinction between the two sites was entirely academic. Although one was supposedly final and connected to the internet, it wasn't visible to the actual public. Although we had practiced pushing things live, and pretended we had real customers using it, there weren't any real consequences. This was all about to change.

For the hundredth time, Eric idly scrolled through on the staging site, pretending to be a customer. "It looks good, it looks good," he said, clicking on the links and filling in fields on our forms. Boris and Vita were acting nervous, too. They knew — as we all did — that things would break, and that they'd have to be on their toes to fix the site when it invariably malfunctioned. They'd planned for things to go wrong. What happened if a user entered his state abbreviation as NF rather than NC, ND, NE, NM, NV, or NY on the checkout page? What would happen if the credit card number didn't start with a 4 (for Visa) or 5 (for Mastercard), or didn't go through at all? Would we fail gracefully, or crash and burn?

One final thread that I knew was still sticking out of the seams of our startup was the confirmation email. We hadn't yet created an automated confirmation email function for users, one that would contact a customer after she placed an order and reiterate information about payment and shipping. We'd have to compose confirmation emails by hand for each individual customer. That wasn't ideal, obviously, but I figured it would be workable.

"Five minutes," Christina said at 8:55. She was drinking coffee out of a huge mug and munching on a scone. That's how I knew she was nervous — a gym rat like her usually stayed far away from buttery pastries.

"How are the nerds?" I asked Corey. He'd been on the forums all morning, reminding some of the heavier users about the Netflix launch.

He shrugged. "Hard to tell. I think they'll show up, but who knows how many."

Jim had his hands on his hips. I could see his mind going through the logistics of shipping, replaying over and over how to fill an order, pack it, and store it until 3:00 p.m. That's when the orders had to hit the post office in Scotts Valley, to ensure that they'd ship that day.

At 8:57, Te tapped my shoulder and said, "Remember, you've got a call in five. So you can watch the ball drop, but then you gotta be by the phone."

I nodded, and out of the corner of my eye saw the door open and then close. It was Reed, slipping in just before launch. I hadn't expected him to come, but I was glad to see him — and somewhat relieved that we were on schedule. He gave me a brief nod when he walked in, but he didn't say anything, just stood somewhat awkwardly behind the huddle of employees in front of the computer.

By 8:59 the office was so quiet that I could hear my watch's second hand. At 9:00 on the dot, Eric leaned over, punched a few keys, and we were live. We held our breath. Eric had hooked up a bell to his computer — not unlike the kind that businesses leave on the counter to alert employees that a customer needs help — and rigged it up so that it would ring each time an order came in. I filled out the day's first order as a test: I, Marc Randolph, requested a copy of *Casino*, to be delivered to my address outside Scotts Valley. I hit Enter to place the order, and moments later the bell rang. Almost immediately, we had three others in the queue, each sounding the bell as credit cards were authorized, inventory decremented, and packing slips printed. I patted Eric's computer for good luck and walked back to my office for press calls.

Within minutes, the bell sounded like a machine gun. Even with the door closed, even as I carried on a conversation with Steve Perez at the *Santa Cruz Sentinel,* I could hear it, pinging in the next room.

We got fifteen minutes.

For fifteen minutes, customers chose movies, inputted their personal information, gave us their credit card numbers, and hit the red button that said confirm. For fifteen minutes, the bell rang, orders were printed out on the pair of laser printers at the back of the office, and Jim's team took them to the vault. For fifteen minutes, each order was matched to its movie, the disc was slid into the mailer, and an address label slapped on. For fifteen minutes, the completed orders grew into a small stack in a box by the door.

Several months ago we recognized an opportunity to create a major commerce brand in a billion dollar market, as well as to be a critical catalyst in the growth of one of the fastest-growing consumer electronics categories. This morning, Netflix opened the world's first Internet DVD rental store: NetFlix.com. The NetFlix store carries every DVD movie — all of which are fully available for rental.

I watched it all through the glass of my office window, giddy with excitement. I'd asked Te to stay in the room with me, and to write down any questions from the press on the whiteboard I kept in my office — the same board we'd used to decide on a name. I liked to use journalists' questions as a jumping-off point for longer, more in-depth stories — even though the beginning of each call was canned, I wanted my answers to be improvisatory riffs that really got at the heart of what we were trying to do. I'd weave in American history, pop culture, and even stories from the outdoors. But I needed an anchor, a handhold to grab — hence the questions on the board, and Te standing next to it, marker in hand, like a Silicon Valley Vanna White.

Marc Randolph

*Despite phenomenal growth in the DVD market, most of the na-
tion's video outlets don't yet carry DVD — and those that do, carry
only a limited selection of titles, often a single copy of each. Netflix,
on the other hand, carries virtually every DVD. While we don't
carry X-rated titles, we do — as of this morning — list 926 titles for
rent, the largest selection available anywhere. And our warehouse
contains hundreds of copies of the most popular movies, virtually
guaranteeing that our customers can rent the movie they want,
when they want it.*

It wasn't hard to get excited, riffing about our business, that day.
I could see it through the window, right there in front of me — the
dream I'd been working on, in full color.

*At the NetFlix web site, we make it fast and easy to find the right
movies, and we deliver them in two or three days. Customers keep
them seven days and get to watch them as often as they like. When
they are finished, they simply replace the discs in the envelope we
provide and drop it in the nearest mailbox. We even pre-pay the return postage.*

Slowly, however, I started to realize that something was wrong. Eric
was frowning at his computer. Boris and Vita were typing furiously.
Suresh was down on his hands and knees, grasping at something underneath the servers. Kho was unplugging and replugging cords into
the wall, and tracing their looping trajectories up to the ceiling.

Eventually, Christina edged into the office, biting one of the few
fingernails she had left. I'd just finished chatting with Jon Swartz at the
San Francisco Chronicle.

*This is a tremendously exciting prospect for us, for our customers,
and most importantly, for the entire DVD community.*

114

I set the receiver down in the cradle. That's when I noticed it — the bell wasn't ringing.

"What happened?"

Christina rolled her eyes. "Servers crashed."

This is another problem that current startups don't really have to deal with. Now, almost every web company runs their business in the cloud. Rather than the long, laborious, and capital-intensive setup that Eric and Kho had to deal with, now companies simply write a check, buying access to somebody else's computers, stored in air-conditioned warehouses with backup power and plenty of storage. But back in 1998, cloud services didn't exist. If you wanted to run an e-commerce site — or any website with high traffic, for that matter — you had to own the means of serving up web pages, storing data, and keeping track of customer information. That meant racks of computers in your own office dedicated to hosting your website.

We'd gone into launch day with a grand total of two of them. Corey, who had spent two years at Netscape, had tried to tell me to stock up on extras. "You're going to need them," he'd said. "If not for the launch, then soon after. Why not buy in bulk, ahead of time? Don't you want to anticipate the best-case scenario?"

I did. But I think a part of me was still superstitious, worried that I would jinx the whole thing. Christina had said it best — launching the company was like throwing a party, one that you weren't sure anyone else would attend. You didn't want to buy extra kegs if no one was going to come.

But Corey had been right, of course. Two servers was like trying to cross the old West with a single mule. Wasn't going to cut it.

When I walked out of my office, Eric and Boris were gearing up to make a trip to Fry's, the electronics store over the hill in Campbell, where they'd buy eight new desktops with a whopping 64 megs of RAM each.

"That should do it," Eric said, looking unconvinced.

"What do we do in the meantime?" Christina asked. "We could be losing dozens of people."

"What a nightmare," Te said. "All these press guys are gonna go to the site and there's gonna be nothing there!"

Then Reed spoke up. It was the first time he'd said anything all morning. "Can't you just put a STORE CLOSED, COME BACK TOMORROW sign up?"

We'd grown accustomed to calling Netflix "The Store." It made sense — what we were trying to offer was an e-commerce version of what Mitch Lowe and his family were doing at Video Droid. But unlike a storefront, a website can't hang an OUT TO LUNCH sign on the door. The internet doesn't have business hours.

"Did we build an error page?" I asked.

Christina's face fell. "No," she whispered.

"Well, let's do it," I said. For the next forty-five minutes, while Eric and Boris were buying new servers, we built a cheeky "We're down but not out" page that would reassure customers that they were in the right place — and that we'd be right back.

That page got a lot of views that day.

An hour later, Kho hooked up the eight new servers, essentially quintupling our capacity for new orders. Everything worked fine — the site was up and running, the orders were flying in — for about forty-five minutes. Then the servers crashed. Again.

And again, Eric and Boris took off for Fry's. I didn't go with them, but I can imagine it even now — the two of them riding sternly to the store in the rusty pickup truck that belonged to Greg Julien, Netflix's company controller. Pushing a shopping cart directly to the computer department, then dealing with the same checkout person as they discussed among themselves whose credit card to use. That clerk had probably seen this exact thing happen dozens of times, with dozens of startups. We were in Silicon Valley, after all.

*　　*　　*

The site crashed all day. And because we had no way to measure site traffic yet, we didn't know how many potential customers we were missing.

It was a disaster. But at the same time, these were *good* problems — we had visitors to the site, we had orders coming in.

"People are coming!" I found myself saying in amazement. "They're coming to the site, and they're giving us their credit card information!"

When we'd moved into the offices, I'd bought a bottle of 1995 Ridge Estate Cabernet Sauvignon — a California wine that was about a hundred dollars more expensive than the bottles Lorraine and I usually bought. (Translation: It was $120.) I'd told everyone that we'd open it once the website had gotten a hundred orders, and took a straw poll about when the rest of the office thought that would happen. The shortest guess was from Suresh, who was working on inventory and order entry. He guessed less than a day.

I guessed a month or two.

Guess who was right?

"Good call, Suresh," I said sometime after 2:00 p.m., when the hundredth order came in. I flipped him a silver dollar, which he caught without even taking his eyes off the screen.

It's what we'd all hoped for, of course. But it still was astonishing, in the moment, to see it. As I watched the orders come in, and listened to the printer printing them out, I had an enormous sense of relief. Our big reveal hadn't been greeted by an orchestra of crickets.

It was popular. In fact, it was a bit too popular.

We ran out of boxes. We ran out of tape. We ran out of paper. We ran out of ink.

After the fortieth printer jam of the day, I walked to Corey's desk and asked him if he could slow things down a little. The servers were down, the printers were jammed, and we had Christina's entire content team typing individual confirmation emails for the orders we'd already received. (Turns out an automated email should have been higher on the to-do list.)

"Think you can hold off the nerds for a little while?" I asked.

Corey laughed. "I'll try."

He paused.

"But they're *really* into it," he said.

Increasingly, as the day went on, one deadline began to loom large: 3:00 p.m. That's when the Scotts Valley post office packed all *their* mail into their trucks and headed over to San Jose. If we wanted our DVDs to go with them, we had to have all of our shipments there — processed, packaged, and addressed — by 3:00, or the same-day shipping we'd promised our users would turn into *next*-day shipping.

That was unacceptable to Jim. But as the day went on and the orders rolled in — as the servers crashed, and the printers jammed, and Christina's team gave themselves blisters writing confirmation emails to everyone who ordered a DVD — he was getting nervous.

"If we get jammed, we can drive everything down to Santa Cruz," Jim said. "Their last pickup is at four."

Jim had done research for weeks on pickup times, post office hours, and routes. He knew that the DVDs we dropped off, presorted by destination, would travel first to San Jose, then to all of the destinations we'd seen on orders that morning — San Diego, Seattle, San Antonio. But first they had to get out of our hands.

"If I leave at two fifty-two," he said, "I can get to the Scotts Valley PO with a minute to spare. If we're not ready by then, I can go to the Santa Cruz post office — but it'll take me twenty minutes to get there, and who knows if there will be parking. So I'd have to leave at three thirty to be safe."

I knew that Jim was just thinking out loud. He'd driven to the post offices a half-dozen times in the weeks before the launch, trying to find the quickest route. Once he was there, he'd familiarized himself with the parking lot and the drop-off location. In an extreme gesture of optimism, he had even put a handcart in the back of his pickup that he could use to wheel up boxes if the orders were too heavy to carry. He'd already scouted out where the handicap ramps were, in case he needed to use them.

"You do whatever you think is best," I said. "But it would be kind of nice to use the hometown PO for the first run, wouldn't it?"

Jim nodded. We'd stepped into the vault by then, and two of Jim's team were busy flipping through the hanging discs, searching for movies to fulfill recently placed orders. I picked up an order slip from the table near the door and joined them, searching the alphabetized wall for a DVD copy of *Heat*. I walked past it several times before I saw it. I bumped into Jim's workers at least twice.

"You're hopeless, Marc," Jim said, grabbing the DVD from me and expertly shoving it into a mailer. He affixed an address label with finesse and expertly sealed the flap. "Now get out of here. We've got forty-five orders more to fill before the post office closes."

The clock on the wall of the safe read 2:24.

It was stressful until 2:52, when Jim left for the post office. Then the whole office relaxed. The day's deadline had passed. Now it was just time to figure out how to make things work better the next day.

We'd expected 15 or 20 people to use the site to order a DVD. We'd gotten 137 — and potentially we'd gotten more than that, since we didn't know how many people had tried to access the site when it was down.

It was an enormously promising start. But that's all it was: a start. There were hundreds — no, *thousands* — of changes we still needed to make.

Did we open the bottle of wine? We didn't have a corkscrew, so I had to push the cork into the bottle using a ballpoint pen, then decant into an empty liter bottle that used to hold Diet Coke. And we had to use red Solo cups instead of wineglasses. But we opened that bottle, and all shared a brief toast in the conference room. I looked for Reed but didn't see him — he'd slipped out sometime in the afternoon.

"To beginnings," I said. "To the work ahead."

And there was a lot of it. We needed to automate confirmation emails. There were dozens of problems with the online ordering form, which, it turned out, was fine at catching bad state codes. Not so good at validating zip codes. And clueless for international orders. (Who knew people would try to order from other countries!) We still needed an algorithm that would ensure that high-demand titles were always in stock — and figure out how to steer customers to lower-demand titles in a way that made them actually want to rent them.

There were thousands of puzzles to solve, and we all knew that we'd spend months solving them. So after the toast, we all crumpled our Solo cups into the recycling bin and got back to work.

Around six or so, someone ordered pizza. I left around ten. The engineers would probably be in the offices all night, working to ensure that the next day's traffic wouldn't crash the site. And of course the site didn't shut down overnight — you couldn't just turn the neon sign off and get back to work in the morning. All of us realized, then, that our work with Netflix was entering an entirely new stage.

That night, I sat again at the table in my unfinished kitchen. The kids were asleep, and so was Lorraine. I was still antsy, high on the adrenaline of the day. When I'm like that, there's no point in trying to sleep. So I pulled out my notebook and started writing down a list of all the things we needed to work on:

- Site Redundancy—how do we gracefully recover from crashes when a server goes down?
- Get better Packing slips—peel off labels keep coming off in the printer.

- *More inventory? How many is too enough? How many is too many?*
- *Need Metrics! Get Suresh to report on today's orders by source and title. What else?*

As I thought of possible solutions, I idly lined up a few slats of wood we'd left on the table. They were 120-year-old pieces of redwood that we had reclaimed from some of the house's original flooring, and Lorraine had been thinking of using them as shelving. I lifted one, felt its heft, the lines of the wood grain. I tried to imagine it on the wall behind me, which was covered in paint samples for the eventual renovation. I could almost see it.

We were still building our kitchen, even as we lived around it. Just like Netflix, I thought — we'd built it, but it wasn't finished yet. It would probably never be finished, truthfully. Every day, we'd have to work to keep it upright — to keep the water flowing, to keep the cabinets filled. To keep the burners clean and the gas bill paid.

But it was there, now. It was out in the world.

Years ago, on a climbing trip, I was hiking across a snow plain just below the summit of a mountain when I felt a peculiar static buzzing around my head. My hair stood on end, and around my helmet there was an ultraviolet glow. It was Saint Elmo's fire — a positively charged electromagnetic field that was about to discharge itself to earth. It was lightning, just before the strike.

That's how Netflix had felt, all that spring — a blue haze buzzing around all of our heads. But starting on April 14, Netflix wasn't just potential energy anymore. It was a live current, positive meeting negative. It was a lightning strike.

And now we had to figure out how to manage it.

9.

A Day in the Post-Launch Life

(summer 1998: eight weeks after launch)

5:00 A.M.

"It's your turn."

After this proclamation, Lorraine rolls over and folds the pillow over her head.

It's two months after launch. I lie in the dark, squinting at the clock radio, waiting for the onslaught. Already it's starting: There's a faint rustling coming from somewhere down the hall, then a series of soft *ploomphs*. Hunter is greeting the morning, hurling his stuffed animals over the bars of his crib. Soon he'll wedge his feet in the bars, grab the rail, and swing himself up and over, onto a landing pad of plush tigers and elephants.

Who needs an alarm clock?

I dress in the weak light, and when I step into the hall, Hunter is there to meet me, a well-loved zebra dangling from his hand by one dingy, furless ear.

"What's up, little man?" I ask as he follows me sleepily down the stairs. In the kitchen, he lifts his arms over his head and lets me hoist him up into his chair. I ritually mix cereal, bananas, and milk in a bowl and set it in front of him. He plunges his hands into the bowl and starts to eat, just as the coffee machine gives three beeps and sputters the last drops into the pot.

Perfect timing.

I sit across from Hunter and open my laptop. The morning monitors are already in my in-box.

In the weeks since launch day, we've learned to take full advantage of the data we can gather through The Store. Our website never misses a thing. Every night, just after midnight, the Netflix servers — which number twenty-four by now — systematically begin grinding through the previous day's business in order to get ready for the next. They balance accounts, adjust inventory, and reconcile payments. They read every one of the previous day's transactions from the production servers and add them to a log, creating a data warehouse. Unlike the over-crowded vault, there is nothing physical about the data warehouse. The entire thing fits onto a single hard drive.

Every customer. Every order. Every shipment of a DVD. Our data warehouse knows where every customer lives, how and when they joined, how many times they've rented from us, and how long, on average, they keep their discs. It knows exactly what time someone visited the site, where they came from, and what they did once they got there. It knows which movies they looked at and which ones they chose to put in their cart. It knows whether they completed checkout — and if they didn't, it knows where they gave up. It knows who was visiting us for the first time and who is a repeat customer.

One hard drive knows almost everything.

With so much data to consider, it's easy to get overwhelmed. That's where the monitors come in.

Monitors are data summaries: short, clear, and easy to digest. The top ten movies in both rentals and sales, how many new customers we've acquired over the previous twenty-four hours, how many orders we've received, how many of those were rentals and how many were sales. That sort of thing.

This morning's monitors — which I scan with one eye, the other trained on Hunter's slowly emptying bowl — contain good and bad news. The good is in the left column: Sales are up 50 percent over May, our first full month in business. Monthly revenue has just passed $94,000 for the month of June. With twelve months in a row like that, we'll hit one of those magic startup numbers: a million dollars of annual revenue. I make a note to myself to bring that up at our company meeting at the end of the week.

The bad news is one column over: Rental Revenue.

I wince when I see that it is still in the four digits.

And that the first digit is a 1.

We have $93,000 in DVD sales. Barely $1,000 in DVD rentals.

"Shit," I murmur to myself. Hunter looks up at me for a moment, then goes back to his cereal, oblivious to anything that isn't a banana.

I pour a second cup of coffee and ponder the numbers. One reason for the great disparity between sales and rental revenue is pricing. Customers pay $25 for a DVD but only $4 for a rental. We make six times as much selling a DVD as we do renting it once. Of course, you can only sell a DVD one time. You can *rent* it hundreds of times.

The problem is, no one is renting from us. And when we *are* able to convince someone to rent a DVD, they almost never come back for a second one.

I methodically lay out bread, peanut butter, and marshmallow fluff, and construct sandwiches for Logan and Morgan. They love it when I make their lunches, because unlike Lorraine, I let them eat garbage. I just have to balance it out with something healthy. Hence the carrots I'm slicing, my mind a million miles away now, pulling up mental images of each of our current round of promotions — imagining how I might be able to tweak the words, the graphics, or the offer itself to make a difference. To make people rent.

I barely even notice when Lorraine glides into the kitchen, an efficient hurry of noise and activity. She herds Logan and Morgan, already dressed and ready for the day, ahead of her and to their places at the table, simultaneously dishing out cereal and yogurt, shoving the lunches I've made into lunchboxes, squeezing Hunter into pants and a shirt, rounding up soccer shin pads, preschool projects, sweaters, and bathing suits — and then, seemingly within seconds, she's swept three children out the kitchen door, strapping them into their car seats in the big maroon Suburban, with a quick kiss good-bye to me.

Talk about efficiency. Talk about project management. Lorraine is a genius.

7:30 A.M.

Christina is scribbling at the whiteboard when I walk into the office. Six months ago, we used the board to brainstorm possible company names. On launch day, it was filled with journalists' questions. Now, it looks like a DVD magazine marketing department got drunk and tried for a rebrand.

- DVD Watcher?
- The Digital Bits
- DVD Express
- ~~Surround Freak~~
- DVD Resource
- Short Cinema Journal
- DVD Insider

"What's all this?" I ask, squinting to make out the names and numbers that follow each entry. "Does *Digital Bits* really have seven hundred readers?"

"Pretty sure," Christina answers, rubbing the side of her hand across one of the entries. We lost the eraser long ago. "But they're far and away the biggest. Some of these are...pretty small. *DVD Insider* has about a hundred readers."

"Let me show you something," Christina says, putting down the dry-erase marker and swiveling to her desk. She flips open her computer, types for a moment, then slides the screen toward me. "Check out all the engagement!"

The screen is filled, top to bottom, with back-and-forth web forum conversations. She points with her marker at a post halfway down the page, from a name I don't recognize: Hamilton George.

Just curious. Anyone try out that new DVD by mail company yet? Netflix? Looks like they have 100s of DVDs. Prices are pretty good, too.

"That's one of Corey's," Christina explains. "He's one of the most active members of this group."

Corey's black-ops tactics haven't stopped, post-launch. He has seventeen different personas, each of them engineered for a different site, and now that Netflix is a go, he can keep track of who is actually visiting the site and ordering from us.

Before launch, he was our pusher. Now, he is our spy.

Christina scrolls through Hamilton's comment history, reading the responses.

"People love him. Or...," she hesitates. "They love Hamilton, anyway."

I'd asked Corey once where he came up with the names for his personas.

"Celebrities," he said. "I just invert the names."

Hamilton George = George Hamilton.

Meet our spy: the perpetually suntanned star of *Love at First Bite*.

9:00 A.M.

I spend the morning in my office, going over the terms of a revised coupon deal with Toshiba and calling dry cleaners in the Santa Cruz area, because I've forgotten where, exactly, I dropped off my "New Media Outfit."

Let me explain. To understand the New Media Outfit, you need some background on one of the biggest issues we faced as a young company. Essentially, it's a version of the chicken and the egg.

How can we market a DVD rental service to people if hardly anyone owns a DVD player?

In direct marketing, if you're trying to reach a group of people, you contact a list broker and rent a list. "Give me two million DVD owner addresses," you might say, and then you do a mailing to that list. But in the case of a brand-new technology, there is no list yet. Because there are hardly any DVD players.

The big consumer electronics companies that make DVD players are in the same boat as we are, but they're rowing in the opposite direction: it's hard to convince people to buy a $1,200 DVD player when there are hardly any DVDs.

Back in January, I'd sensed an opportunity. We needed a way to reach people who owned DVD players. The manufacturers needed a way for their new customers to access DVDs. What if we could come up with a promotion that would link our interests?

In January, I'd flown to Vegas for the Consumer Electronics Show. At that time the largest trade show in the world, it made VSDA — which to me had seemed like an acid trip — look like Sunday school. Every major consumer electronics company was there. They rented out entire hotels to house their employees. The booths were the size of football fields, and they were filled with hi-tech gadgetry. Think 3-D. Think robots. Think PlayStations. Think 3-D robotic PlayStations. All months before their release dates.

In addition to Mitch, my companion through this foreign land was Kirby Kish, Christina's husband, who worked in consumer electronics and had volunteered to act as a so-called jungle guide — someone who could make introductions and show me how to navigate the complex hierarchies of the multinational conglomerates we'd be dealing with. "It's a different world, man," Kirby warned me before we stepped off the plane at McCarran International Airport. "Buckle up."

It was a true East-meets-West moment — not just because most of the companies were headquartered in Asia, or because their American offices were all on the East Coast, in suburban office parks in New Jersey. It was a difference in culture. Employees at Sony or Toshiba went to work in suits. They parked their cars in front of anonymous office parks in Secaucus or Wayne or Park Ridge and entered drab, sterile buildings with thousands of other people. They obeyed a rigid hierarchy, in which each employee had clearly delineated responsibilities and tasks to accomplish. They answered to their superiors along vast and complex chains of command. They worked from nine to five every day and got paid overtime if they stayed late. Once a month, they came to work in khakis and polos for casual Friday. But only once a month.

In other words, the ethos of a consumer electronics company was about as far from the startup mentality as possible.

That was understandable, though. Consumer electronics companies were selling products with an incredibly long lead time. From research and development to packaging to marketing to shipping, it took years to roll out a new TV, VCR, or CD player. There were quite literally hundreds of thousands of tiny decisions that had to be made, and they all had to be made in concert. Coordinating these decisions across a multinational company with tens of thousands of employees and hundreds of products took time, and more than a few product managers. We had one Christina. Sony must have had thousands.

A major challenge that the consumer electronics companies were facing was how to standardize the technology behind the DVD.

Details like storage space, dimensions, and user-facing functions were still different from company to company. To simplify things — and to prevent a format war — representatives from the three biggest companies formed an uneasy alliance, agreeing to a set of specs for the nascent technology. They called it the DVD Video Group.

The 1998 CES conference was one of the first public appearances by the DVD Video Group, and I'd been there for it. The occasion was not exactly auspicious. In contrast to the gaudy displays of the rest of the conference, there was just a small area, about the size of my kitchen at home, surrounded by a velvet rope. Inside of it, a couple of dozen people milled around, among them representatives from each of the major manufacturers: Toshiba, Sony, and Panasonic. The whole event had a kind of Yalta Conference feel — three uneasy allies, unaccustomed to collaborating with each other, circling with tiny plates of cheese.

I was angling to meet three people: Mike Fidler from Sony, Steve Nickerson from Toshiba, and Rusty Osterstock from Panasonic. Between the three, they controlled roughly 90 percent of the DVD player market. I knew that if I wanted to cut any sort of deal, I'd have to get my foot in the door with one of them.

Easier said than done. After all, I ran a seventeen-person startup that hadn't even launched yet. Nickerson, Fidler, and Osterstock worked for corporations so large they needed their own phone books. I was a gnat. They were elephants whose tails I wanted to ride.

Still, I was confident. For one thing, I was wearing the aforementioned New Media Outfit. I'd bought it for IBMs (Important Business Meetings) outside Silicon Valley — for times when I needed to wear something nicer than jeans and sneakers. I thought it was important to never be seen wearing a tie, and to also look like I could navigate entertainment circles. To that end, I'd bought a pair of greenish khaki pants, a blazer with a fluorescent glow, and a shirt with a subtle geometric print that a salesperson told me was "moiré."

It was absolutely hideous. When Lorraine saw me trying it on for the first time, she couldn't stop laughing. "You look like a chameleon," she said.

In a way, that's exactly what I was. I needed to be able to adapt to a number of different environments — media, consumer electronics, tech. Wearing the New Media Outfit — or NMO, as I sometimes called it — gave me a way to blend in with companies and entities far larger and more powerful than my own.

That afternoon I sweated through my NMO many times over. I gave every one of the manufacturers the same pitch: What if I could, in one fell swoop, eliminate their biggest obstacle to selling more DVD players? What if they could assure every one of their customers that if they bought a DVD player, they would have immediate access to every DVD available?

And then the real heart of the pitch: What if every new player they sold came with a coupon offering three free Netflix rentals?

Chicken.

Egg.

Simultaneous!

We'd get traffic to our site, and they'd help grow the DVD user base. Sounds good, doesn't it?

I got polite demurrals from all three.

"This sounds interesting," Mike Fidler said. He was a California guy. Easygoing, well dressed, and with a better haircut than most of the other suits at CES, he exuded confidence. And why shouldn't he? Mike worked for Sony, the industry leader. He told me it would be a hard sell but that he'd think about it.

Rusty Osterstock, who was in charge of the DVD operation at Panasonic, turned out to be a short man in a blue oxford shirt who looked older than his thirty-five years — one of those men who has looked like his dad since age twelve. He was noncommittal.

"Hmm," he said, maybe just because he'd seen me talking to Fidler five minutes prior. "Let's set up a call."

Steve Nickerson sounded the most interested. A former college lacrosse player, he was dressed in a style I recognized from my preppy East Coast upbringing — conservative and obviously expensive suit, glossy wingtips, a class ring from Drexel. His entire bearing was athletic and animated. I pegged him as a risk-taker.

"Let's talk," he said.

I left CES that afternoon with a pocketful of business cards, a DVD swag backpack with ten DVDs, and a head of steam. When Mitch said he had some friends he wanted to say hello to before dinner, I thought nothing of it — until we were outside, walking to a different corner of the Las Vegas Convention Center and into a parallel universe.

"Hi, Mitch!" giggled a beautiful young woman in a halter top.

"Mitch! It's been so long!" said another, pressing her impossible curves into Mitch's chest for a hug.

He just beamed. "Meet Helen," said Mitch. "And Juliet."

That's when I finally looked around me. All around, buff, suspiciously tan men walked arm-in-arm with peroxide blondes wearing a lot of makeup and not much else. A huge sign over the check-in desk read, in seductive cursive letters the color of lipstick: AVN.

AVN stood for *Adult Video News*, the trade publication for the porn industry. We were at the Adult Entertainment Expo — held, every year, the same week as CES.

Mitch, it turned out, was a veteran attendee. Years running a chain of successful video stores meant that he was well-acquainted with the porn business. He knew all the major players and was as at home here as he had been at VSDA. Over the next four hours, as I nervously stammered out my name and made copious eye contact — all the while brainstorming ways to explain the whole thing to Lorraine — Mitch glad-handed, greeting studio heads, major distributors, directors, and on-screen talent like old friends. The executives here didn't look that much different from their counterparts at CES. If it weren't for the scantily clad women flocking to Mitch, I would have thought we were still back with the suits at Sony.

"You know *everybody*," I said a couple of hours later, as we headed back to our hotel. My DVD backpack had a couple of new titles in it.

Mitch just grinned. "Pays to have friends in high places," he said.

As January turned to February and then March, I hadn't heard anything from Fidler or Osterstock. And to be honest, I wasn't all that surprised. It was a hard ask for them. Companies like Sony and Panasonic had years-long product development timelines. To put a sticker or a coupon into one of their boxes would require months of negotiation with dozens of different project leaders. Going by the normal processes, to have any chance of getting our coupon into a Sony DVD box, you'd need to start about a year ahead of time. To jump into the middle of a new release, as I was hoping, you'd have to really stick your neck out. It was a big risk for them. And CES companies didn't usually reward risk.

I still don't really know why Steve Nickerson called me. I think it was because he saw — even in the risk-averse field he worked in — an opportunity for a big risk to have big rewards. Yes, it would be a night-mare to navigate the chain of decisions. Sure, if it backfired his job might be in danger. But if a promotion with a new company called Netflix helped him connect with DVD customers, it could grow the base for a new, fledgling technology.

Plus, Nickerson worked for Toshiba, the perpetual second banana. In the CES world, Sony was the undisputed king. They didn't need to take risks. But for a company like Toshiba, always vying for market share, a risk or innovation *could* help set the company apart.

Whatever his reasoning, I'm eternally thankful to Steve Nickerson for taking the plunge. In my estimation, he's one of the single most important players in the Netflix story. Without his help, there is ab-solutely no way the company would have succeeded.

I'd flown up to New Jersey, the NMO in tow, and over the course of a few days in April, Steve and I had settled on a deal. In every DVD player Toshiba sold, they'd allow us to include a small promotional flyer, offering three free DVD rentals through our site. All a customer would have to do would be to visit Netflix.com and enter their DVD player's serial number, and they'd have three free DVD rentals.

It was a win-win. We got direct access to DVD player owners, at precisely the moment when they needed us most. And Toshiba solved its biggest problem: convincing reluctant buyers that they'd actually be able to find something to play on their new machine. The promotion was advertised right there, on the outside of the box: 3 FREE RENTALS WITH PURCHASE!

But it was more than a win-win. It was a revelation. You see, a startup is a lonely place. You are working on something that no one believes in, that you've been told time and time again will never work. It's you against the world. But the reality is that you can't really do it on your own. You need to enlist help. Bring others around to your way of thinking. Let them share in your enthusiasm. Give them the magic glasses that will let them see your vision of the future.

Steve Nickerson had glimpsed and believed. And it was already paying off. Within days, we'd seen an immediate uptick in traffic, and we knew where it was coming from. Corey, using his moniker Damon Matthews, had been listening to the chatter on the Toshiba message boards, and it seemed like our promotion was resonating with their customer base.

So why, once they used their three free rentals, weren't they coming back?

11:15 A.M.

After making a few small changes to our agreement with Toshiba — minor stuff — I call Michael Dubelko, from DVD Express. I've spent countless hours trying to convince him that we can help each other.

"It just doesn't make sense, Marc," he says. "We sell DVDs, too. Why would we partner with a competitor?"

"We just need you to push rentals," I said. "Different ball game."

"How?"

The conversation doesn't really go anywhere. It often doesn't. Sites that sell DVDs don't really want to do business with a site that could chip away at their market share.

I understand, I tell him. But I know it's possible. As I hang up the phone with Mike, I think about Steve Sickles, administrator of DVD Daily, one of the largest DVD sites, whom I'd convinced to do a deal with us over raw yellowtail at Nobu in New York City. Every mention of a movie on his site would now be a link to Netflix. I think about Bill Hunt, of *Digital Bits*, who, in a hallway of the gaming industry trade show in Atlanta, had agreed to pump our service in his editorials provided we gave him an online shout-out now and then.

Maybe the key is meeting in person.

I'm leaning back in my chair, brainstorming new places to wear the NMO — I've just tracked it down to Mission Dry Cleaners in Santa Cruz — when Eric pops his head in. "You almost ready? I've got Ishaan and Dev out front. They're ready to go, but they're both really nervous."

"Nervous? Why? Am I really that intimidating?"

Eric shrugs and tilts his palms up. "Not to me," he says. "But those guys are freaking out about everything here. They don't know what to expect from lunch with the CEO."

Nearly a year after Reed and I had mailed that Patsy Cline CD, the company is growing beyond its founding team. When it comes to hiring, I'm not just hitting my own Rolodex anymore — which means new faces. To ensure that we remain a tight-knit group, I've instituted the monthly ritual of taking all new employees out to lunch. This serves a number of purposes. At a minimum, it's a chance to get to know everybody. I'm present for nearly all of our job interviews, but it's hard to get past someone's nerves and ambitions in an interview setting, and a lunch allows me to see past all that.

More importantly, though, lunch is a chance to start imprinting culture: to explain the most important aspects of working at Netflix, what we expect of people, and what they can expect of us.

In today's lunch, though, "culture" is going to take on a different meaning. That's because I'll be eating with two of our newest engineers.

Two months in, hiring engineers is shaping up to be a bigger problem than we'd imagined. In Silicon Valley, the fight for engineers is always intense, with hundreds of companies competing for top talent. I have some experience in the recruitment fight, and over time have recognized a key truth: For most engineers, it's not about the money. That's a good thing for Netflix, since our pile of chips is quite a bit smaller than the more established companies'.

Most engineers can choose where they want to work, and the way they make their decision boils down to two questions:

1) *Do I respect the people I'm working for?*
2) *Will I be given interesting problems to solve?*

We have an answer for question #1: Eric Meyer, a certified genius who commands respect. And if you ask me, the answer to question #2 is a resounding *Yes*.

Pre-launch, I'd also counted on another recruiting advantage: Location. About 19,000 people per day commute from Santa Cruz "over the hill" to tech jobs in Silicon Valley. Probably 18,997 of them hate it. (And I can't imagine what those other three are thinking.)

I'd assumed that there would be plenty of local engineers so fed up with their commute that they would jump at the chance to take a job closer to home. I'd been so confident about it that I'd run pre-movie advertisements — HELP WANTED — in the Scotts Valley movie theater.

But I'd made a deep miscalculation. I had assumed that we would need a lot of "front-end" engineers — people with the skills to build web pages designed for e-commerce. But it turns out that what we really need is help with "back-end" problems — processes having to do with order processing, inventory management, analytics, and financial transactions.

And if you want engineers for *that* kind of work, no amount of pre-movie advertising in Scotts Valley will do the trick. Most of the good back-end engineers live near San Francisco, and despite Eric's reputation (and my powers of persuasion), it is virtually impossible to convince someone to drive 75 miles each way to work.

Eric has come up with a solution, though. Forget engineers from 75 miles away. How about engineers from 7,500 miles away? Turns out, there's a large population of recently arrived Indian engineers in Silicon Valley, looking for work and eager to join a fledgling startup. With Suresh's help, Eric has hit the cultural centers and cricket fields of Silicon Valley, recruiting talented immigrant programmers like Dev and Ishaan, who are waiting for me now. As I rush out to say hello, I'm already thinking about what I can say to make them more comfortable in their new life, how I can ease the transition to the United States, and how I can ensure that their job is rewarding.

And what I'm going to order at Zanotto's, the Italian restaurant across the street.

12:45 P.M.

When I get back from lunch, I see that Lorraine has called to check in. I'm not looking forward to talking to her, because I'm pretty sure I know what's coming. Financial worries. Morgan is getting ready to start kindergarten in the fall, and we are planning on having her join Logan at the private school down by the water in Santa Cruz.

And kindergarten at a private school is much more expensive than preschool.

"How are we ever going to afford this?" Lorraine starts in when I finally reach her. In the background, I can hear kids, and what sound like seagulls.

"Are you at the beach?"

"I'm with a bunch of Logan's school friends. I know Morgan's really excited about going to Gateway, but I think we're making a big mistake."

She pauses, and I hear the crash of a wave, followed by a child's delighted squeal.

"We should sell the house," she says.

This is a common refrain. Almost as common as a reminder that Montana — and my dream life as a postman — beckons, should everything go south with Netflix. It has gotten more frequent lately. It is as close to an argument as we usually get.

"We're going to be fine," I remind her. Through the glass I can see Dev and Ishaan ripping open boxes containing brand-new Gateways. Eric is watching them, a smile on his face.

"I just want you to be realistic," she says. "We can do without a lot of stuff. Maybe we should think about cutting back more."

"We're making great progress here," I tell her. "As of today, we're officially a million-dollar company."

I don't tell her that we're a *projected* million-dollar company, or mention how concerned I am about where that money is coming from. I just say we can talk more about it at dinner — as usual, I'll be there.

2:00 P.M.

"Are you off the phone?"

Without waiting for an answer, Te swooshes into my office. As always, she knows the answer to her question before she even asks it.

"We're trying to finalize the press announcement for the Sony promotion." She pauses, pushing her lips together in an exaggerated pout. "It's going to be almost impossible to get them to approve our release."

Sony hadn't really given me the time of day when I first approached them about a coupon deal. But once they'd seen that we were working with Toshiba, they felt like they had to keep up with the Joneses. You see this all the time in business and in sports — a younger upstart tries something new, and when it works, the industry leader co-opts. Why? Because they can.

Plus, their own promotion — bundling a free copy of *James Taylor in Concert* with every DVD player — hadn't really moved the needle. James Taylor is a Sony artist, so it had cost them almost nothing. But they should have known better. It's 1998, a full twenty years after "Fire and Rain." Sweet Baby James isn't really all that enticing to tech geeks.

Te spreads a sheaf of papers out across my conference table.

"Look at this mess," she says, shaking her head so hard that I get a whiff of hairspray. "I don't know how they ever get anything done. There doesn't seem to be anyone with the power to make decisions. I'm starting to think we should just say *screw it* and announce, whether they approve the release or not."

"That's a terrible idea," I say, coming around from behind my desk and bending over the pages. "I've spent weeks trying to get them comfortable trusting a startup. If we go Wild West on them now, it'll screw everything up."

But she isn't lying about their nit-picking. The draft of the announcement is spattered with revisions and cross-outs. "What are they having a problem with now?"

"Everything!" Te throws up her hands, then grabs the release and stabs at it with her bright red pen. "Everything we bring up — the growth of the DVD market, the number of movies coming out, even *how excited we are, blah, blah, blah* — everything needs to go through about six layers of approval. And that's not even talking about legal."

"I'll call Mike," I answer. But I'm not optimistic. Mike Fidler is famous for delivering "the smiling screw": asking you for a deal point that will be brutal, expensive, and difficult, all with a big smile on his face. That's exactly what he did to me three weeks ago. He'd caught wind that Toshiba was interested, he said, and he thought we could work together, too. But he didn't want *three* free DVD rentals: He wanted *ten*. And that wasn't all. In addition to the free rentals, he also wanted *five totally free DVDs*.

This had been an enormously expensive proposition for us. Five free DVDs from our library was essentially a hundred dollars. So, under the terms of his deal, we were basically paying Sony a hundred bucks just for one person who owned a DVD player to visit our site. And that was on top of the cost of fulfilling the five free rentals. Worst of all — I'd promised exclusivity to Toshiba.

But the opportunity to work with Sony, the largest player in the game, had been too good to pass up. It was worth it. I'd given Mike what he wanted.

Pushing him now might piss him off. But calling Mike to argue about the language of the press release would be a lot easier than calling Steve Nickerson, tail between my legs, to admit that I'd been cheating on Toshiba with its hot older sister. Now *that* is a call I'm dreading making.

"Give me twenty minutes," I say to Te. "Let's see if I'm any good at the smiling screw."

4:00 P.M.

Crisis averted. No hard feelings. Just promises from Mike.

"We'll try to be a little speedier, a little more proactive," he says to me. "We're being careful on this because we think it can really work."

Music to my ears.

Now, I just have to figure out some way to get people to rent when it *isn't* free. It's taken all day, but I finally have a moment to pull up the data from the morning and begin digging.

Turns out, it's even worse than I thought. We aren't just stagnating. We're losing ground.

Don't get me wrong — it's great that we're doing so much business, two months in. The $100,000 coming in every month from DVD sales not only pays a few of our bills, it demonstrates to our suppliers and partners that we're real. It gives Eric and his team a chance to stress-test the site under the load of real customers, not projections. It gives our operations team the thrill of seeing real packages going out the door each day. It gives the entire company a sense of momentum.

But it's a sugar high.

Right now, we're the only game in town. But it won't be long before Amazon expands into selling DVDs. And after Amazon, there will be Borders. Then Walmart. And then virtually every other store — online or brick-and-mortar — in America.

When you get down to it, selling DVDs is a commodities business. Looking at the figures, I know that once everyone is selling the exact same thing, pretty much exactly the same way, it will only be a matter of time before our margins shrink to nothing. It might not happen next week, next month, or even next year, but it is inevitable. And when it happens, we'll be toast.

DVD *rental*, on the other hand, has real potential. It's hard to find places to rent DVDs in person, much less online — and it might be a while before that changes. As we've found out the hard way, renting DVDs online is operationally difficult, which means that it will be difficult for potential competitors to figure it out. We have at least a year's head start. Plus, the margins are higher, since you can rent the same disc dozens of times.

The monitors show that we're selling a lot of DVDs. We just can't convince anyone to rent from us. And doing both rentals and sales at the same time is really hard. It's complicated for our inventory: there are some titles that, legally, we can both rent *and* sell, but others we can only rent, or only sell. Our warehouse and shipping procedures have to accommodate some movies that go out and come back, while others go out and stay out.

Offering both DVD sales and rentals is confusing for our customers, who arrive at Netflix.com unsure of what, exactly, we do. We have to explain on our home page that users can either buy *or* rent most titles — and a general rule of web design is that if you have to explain something, you've already lost. The checkout process is cumbersome, too.

Everything is harder than it needs to be, I think, leaning back in my chair. *We have to focus.*

But on what?

Should we focus on selling DVDs, which is bringing in 99 percent of our revenue, but will slowly — inevitably — evaporate as competitors crowd the field? Or should we throw our limited resources behind renting DVDs — which, if we can make it work, could be a hugely profitable business, but at this point is showing absolutely no signs of life?

There's no easy answer.

5:15 P.M.

As I pull into the driveway, I can already hear the murmur of kids in the kitchen, and before I've even gotten up the steps to the porch, Logan is running out the door to throw himself into my arms.

"Did you bring home the bacon?" he asks, with a big grin, six years old and in on the joke.

When I carry Logan inside, Morgan looks up from the tiny toy kitchen that she likes to set up while her mother busies herself in the real one. Lorraine is heating up a frozen lasagna, and Morgan appears to be scrambling eggs. "Did you climb the ladder?" she asks, as she always does, knowing by my smile that there is something funny about it, but not exactly sure what.

Lorraine turns away from the oven, blowing a strand of hair away from her face. She kisses me on the cheek and winks. Whatever anxiety about money and the future she was feeling earlier in the day seems to have calmed — money worries and private school tuition can wait. I set Logan down and pick Hunter up out of his high chair, feeling applesauce on my neck as he snuggles himself against my collar.

For the moment, Netflix seems very far away.

8:00 P.M.

The only light in the office spills out of the open door to the "warehouse" — even two months in, we're still storing all the DVDs in the safe. When he hears the front door open, Jim steps out, a piece of pizza in one hand and a grease-stained paper plate in the other.

"We're in trouble," he says, wiggling his arm in a way that signals I should grab the manila folder tucked under his arm. He puts down his pizza, wipes his hands on his jeans, and grabs the folder back. He pulls out a page and points to a column of numbers. "You've seen this before, but it's getting worse."

All our budgets are based on a 32-cent postage stamp. That's what you need for a one-ounce letter in 1998. That's what we'd been aiming for when we designed our mailers. But Jim's latest analysis shows that only a handful of the previous month's rentals had made the one-ounce cutoff. Worse, more than half of our mailings had clocked in at two ounces or more.

"It gets worse," Jim explains, pulling another page from his folder. "Look at our packaging costs."

My eyes scan the numbers. We are wildly over budget. Our original test — that Patsy Cline CD, stuffed into a greeting card envelope — had been the guiding force behind our budget, but it is clear now that as we moved from concept to scale, it had been a gross oversimplification.

Although I'm upset, I'm not entirely surprised. The second your dream becomes a reality, things get complicated. You simply can't know how things are going to behave until you've actually tried them. Go ahead and write up a plan, but don't put too much faith in it. The only real way to find something out is to do it.

We'd been lucky that the CD had arrived unscathed at Reed's house. But when you ship thousands of DVDs across the country, you can't rely on luck. To protect the DVD from scratches, fingerprints, and other general abuse, the disc needs to be in some sort of sleeve. The plastic sleeve we've decided on is sturdy, reusable, and transparent. But it is also expensive and heavy. And it has gotten even heavier (and more expensive) with the addition of a 3″ × 3″ paper label for the movie info and unique serial number.

The mailing envelope has evolved from a simple pink greeting card envelope into a total chimera, made up of disparate parts and scraps. We've moved from paper to heavy cardboard, adding a third layer of paper that doubles as the return envelope. The current version, in stacks in the vault behind Jim, has two adhesive strips, and has grown in size (and weight) to accommodate *multiple* DVDs if needed.

Jim gives me a sheepish grin. "Just one more thing to worry about," he says, picking up his pizza and turning back to the safe.

I grab one of our mailers, walk across the office, and settle into one of the aluminum lawn chairs that Eric Meyer uses as his "guest chair" next to his desk. Above me, cables snake down through a crack between two ceiling tiles. "There has to be a better way to do this," I think to myself, idly passing the mailer from hand to hand, opening and closing the flaps.

The flaps. Maybe they could be a different shape. I rifle through Eric's desk, pulling open a drawer to look for scissors or a knife, or anything I can use to make cuts in paper. No dice.

But I have an idea.

Out in the parking lot, I open the back hatch of the Volvo and grab the beach bag tucked behind the rear seat. Lorraine and I call it the "restaurant bag." It's stuffed with all the distractions needed to get through a meal in public with three children under the age of seven: crayons, coloring books, scissors, tapes, modeling clay, pipe cleaners, construction paper, and cardboard. Lots of cardboard.

I tuck the bag under my arm and head into my office, ducking briefly into the warehouse for another handful of mailers. I pour the contents of the restaurant bag onto the conference table, find the cardboard, pull out some scissors, and get to work.

10:00 P.M.

Jim is still bent over the workstation, stripping DVD cases of their cellophane, pulling out DVDs, inserting them into sleeves, adding labels, and neatly hanging them in tight rows on the Peg-Board. A pile of discarded DVD cases lies at his feet. He'll take them out to the Dumpster at the end of the night — there's no room for them here, and no reason to keep them.

Jim looks up as I drop my cardboard mock-ups on his desk. "Meet Frankenstein's mailers," I tell him. "Or the turducken, if you're still hungry."

The new mock-ups are crude: flaps torn off, taped into new positions, new folds made, windows roughly cut, crayon markings — but they're enough for Jim to go on. He can use them to have some real mock-ups made, weighed, and priced.

I'd had an afternoon espresso and a cup of coffee after dinner with

Lorraine, but by now my eyes are drooping, my brain fried. It's time to go home. I hadn't even meant to work on the mailers when I returned to the office. But that's how things are — there is always so much to do that making plans and to-do lists is a waste of time.

Before I leave, I catch Jim walking over to the back of the office. Suresh is there, printing packing slips — I hadn't noticed him earlier. Next to him is a woman wearing a Salwar kameez and headphones, watching DVDs on a portable player. I've encountered her before — she's Suresh's wife. A month before launch, Suresh had surprised Eric by saying that he needed to fly back to India to get married. Ever since then, when Devisree, his wife, knows it will be a late night, she keeps him company in the office, sometimes sleeping on one of the couches near his workstation.

True love, startup style. It makes me smile.

I'm lucky to have a much shorter commute to see my family. I drive back home, winding my way up the hill and down the long driveway until the house comes into view. Lorraine has left the porch light on for me. It casts light on the new orange trees I've planted in the back, near where I think a garage might eventually go. But all that is far, far in the future.

I sneak inside, taking my shoes off at the door. The house is quiet — the kids are asleep, the kitchen is clean, and Luna, the useless guard dog, is curled at the foot of the stairs. I step over her and skip the fourth step, which always squeaks. Still, Lorraine stirs and opens her eyes as I climb into bed. "How did it go?"

"Making progress," I say as I put my arm around her. I'm drifting off. But suddenly I have a premonition: Hunter in his crib, in less than six hours, throwing animals over the bars and onto the floor. I nudge Lorraine.

"Your turn tomorrow," I remind her.

10.

Halcyon Days

(summer 1998: two months after launch)

"Jesus, Reed, where are you taking us?"

The street we were walking on looked like a movie set of skid row. There was trash on the sidewalk, broken glass in the window casements. Most of the businesses were closed, or if they were open, it was hard to tell: Liberty Loans Pawn Shop. Fair Hair Wig Store. And then, a few doors down, a plain doorway with a red awning reading ADULT ENTERTAINMENT CENTER.

"Joy said 1516 Second Avenue," Reed replied, squinting down at the map he'd printed out that morning. "Should be right around the corner."

I glanced toward a group of shabbily dressed young men huddled in the doorway of a large building. The sign on the window read DEPARTMENT OF PUBLIC HEALTH — NEEDLE EXCHANGE PROGRAM. "Somehow I think I expected something a little more...I don't know, modern?"

"There it is," Reed said, pointing to a run-down four-story brick building across the street. The windows were dusty and streaked. A faded sign over the front door said COLUMBIA. Maybe this building had *once* housed a world-changing company, but it was clear that if so, it had been many years in the past. "See! 1516."

We crossed the street and Reed stepped up to the door. He seemed unsure now, less certain — despite what his map told him — that this could actually be the place. I leaned in toward one of the tall glass windows that made up the front of the building. If I cupped my hands around my eyes, I could just see into the dimly lit lobby. On the wall, behind a faded wood desk, was a large sign reading AMAZON.COM.

Reed had gotten the call a few days earlier from Joy Covey, Amazon's CFO. She wondered if we would be interested in coming up to Seattle to meet with her and Jeff Bezos, Amazon's founder and CEO. She didn't say why she wanted to meet, but she didn't need to. It was obvious.

Although Amazon was only a few years old, and still strictly a place to buy books, Bezos had decided early in 1998 that his site wouldn't just be a bookstore. It was going to be an *everything* store, and we knew that music and video were going to be his next two targets. Although it was unlikely that Jeff would be interested (or foolish) enough to rent DVDs, it was clear that he was soon going to start selling them. And once that happened, we'd be out of business. Fast.

We'd also heard from our VC connections that Bezos planned to use a good chunk of the $54 million raised during his company's 1997 IPO to finance an aggressive acquisition of smaller companies. That's normal — most companies looking to enter a new business arena do what's called a "make-or-buy analysis," in which they consider the cost, timing, and difficulty of starting a new business from scratch, then evaluate whether it would be cheaper, faster, and better to simply *buy* another company that's already doing it.

With that in mind, it didn't take us long to figure out why Jeff and Joy wanted to meet. Netflix was in play.

I'd be lying if I said that the feeling — although thrilling — wasn't also a little bittersweet. In the summer of 1998, we'd finally gotten the engine to turn over, and we were just starting to pick up some speed. I wasn't quite ready to put it in park and hand over the keys.

But when Amazon calls, you pick up the phone. Even if it's 1998, and Amazon is nowhere near the powerhouse it is today.

The building we were winding our way through certainly didn't look like it belonged to a powerhouse. The stairs to the second floor were warped and creaky. The reception area was cluttered and dusty. Piles of Amazon boxes were pushed into the corners. The chairs against the wall were mismatched. On the desk was a telephone with a printed directory of numbers under a piece of glass. Reed leaned over, squinted at the glass, and dialed a number.

Within seconds, Joy swept into the lobby, giving Reed and me huge smiles, like we were long-lost friends. Pretty and athletic, with shoulder-length dark-blond hair falling over a string of huge pearls, Covey was younger than either of us. But she was already a respected and successful businesswoman, a dynamo who had taken Amazon public just twelve months ago, convincing skeptical investment bankers that a company that wasn't remotely profitable — and didn't plan to be anytime soon — was worth $20 billion.

Joy was sharp. She reportedly had an IQ of 173. She'd dropped out of high school at fifteen, bagged groceries to pay her bills, gotten her GED, and then graduated from Cal State–Fresno in two and a half years. After a brief stint as an accountant, she'd gotten dual master's degrees from Harvard, in business and in law.

When Bezos had recruited Covey to Amazon, she'd casually mentioned that after college she had managed to get the second-highest score in the country on the CPA exam — a test taken by nearly seventy thousand other aspiring accountants. When Bezos had teased her — "Really, Joy? The *second*-highest?" — Covey had shot back, "I didn't study."

As Covey led us back into the warren of cubicles that made up the Amazon offices, it was hard for me to believe that *this* was the company reinventing e-commerce. The carpeting was stained; the partitions used to separate the cubicles were dirty and torn. Dogs roamed the hallways.

There were multiple people per cubicle, desks under the stairs, desks pushed to the edges of hallways. Almost every horizontal surface was covered: by books; by gaping Amazon boxes; by papers, printouts, coffee cups, plates, and pizza boxes. It made the green carpeting and beach chairs of the Netflix offices seem like the executive suite at IBM.

We could hear Jeff Bezos before we saw him. *He-huh-huh-huh-huh.* Jeff has a . . . distinctive laugh. If you've seen any video of him speaking, you'll have heard a version of it — but not the true, untamed thing. In the same way that he's definitely hired a personal trainer since the late nineties, I think he's also worked with someone to tame his laugh. Now it's polite, a little giggly. But back then, it was explosive, loud, hiccupping. He laughed the way that Barney Rubble laughs on *The Flintstones.*

He was in his office, just hanging up the phone when we walked in. His desk, and the desks of the two other people he shared the office with, were made of doors that had been mounted atop 4 × 4 wooden legs, braced with triangular metal pieces. I suddenly realized that every desk I'd seen in that office was the same: all made from doors, all on top of simple repurposed 4 × 4s.

A short man, Bezos was wearing pressed khaki pants and a crisp blue oxford shirt. He was already well on his way to being completely bald, and the combination of the huge forehead, a slightly peaked nose, a shirt that was a little too big for him, and a neck that was a little too small all had the effect of making him look like a turtle that had just popped its head out of its shell. Behind him, hanging from an exposed pipe in the ceiling, four or five identical pressed blue oxford shirts fluttered in the breeze provided by an oscillating fan.

After the introductions had been made, we filed into a corner of the building where enough space had been cleared to fit a bigger table with eight chairs around it. This table, too, was made from recycled doors. I could clearly see where the holes that used to hold the doorknobs had been neatly patched with circular plugs of wood.

"Okay, Jeff," I said, grinning. "What's with all the doors?"

"It's a deliberate message," he explained. "Everyone in the company has them. It's a way of saying that we spend money on things that affect our customers, not on things that don't."

Netflix was the same way, I told him. We didn't even provide chairs.

He laughed. "It's like this building. It's a mess. We barely have room to turn around in it. But it's cheap. I've held out as long as I can, but even I admit that we need more space now. We just signed a lease on what used to be the Seattle Pacific Medical Center. It's huge — but we got a great deal, because no one else wanted it."

I wasn't surprised to hear any of this. Bezos was notoriously frugal — even cheap. He was famous for his "two-pizza meetings" — the idea being that if it took more than two pizzas to feed a group of people working on a problem, then you had hired too many people. People worked long hours for him, and they didn't get paid a lot.

But Bezos inspired loyalty. He's one of those geniuses — like Steve Jobs, or like Reed — whose peculiarities only add to his legend. In Jeff's case, his legendary intelligence and notorious nerdiness mix into a kind of contagious enthusiasm that pushed him headlong into every challenge. He didn't look back — or, as he put it, he "evaluated opportunities using a regret minimization framework." He showed Reed his wristwatch, bragging that it updated itself thirty-six times a day by picking up the radio signal from the national atomic clock in Fort Collins, Colorado. A *Star Trek* fan, Bezos had spent his entire childhood acting out scenes from the show with his friends. His pals would play Kirk or Spock. Jeff was always the *Enterprise*'s computer.

When he spoke, I noticed that unlike me, Jeff didn't gesture with his hands. Instead, he used his head for emphasis, lifting his chin up for questions, dropping it down suddenly for emphasis. Twisting his head at a 45-degree angle meant he was curious. At thirty-four, his demeanor still retained a strong dose of "gee whiz" enthusiasm, but all the childlike delight in the world couldn't mask the analytical and ambitious brain constantly at work behind his unblinking eyes.

As I started to bring Jeff up to speed about Netflix, detailing the efforts we'd made to get the site off the ground, he peppered me with questions. How could I know that I had every DVD? How could I forecast expected turns? What did I expect the ratio of sales to rentals to be? But it was clear to me that what he was most excited about were the stories about launch day — particularly, the story of that ringing bell.

"That's fantastic!" he exclaimed, so excited that he almost moved his hands. "We had the exact same thing! A bell that rang every time an order came in. I had to stop everyone from rushing over to the computer screens to see if they knew the customers."

We traded beta names: he laughed at Kibble and told me that Amazon had originally called itself Cadabra, which he had thought evoked the sense of magic that online shopping could produce. "The problem is that Cadabra sounds a little too much like *cadaver*," Bezos said, barking out a laugh.

Although Amazon was still relatively small in 1998, they already had over 600 employees and were doing more than $150 million in revenue. They were a real company now, with real pressures, but as Jeff and I chatted about our launch days, I could see in his face and hear in his voice that in many ways he missed those simpler, more exciting times.

Reed, on the other hand, was obviously bored. Forget "regret minimization framework" — Reed has never been someone who dwells, *at all*, on the past, so these stories of early struggles and frenetic launch days were of little interest to him. His placid stare had turned stony, and he was impatiently jogging his leg up and down. He wanted, I knew, to direct the conversation to the topics at hand: what Netflix was doing, how it could potentially fit with what Amazon was doing, and how some kind of "arrangement" could be a win-win situation for both parties.

I was just finishing bringing Jeff and Joy through my professional résumé, and was about to brief them on Christina, Te, and other key members of our team, when Reed decided he'd had enough.

"We don't need to go through all this," he said, exasperated. "What does this have to do with Netflix and Amazon and possible ways we can work together?"

Everyone stopped. It was quiet.

"Reed," I said after a few seconds. "It's obvious that Amazon is considering using Netflix to jump-start their entry into video. Our people would be a huge part of any possible acquisition, so it's entirely appropriate for them to want to understand who we are."

I was relieved when Joy jumped in to help. "Reed," she suggested, "can you help me understand a bit better how you're thinking about your unit economics?"

This was exactly what Reed wanted to hear, and with obvious relief that we were finally on topic, he began running Joy through the numbers.

An hour later, after the meeting was over and Bezos had headed back to his office, Joy lingered behind to wrap things up. "I'm very impressed with what you've accomplished," she started, "and I think there is lots of potential for a strong partnership to jump-start our entry into video. But…"

Now, let me interject something here. I'm not a "but" man. Nothing good ever comes of that word. This time was no exception.

"But," Joy continued, "if we elect to continue down this path, we're probably going to land somewhere in the low eight figures."

When someone uses the term "eight figures," they are referring to digits. Eight figures translates to tens of millions of dollars. When someone uses "low eight figures," that means *barely* eight figures. That means probably something between $14 million and $16 million.

That would have been a pretty good outcome for me, since at the time, I owned about 30 percent of the company. Thirty percent of $15 million is a pretty nice return for twelve months of work — particularly when your wife is broadly hinting that it might be time to pull the kids out of private school, sell the house, and move to Montana.

But for Reed, it wasn't enough. He owned the other 70 percent of the company, but he'd also invested $2 million in it. And he was fresh off the Pure Atria IPO. He was already an "eight-figure guy." A *high-eight-figure guy.*

On the plane ride home, we discussed the pros and cons. The pros? We'd find a solution for our biggest problems: We weren't making any money. We didn't have a repeatable, scalable, or profitable business model. We were doing plenty of business, most of it through DVD sales, but our costs were high. It was expensive to buy DVDs. Expensive to ship them. Expensive to give away thousands of DVDs in promotions, hoping that we'd convert onetime users into return customers.

And of course there was the bigger problem. Which was that if we *didn't* sell to them, we would soon be competing with them. So long, DVD sales. So long, Netflix.

Selling to Amazon now would solve all those problems — or at least it would hand them off to a larger company with deeper pockets.

But . . .

We were also on the brink of something. We had a working website. We had a smart team. We had deals in place with a handful of DVD manufacturers. We had figured out how to source virtually every DVD currently available. We were unquestionably the best source on the internet for DVDs.

Amazon's entry as a competitor would undoubtedly make things more complicated and difficult. But we had a bit of time. And it still didn't seem like the right moment to give up.

"Listen, Marc," Reed said over airline peanuts and ginger ale, as we watched Mount Rainier scroll by outside the window. "This business has real potential. I think we could make more on this than on the Pure Atria deal."

I nodded in agreement. And then, for some reason, I chose that moment to tell Reed that we should abandon the only profitable part of our business. I think it was the afternoon with Bezos — seeing Amazon in the flesh, dingy office and all, just reinforced for me that we could never compete in the DVD retail sales market. Better to focus on what made us different and unique.

"We just have to figure out some way to get out of selling DVDs," I said to him. "Doing rental and sales is confusing for our customers and unnecessarily complex for ops. And if we don't sell, Amazon will *destroy* us when they enter the field. I think we get out now. Focus on rental."

Reed arched his eyebrows.

"Kinda puts all our eggs in one basket," he said.

"That's the only way to make sure you don't break any," I replied.

That's true, by the way. One of the key lessons I learned at Netflix was the necessity not only of creative ideation, or of having the right people around you, but of *focus*. At a startup, it's hard enough to get a single thing right, much less a whole bunch of things. Especially if the things you are trying to do are not only dissimilar but actively impede each other.

Focus is imperative. Even when the thing you're focusing on seems impossible. Especially then.

But Reed agreed with me. "You're right," he said, throwing back a few peanuts. "If we get funding this summer, that'll buy us some time. It's a difficult problem."

He frowned, but I could tell he was pleased to have something new to chew on.

"What percentage of revenue comes from rental right now?"

"Roughly three percent," I said, signaling to the flight attendant for a much-needed gin and tonic.

"That's horrible," Reed said. "But sales are a Band-Aid. If we rip it off…"

"Then we have to focus on the wound," I said, squeezing my lime into the drink.

We went back and forth like this for the rest of the plane ride, and it was only when we landed that I realized we hadn't actually formally decided not to take Bezos's offer. We'd just naturally gone back into our carpool-on-17 mode, lobbing ideas back and forth and shooting them down. Without deciding, we'd decided: we weren't ready to sell.

Before we landed, we agreed that Reed would let Amazon down lightly — and politely. We'd be better off having Amazon as a friend, not an enemy. And once they entered the DVD sales business, there might still be a way to make it work.

In the meantime, we needed to figure out a way to get people renting from us.

When an opportunity comes knocking, you don't necessarily have to open your door. But you owe it to yourself to at least look through the keyhole. That's what we'd done with Amazon.

As the weeks went by that summer, that glimpse started to look a lot more enticing. Because not all the meetings I attended with Reed went as well as the one with Bezos.

Our number one problem, after launch, was money. We had taken on an additional $250,000 just before the launch from Rick Schell, an old colleague of mine from Borland, but that had quickly been absorbed by the steadily increasing pile of DVDs that we were shoehorning into our warehouse. We still had cash in the bank, but we were rapidly approaching the point where we'd need more. That money was definitely not coming from our own profits — it was still far too early for that. But to raise our Series B round of funding, we were going to have to convince some people that our business wasn't just shiny and new, but that it had the potential to be profitable. Massively profitable. And fairly soon.

We weren't approaching friends and family this time. We were approaching professional investors. Real venture capitalists. And they would need more than a sincere look communicating how hungry I was. They needed data.

Sounds easy, right? Wrong.

Flash-forward to my Volvo station wagon idling in a parking space in front of the Sand Hill Road offices of Institutional Venture Partners, a prominent Silicon Valley venture capital firm. In just twenty minutes, we will be ushered into an opulent conference room, where we'll make the case for why IVP should invest in us. We're asking for $4 million. I'm freaking out, and even Reed, who normally isn't one to show emotion, is visibly concerned. It is obvious to both of us that my numbers aren't adding up.

For the previous three nights, the lights have stayed on late in our small conference room. Duane Mensinger — the interim CFO who isn't even confident enough about the numbers to come on full-time — and I have burned the midnight oil coming up with multiple financial scenarios, trying to make the numbers show that, with just a nominal investment, we can get our company to a place where we could actually make money.

But it's not looking good.

Reed is hunched forward in the passenger seat, looking at the numbers for the first time and seeing clearly what will also become evident to the IVP partners just a short while later: that without some tectonic change in the market landscape, our company won't make it.

"Okay," I say, flipping open my laptop and rehearsing my pitch. "As you can see, our user growth has exploded in the weeks post-launch. Site traffic is up three hundred percent, with at least half of all visitors to Netflix.com trying the service out. We expect that, pursuant to our deals with Toshiba and Sony, we'll see a two hundred percent uptick in user acquisition by the New Year, when DVD player sales..."

"These numbers don't make sense, Marc," Reed interrupts. "You still aren't capturing enough revenue from each new user to cover the expenses of the promotion. It's like a taxi driving all the way to another state just to pick up a four-dollar fare."

He's right. Our promotions with Toshiba and Sony are reaching new DVD owners, but they're enormously expensive. We are spending a lot of money up front to get people in the door. Factoring in two-way shipping, the mailer, the labor, and the DVD, each of those three-free-DVD rentals is costing us more than $15, and the Sony deal — with its ten free-rentals — is even more expensive.

None of this would be so bad if every free trial eventually turned into a return renter (read: paying customer), but most of our free-trial users are only tire kickers. In fact, only about 5 percent of them actually return and rent again. That means that we have to subsidize twenty freebies (at $15 apiece) for every actual customer we get out of the deal. Do the math: every paying customer is costing us $300. We call that CAC. Pronounced *kack*, it stands for "cost of acquiring a customer." It's also the noise you make when you realize that you'll never be able to make enough money to justify CAC being so big.

I pivot, laying the charm on thick. "We're seeing a thirty percent increase, month over month," I say, pointing to a graph, its columns growing, April to July, like an in-progress skyscraper. "That number will only increase, as the format grows more popular. Already, DVD players are half as expensive this year as they were last year. People are buying the technology — and when they do, Netflix is one of the first things they see. Christmas this year will be *huge*."

"It won't matter if Santa Claus himself rides into Scotts Valley," Reed says, "if we're just giving away the house on promotions."

"I know," I say, frowning. I've been so focused on the launch, on growing the company, on making it exist *at all*, that I've lost sight of the reason we're doing this in the first place: to create something real that can stand on its own.

I've missed the forest for the trees.

Reed looks at me curiously, cocking his head, then shaking it. He's not accustomed to seeing me this rattled. Historically, *I've* been the one to help him out with presentations, with pitches. I've helped him soften his message, helped him pivot from inconvenient problems. I've tried (mostly unsuccessfully) to teach him to lighten tension with a joke. The key to these pitches is to read the room, sense what they want to hear, and then give that to them — without lying, obfuscating, or distorting the truth. In a pitch, perfection isn't always the goal: projection is. You don't have to have all the answers if you appear to be the sort of person to whom they'll eventually come.

I am not that person, sitting in the parking lot. And Reed can see it.

"Come on," he says, opening the door. "Let's go."

I sit for a while, clicking through the slides one more time, chugging a few last gulps of coffee.

"Get your shit together, Marc," Reed says. Then he shuts the door.

The pitch did not go particularly well. Though they didn't question my slides the way Reed had, the firm seemed dubious. And within a few days, one of their analysts was calling the office, asking questions that I didn't have great answers for yet.

Eventually, they decided to fund us. But that had less to do with my pitch than Reed's presence. Reed was a known quantity, venture capitalist catnip. He'd orchestrated major deals, he'd appeared — reluctantly — on the cover of *USA Today* next to his Porsche. People with money trusted him because he had a track record of making *them* money. Even in 1998, he had around his head the halo of Silicon Valley success: when Pure went public, well before the merger with Atria, he made a lot of people rich.

More importantly, he had a track record of solving seemingly unsolvable problems. Investors and VCs knew this even then. They definitely know it now. That's why the second he walks into a room, people whip out their checkbooks. They know that what he does isn't teachable, isn't reproducible — hell, it's barely even *explicable*. He's just got it.

That's what great entrepreneurs do, in the end: the impossible. Jeff Bezos, Steve Jobs, Reed Hastings — they're all geniuses who did something that no one thought was possible. And if you do that once, your odds of doing it again are exponentially higher.

IVP funded us not because our forecast was good, or our pitch was perfect, or because I'd wowed them with my slides and enthusiasm. IVP funded us because, despite how impossible things looked, Reed was a miracle worker, and Reed was on board.

I was thankful for that. And I was thankful, too, that even though Reed was still running TechNet that summer, he had started taking a daily interest in what we were doing in Scotts Valley. But in retrospect, I can also now see that that's when everything started to change.

One of the paradoxes of memory is how it distorts time. If you'd asked me, before writing this book, how long the truly early days of Netflix lasted — the days of lawn chairs and pathetic Christmas parties, heated arguments and hash browns at Hobee's — I would have scratched my head and said a year and a half, two years.

Really, it was about a year. But those eleven or twelve months were crucial. They exist in a kind of peaceable vacuum, set apart from what came before and what came after. Before we almost sold ourselves to Amazon, we were just trying to make something happen that no one else had ever done. We were working independently of competition. We were, in a sense, protected by the walls of that bank vault. We had a stinky, green-carpeted place to dream.

The ancient Greeks had a term for this: halcyon days. I won't bore you too much with the mythology, but essentially, they referred to the seven days each year when the winds were calm and Alcyone, a king-fisher, could lay her eggs.

The halcyon days of Netflix ran from the summer of 1997 to the summer of 1998. There wasn't a moment, that fall or afterward, when I realized that they were over — transitions rarely work like that. When change is incremental, it's hard to put your finger on the end point. The ironic thing is that change is what you wanted all along. It's the point of any startup, and it's what we worked so hard to have happen. But that doesn't make it any easier when it does.

Still, with the benefit of hindsight, I *can* pinpoint a high-water mark, and tell you that the halcyon days of early Netflix were at their apogee in June, during our summer company picnic at Hallcrest Vineyards. I remember it so clearly: picnic tables topped with pizzas, an open field surrounded by redwoods, glasses of wine in all our hands. Luna and a pack of other people's dogs ran free in the grass, and all our kids were shooting each other with brand-new Super Soakers, bought for the occasion. With Reed's help, we'd just raised $6 million to get us through to the end of the year, and we were expanding daily, hiring new engineers and web designers, building our inventory, and acquiring thousands of new customers per month. I'd given a toast to our employees and bored kids, and at the end of it, Mitch Lowe had proudly presented me with a NETFLIX vanity license plate. I was holding it with one hand, and with the other I was holding a glass of Pinot Noir, looking down into the Valley and thinking, *You know, this is going pretty well.*

A year, maybe a little more. Doesn't sound like a lot. But those twelve months or so determined so much about the company's culture, direction, and ethos. Netflix today wouldn't exist without them — or if it did, it would look a hell of a lot different.

Netflix also wouldn't exist today without what happened after. That's the thing about halcyon days: you need them, but if you want your egg to hatch and the bird to fly away, you need a little wind.

11.

Two Cents for Bill Clinton

(September 1998: five months after launch)

WE HAD A PROBLEM.

Remember those deals I was so proud of, the ones with Sony and Toshiba that would direct new owners of DVD players straight to Netflix? The deals that required me, Marc Randolph, startup guy to the core, to don the NMO like a superhero and convince a bunch of hidebound Japanese consumer electronics companies to fast-track a promotion? Well, it turns out that when a big company accustomed to long lead times and reliant on a careful, methodical rollout does something on the fly, things go wrong.

Remember? For users, our promotion was pretty simple. If you bought a Sony DVD player in the fall of 1998, there was a promotional sticker on the outside of the box, promising ten free DVD rentals and five free DVDs. All you had to do was head to Netflix.com, enter your DVD player's unique serial number, and bingo: ten free DVDs to rent, five free DVDs to keep.

It would have been better if the coupons were on the inside of the box, but Sony's methodical production schedule didn't allow for it. Besides, you still had to buy the DVD player to get the serial number, right?

Wrong.

A few weeks into the promotion, Jim's guys in the vault started to notice a repeat customer. This guy was ordering truly massive quantities of DVDs. Hundreds of them per week.

Now, back then we had no cap on rentals. We were desperate for renters — we weren't going to turn them away. The problem was, this heavy user wasn't renting. He was just raking in free DVDs from the Sony promotion.

"Either this guy really loves DVD players and is buying a metric shit-ton of them," Jim told me in the vault, frowning down at a pile of mailers, all of them addressed to the same address, "or he is scamming the hell out of us."

That afternoon, Mitch and I drove out to Fry's. We wanted to see exactly what a customer would see. There they were, the Sony DVD players, our yellow Netflix stickers neatly pasted to every top-right corner. So far, so good. Mitch picked up one of the boxes, turned it over, put it back down. He tugged on the promotion, and it came off easily. He walked halfway down the aisle, looking at the identical DVD players. I was scanning the information on the bottom of the box closer to me when I saw it.

"Shit," I said.

"What?" Mitch asked.

I pointed to the fine print on the bottom of the box: Sony mailing address, DVD player technical information in English, French, and Japanese. And there, right at the end? The unique serial number. It was on the outside of the box. All our scammer had to do was walk down the aisle of his nearest Best Buy, pad and pencil in hand, and he'd have dozens of serial numbers to type into our promotional form. He didn't have to buy a single thing.

An easily duplicated scam, unreliable servers, mailers that sometimes got stuck in post office machinery, a business that lost money on every transaction. Slide after slide of graphs, with no path to profitability.

Things might sound dire to you at this point. But that's the thing about startups — you're almost always on the razor's edge between total success and total failure. You learn to live there. I imagine it's how the Flying Wallendas feel, when they're stacked on top of each other over Niagara Falls, or between two skyscrapers, riding bicycles across a chasm, the only thing under them a thin metal cord. Sounds terrifying to most people. But do it enough times, and that's just the life you lead.

Plus, success in Silicon Valley often has quite a long tail. We got a lot of press on launch day, but it was really for work that we'd done a month, three months, six months, *a year* prior. The life span of a startup is often so short that by the time people notice what you're doing, you're hanging on by a thread.

That's true of most things, really. When you're busy making your dream into reality, no one praises you until the work is done — and by that time, you've long since moved on to other problems.

We were growing that fall — and fast. We had hundreds of new users every day, and DVDs arriving by the truckload every Tuesday. The vault was stuffed — it looked less like a bootleg Blockbuster than a hoarder's lair. We were chasing a market, and if we wanted any chance of surviving, we had to expand with the DVD user base. That meant growth. That meant more space — a lot of it.

I didn't particularly want to leave our Scotts Valley home. I'd grown to love its money-green carpet, its humid stench of Diet Coke and Zanotto's takeout containers. And I was deeply invested in Netflix being a "Santa Cruz company." I'd been on the Silicon Valley startup roller coaster, and I wanted us to be different, set apart. I wanted something of Santa Cruz's laid-back ethos to seep into our office culture. Santa Cruz felt like a respite from the boom-and-bust cycle in San Jose. I wanted to keep a mountain range between my company and the prying eyes of the VCs keeping it afloat.

But in 1998, we were more dependent than ever on those VCs. And our newest one, IVP's Tim Haley, was adamant that we move closer to the Valley. In a previous life he had been an executive recruiter — he knew what he was talking about.

"You're making it overly hard on yourself," he told Reed and me. "You're already unusual — your *idea* is unusual. Let that be the only weird thing about your company. Don't make it hard for people to give you money. Or to work for you."

He had a point. Aside from Eric's hires, we were still finding it difficult to recruit top tech talent. We were losing potential hires to less interesting but more conveniently located companies. Engineers didn't want to spend an hour and a half driving to work every morning.

Our own employees didn't relish their commutes, either. Other than Te and I (and Reed), most of the founding team lived elsewhere: Christina in Redwood Shores; Eric, Boris, and Vita in the Valley. Working in Santa Cruz was really only convenient for me and a handful of others.

Companies establish concentric circles around themselves — a sort of radar range of overlapping environments. The center of the circle in large part determines the company's guiding philosophy, which is in turn modified by what people bring to it, from the outer boundaries of the orbit. Moving our offices from Santa Cruz to Silicon Valley would, I thought, fundamentally change who we were. I didn't want to do it.

But one of the things I was learning, that first year, was that success creates problems. Growth is great — but with growth comes an entirely new set of complications. How can you preserve your identity even as you include new members on your team? How do you balance continued expansion with coherent identity? How do you ensure that you continue to take risks, now that you have something to lose?

How do you grow gracefully?

Early Netflix was a small, tight-knit group. I knew everyone — I'd hired them. I knew what they were good at and what they didn't know they were good at *yet*. I knew how they thought, how they worked.

Most of all, I knew they were brilliant — that they could learn new things if needed. Jim had no experience in operations when I hired him. Boris wasn't even a web designer. But I knew that both of them had the necessary drive and malleable creativity to make a go of it. And that's how startups typically run, in the early days: You hire a bunch of brilliant people to be jacks-of-all-trades. Everyone does a little bit of everything. You're hiring a *team*, not a set of positions.

That fall, I was trying to manage the growth of that team — to make sure that the culture we'd forged over the previous twelve months survived a scale-up. We'd built a company where freewheeling discussions sometimes turned heated — and it was *okay*. Where ideas were more important than chain of command. Where it didn't matter who solved a problem — only that it got solved. Where dedication and creativity mattered a lot more than dress codes or meeting times.

It was special, and I knew it. Even then.

Here's an example. Te would ask each new hire what his or her favorite film was. Then, the day before our monthly company-wide meeting, she'd instruct the person to come to work the next day dressed as a character from that film. The new hire would spend the day dressed as Batman or Cruella de Vil or Humphrey Bogart as Rick Blaine in *Casablanca* before being introduced in front of the entire company.

Was this silly? Yes. Was it a waste of time? Arguably. Was it pointless? Not at all.

Small, semi-improvised rituals like this kept things light. They reminded us that no matter how stressful the job was, at the end of the day we were renting movies to people. And nothing forces people to bond like shared embarrassment.

But as the company grew past its founders and initial small team, I didn't know if traditions like that would survive. Our hires from India seemed totally bewildered by the practice. The whole thing had "hazing" and "possible HR violation" written all over it. But that's how small we were: we didn't even have HR guidelines to violate yet.

We'd need them, if we continued to grow. And we'd need to codify a lot of things, to make sure our business continued to run smoothly, once the founding team wasn't doing all the work. Navigating those challenges was a lot of what I spent the fall of 1998 doing. That, and looking for new office space.

Oh, and dealing with a massive international porn scandal.

It was supposed to be a stunt, something viral, something that would get traction well beyond its cost.

It was supposed to be Bill Clinton.

When you're trying to build a product, sometimes it doesn't matter how many promotions you run or how many deals you offer. Sometimes, you just need to get attention. Blockbuster would use this tactic in 2006, when they launched Total Access, a combined in-store and online rental service meant to compete with Netflix. They hired Jessica Simpson for a huge unveiling and made her gush, in front of the press, about how much she loved renting movies on the internet.

But in the fall of 1998, we didn't have Blockbuster money. And we *certainly* didn't have Jessica Simpson's number.

But we did have Mitch Lowe.

Mitch was spending more and more time in the Netflix office in Scotts Valley. Despite the draw of his presidential biographies on audio, he was tiring of the long commute to his house back in Marin, so he would frequently stay overnight in a small hotel by the golf course in Aptos, half an hour south of our offices. It certainly wasn't the closest place he could stay, but he had two reasons for choosing Aptos for his pied-à-terre. First, Mitch had become a regular at the Tuesday night wine tasting group that Lorraine, Te, and I had started up. Our usual locale for the tasting was Theo's restaurant in Soquel, and after doing his part to help us finish off six bottles or more of wine each Tuesday night, Mitch had ample incentive to shorten his commute.

The other reason was an old friend, Arthur Mrozowski, who lived in a small house off the third fairway in Aptos. Arthur was another of the colorful characters in Mitch's past, and he shared a fondness with Mitch for staying up late, tasting wine, and talking movies.

Arthur had fled Poland for the United States at nineteen. He'd found a niche importing Polish videos, which he sold to any video store he could convince to carry them. It wasn't long before he realized it would be considerably more lucrative to move videos in the opposite direction, which led to a video export business. By the time he landed in Aptos, Arthur was CEO of a DVD post-production company called Media Galleries. From this perch, Arthur had a bird's-eye view of all the new video technologies coming out of the Valley, and had recently discovered a startup called Mindset that was developing new video codecs, the software that converts and compresses analog video into digital media — a critical part of the technology that goes into creating a DVD. Late one Thursday night, after a bit of "tasting," Arthur told Mitch about a new breakthrough that Mindset had made: their encoding and compression processes were now so fast that they could essentially transfer analog tapes to DVDs in real time. This increased speed, Arthur said, was going to revolutionize the DVD mastering process. They were looking for a project with a quick turnaround time that they could use to "live-test" their process and make sure it worked as fast as they thought.

It took less than twenty-four hours — and a few bottles of wine — for Mitch to come up with the perfect candidate.

For the previous eight months, the country had been gripped by the investigation into President Bill Clinton's affair with Monica Lewinsky. In mid-August, the scandal had reached a critical moment: for the first time, a sitting president had been compelled to testify in front of a grand jury. Although his testimony was secret, the session had been videotaped, and now, a month later, on Friday, September 18, the Republican-controlled House Judiciary Committee had announced that in the interest of public transparency, it would be releasing the video to all the major broadcast networks. The testimony would be made public after the weekend, three days later: at 9:00 a.m., Monday, September 21.

When Mitch got to the office later that morning, he could barely contain himself. "This is it," he said, throwing a printout of a page from Yahoo! News onto my desk. "Look at this. It's the perfect thing. Clinton! Let's make our own DVD."

He stared at me expectantly, and then, realizing that I had no idea what he was talking about, began filling me in on his conversation with Art.

"I've already talked to one of my friends at KTVU," Mitch went on, referring to the Bay Area Fox affiliate. "He said that he could make us a three-quarter-inch master copy directly from the broadcast. It's only four hours long. I'll be there waiting, I'll drive it straight to Mindset, and they can have a DVD master ready to start pressing discs by that afternoon. We can begin shipping them the next morning."

"Okay, hold on, Woodward," I said. "Let's slow down a sec and figure this out."

But I had to admit it: Mitch's idea was good. It wasn't Watergate, but it was good.

While Mitch ran off to set the wheels in motion, I rounded up Te and Christina and filled them in.

Predictably, Te loved it. She pulled out one of the pencils she regularly had in her hair holding things in place, and used it to make notes on a yellow pad while she spoke. "We can probably get national press on this. The *Times*. The *Post*. Even the *Journal*."

"What's wrong, Christina?" I asked. She was chewing on her thumbnail and frowning.

"It's a cool idea, but we can't just jump into this without thinking it through," she explained, her voice rising. "What is the disc art going to look like, how are we going to ship it, how much are we going to charge? We have to get it all set up in the system!" She shook her head in frustration. "There's just no way we can have this ready to go by Monday."

"But this is all about the timing," I countered. "We don't have time to do a full release of this. And we don't have to. We can do very minimal disc art, we can mail it in any envelope. It's a sale, not a rental. It doesn't need to come back."

I paused. An idea was forming.

"And let's not charge anything. Let's make it free. No charge. A public service from your civic-minded friends at Netflix."

"That's crazy," Te said, shaking her head. "So crazy that it just might work."

"We've got a problem."

It was two hours later, and Christina was clearly in problem-solving mode. Her happy spot. She had that smile on her face that said she was excited to tell me what the problem was, and even more excited to tell me the clever way she had already solved it.

"I've been working with Eric on getting a free DVD set up in our system," she explained, preparing to walk me through the process. I normally would have pushed her to cut to the chase, but I decided to let her have her moment. "Well, we had no problem getting it all set up on the development server, but when we tried to actually ship the order? No go."

She paused for effect.

"Eric and Boris played with it for a while and finally figured out that the software can't sell something for nothing. Our system literally doesn't know how to give something away for free. So Eric and I decided to try something. We priced the DVD at one cent and it worked. As long as we charge something for it, we're fine."

She sat back, grinning. There was more. I knew she had something up her sleeve.

"Then I had an idea. Two cents. Let's charge everybody two cents. Then we can do some crazy promotion about 'putting in your two cents' or something like that."

She dropped her hands in her lap, clearly proud of herself. There was nothing else to say. We had the tag for our press release, which would go out first thing Tuesday morning.

Mitch had problems too, but he wasn't quite as happy about them as Christina was.

At first everything had gone smoothly. At the conclusion of the broadcast Monday morning, Mitch's contact at KTVU had been true to his word and immediately transferred the four hours of testimony to tape. Mitch had driven it from Oakland to Aptos, and within a few hours, Mindset had the tape mounted and encoding was under way.

But when Mitch gave me an update call at 5:00 p.m., it was clear that things had begun to go awry.

"The technology is actually really good," he started in, but as he struggled with what to say next, I could hear his enthusiasm fading. "But, uh... it's clearly not ready for prime time. All kinds of bugs. Every time they start the encoding it runs for a bit, then stops. They're running it now, but it's really slow."

There was a long pause. "It might be considered real-time encoding — but only if they were encoding a video of a turtle."

By the time we left the office, we were all set for a Tuesday morning announcement. Te had drafted a press release, headlined "Netflix Lets Consumers Put in Their Two Cents Regarding Clinton Testimony."

Scotts Valley, Calif. —

Netflix, the world's first online DVD rental store, announces the immediate availability of "President Clinton's Grand Jury Testi-mony" on DVD for $.02, plus shipping and handling, exclusively

at its Internet store, www.netflix.com. The leading online DVD re-
tailer had originally offered the title to its customers for a $9.95
purchase and $4 rental price, but decided Tuesday to offer it for
sale only at a lower price to encourage public education regarding
these history-making events.

"Congress released this material with the intent that it be made
available to the widest possible audience," said Marc B. Randolph,
president and CEO of Netflix. "By offering the complete Clinton
testimony on DVD for only $.02, we believe we are making it pos-
sible for virtually every DVD owner to easily review this material
and form their own opinion. In addition, we believe that the abil-
ity of DVD to let a user easily jump from topic to topic makes the
DVD format uniquely suited to reviewing material such as this."

Is this a great country or what?

Meanwhile, Christina had built a custom page for the website, and
Eric had finished setting things up to handle incoming orders. Jim
had put together a special shipping envelope that was cheap and light.
Mitch was standing by at Media Galleries, ready to get the discs duplicated as soon as the master was ready. He would drive them straight to
the office.

We were ready to go.

When Mitch called at 7:00 a.m. Tuesday, he sounded tired.

"Do you want the good news or the bad news?" he asked. Without
waiting for an answer, he continued: "We finally got the encoding
finished a few hours ago, and it works fine on Sony and Mitsubishi machines. But it doesn't work on Panasonic and Toshiba. We're running
it again."

At 10:00, he reported: "Now it works on Panasonic and Toshiba, but
not on Sony. We're running it again."

When I checked my phone early that afternoon, I saw that I had missed a call from him. It had come in at 2:00. The voicemail was short. "We're finally finished. We've gotten a working version and they just finished the silver master platter." I could hear the exhaustion in his voice. "I'm heading down to Fremont to get it duplicated."

When I finally reached him, it was 4:30. In the background I could hear the clatter of machinery. "Almost there," he shouted, sounding almost upbeat. "I'm just about to get the first 2,000 copies. I just need to bring them over to the labeler and then we're ready. You should have them by late this afternoon."

"Mitch!" I hollered. "Just come home. We'll send them out without disc labels."

There was a long pause. The machinery was still humming.

"Okay. I'll be there soon."

The press release was out, the news sites had already picked it up, and Reed and I were in the middle of a company meeting when, at 5:30, the door opened and Mitch walked in. His shirt was stained and wrinkled. He had a three-day growth of beard. His hair sprung in every direction. I'd say it looked like he'd just woken up, but the truth was just the opposite: he hadn't slept in almost seventy-two hours.

But he did have something in his hand I had never seen before. It looked like a roll of crackers, wrapped in foil — but supersized. It was two feet long and five inches in diameter. Only when I looked more carefully could I see that it was actually fifty DVDs threaded together on a long, narrow tube of plastic. A spindle: the first one I'd ever seen.

Mitch looked like shit, but he had enough energy left to smile broadly as the entire company erupted in applause. He'd managed to bring Bill Clinton home.

I wish the story ended there. With good news: nearly 5,000 new customers (all of whom owned DVD players) had been obtained at a total cost of less than $5,000. With press exposure in the *New York Times*, the *Wall Street Journal*, the *Washington Post*, and *USA Today*. With the kind of attention even Jessica Simpson would have been hard-pressed to drum up.

Instead, the following Monday, I was just walking into the office when Corey grabbed me.

"Hey, there's some funny comments that have been running across the board this weekend." He spun around to his computer, where one of his DVD forums was on-screen, and scrolled furiously with his mouse. "See? Here. And here. And here. They're saying we sent them some kind of porno?"

I sat down to look. Immediately I had a sinking feeling in my stomach.

People were certainly talking about the Clinton DVD. But when they said that their DVDs were pornographic, they didn't mean that Clinton's testimony was occasionally X-rated. They were saying that we had sent them real, honest-to-God pornography.

"See if you can figure out how widespread this is," I shouted at Corey, then jumped up and ran back to the safe, where Jim and his guys were just starting to make sense of the orders that had come in overnight.

"Jim," I gasped, trying to catch my breath, "hold up on sending out any more Clintons."

"What's up?" He gave me that smile. "We've got about forty of them packed up from yesterday afternoon ready to go out today. Want to hold them up, too, or can they go out?"

"Hold everything," I said, then gave him a quick rundown before heading to Christina and Te.

"Here's your problem, boss," Jim said about half an hour later, walking over to where I sat with Christina. "See these?" He held out two DVDs. They looked identical to me. "They came off two different spindles, and they both should be the same, but if you look closely, you can see where this one" — he handed me one of the two DVDS — "is *slightly* different. This is the porn one. Looks like we got two spindles of these. One of them has been completely sent out. The other still has a dozen or so discs left."

"Have you" — I didn't know how to ask this — "watched it yet?"

There was that smile again. "Yep. Let's just say we watched enough to know that this is the culprit."

That night when I got home, the house was already dark. Thank goodness. I didn't want to have to explain to Lorraine what I needed to do. I turned on our TV, powered up the DVD player, and slid the DVD into the slot. As it spun up and the image started, I knew in a second that what I was watching didn't star Bill Clinton, Monica Lewinsky, or even Ken Starr. It was porn, all right. And nasty stuff, too. I didn't need to watch anymore. (I promise.)

It was a big swing. And a big miss. But if you're trying to make a dream into reality, you have to be willing to swing at a lot of pitches.

The next day we did the only thing we could. Like Bill, we came clean. We sent out a letter to every one of the nearly 5,000 people who had put in their two cents. We explained what had happened, and we apologized for the confusion and any possible offense. And if they had received the porn version, we asked that they return it to us, at our expense, after which we would gladly send them out the proper DVD.

But you know? Funny thing. Not a single person did.

12.

"I'm Losing Faith in You"

(fall 1998)

BACK IN THE STONE Age, when I was a kid, there were no video games. There was no Instagram, no Facebook, no Snapchat. There was no way to watch movies at home, unless you wanted to set up the old reel-to-reel and watch yourself as a baby. There wasn't — in the Randolph household at least — even cable TV. The only way to rot your brain back then was by watching whatever was on the major networks. And on Saturday mornings and after school, that meant cartoons.

Back then, I'd watch anything: superhero cartoons, cartoon sitcoms like *The Flintstones* or *The Jetsons*, anything by Hanna-Barbera. But now, when I think of cartoons, I mostly remember the old stuff: Bugs Bunny and Elmer Fudd, Wile E. Coyote and the Road Runner, Tom and Jerry and Tweety and Sylvester. All of those cartoons, it strikes me now, are about pursuit — about one character chasing another, often to his doom. Elmer Fudd wants the wascally wabbit. Wile E. Coyote pants after the Road Runner. Tom and Sylvester, cats to the core, spend their lives stalking Tweety and Jerry.

Sometimes chasing a dream is like that: a singular pursuit of something nearly impossible. In the startup world, where the money is perilous and the timeline is unbelievably compressed, the day-to-day pursuit of your dream can appear frenzied — even manic — to outsiders. To your friends and family you'll sometimes look more like Yosemite Sam than, say, Marc Randolph, successful CEO of a young e-commerce company. You'll lose sleep, you'll mutter to yourself while driving. When you try to explain your dream to other people, they won't understand that it isn't just about raising funds or customer conversion or daily monitors. It's a surreal chase, a pursuit that gives your life meaning.

Funny thing about those cartoons — they never end in capture. They're about evasion, disappointment, near misses. You get the feeling that if Wile E. Coyote ever actually caught the Road Runner, he wouldn't know what to do. But that's not the point. The point is the pursuit of the impossible.

Pursuing the impossible is a setup for pratfalls and comedy, drama and tension. Also absurdity. Because despite all the best-laid traps of Elmer Fudd or the most elaborate snares of Tom or Sylvester, a lot of those cartoons end suddenly, with anvils and pianos falling out of the sky.

Follow your dream, spend a year chasing it, and one day you might find yourself sitting dazed in a wreckage of black and white keys, bluebirds chirping around your head, with no idea of how you got there.

It was mid-September. We'd had an Indian summer in Scotts Valley, and even though it was early, I could already feel the heat coming off the pavement as I pulled the Volvo into the parking lot. The gardener must have gotten an early start to beat the heat: a hundred feet of freshly planted flowers already filled the beds lining either side of the driveway to our offices. I wasn't sure what they were — tulips, maybe — but I couldn't help but admire the neat rows and bright colors, every plant healthy and vibrant and new. I parked next to his wheelbarrow and noticed it was loaded high with last week's flowers: uprooted daffodils, browned and wilted, dirt clinging to their shredded roots.

The circle of life.

A few parking spots over, Eric was struggling to load four new PCs onto an office chair, which he was using as a makeshift handcart. With the injection of money from IVP, as well as Tim Haley's recruiting expertise, we'd been on a hiring spree. Each week brought a few new faces to the office. We were only at forty employees, so I still knew everybody — but I was starting to realize that there would soon be a day I didn't.

"Let me give you a hand," I said, picking up one of the boxes and balancing it between my briefcase and my hip.

"We really should invest in a real handcart," Eric said as we squeaked up the ramp and into the offices.

Christina looked up from her computer when we passed, then went back to typing. "Reed stopped by this morning," she said, tilting her head toward me but keeping her eyes angled at her screen. "Superearly, like six a.m. Said he was going to stop by again on his way back from the Valley tonight. He wants you to stick around until then."

"That it?"

Christina nodded. "That's it."

I didn't have much time to dwell on what Reed wanted, but I could guess. Most likely it was the Sony deal. Scammer aside, we were starting to see real returns from it — people were redeeming their coupons. It was by far the biggest bet we'd ever made, and considering all the chips we'd pushed into the middle, we needed it to pay off.

Or it could be an agreement with Amazon we'd been finessing ever since meeting with Bezos in June. We hadn't been ready to sell then, but Reed had been ready to partner with Amazon in a different capacity. Reed agreed with me that if we were going to make it as a company, we'd have to focus on renting DVDs, not selling them. So he'd engineered a soft exit: Once Amazon moved into DVD, we'd push our users who wanted to buy DVDs there. They could rent through us, and buy through Amazon, via a link. In exchange, Amazon would direct traffic our way.

Nothing about this deal was official yet. In fact, in September, I think I was the only one who knew about it. Reed and I had been going back and forth on the subject for weeks. Even though halting DVD sales had been my idea, the thought of jettisoning the only profitable part of our business still made me nervous. But Reed and I were both convinced that we had to choose what we were going to focus on, and partnering with Amazon would not only reinvigorate our rentals, it would be a real feather in our cap. It would validate us.

We were thinking a lot about validation in those days. That's how Tim Haley saw the Sony deal: if they were willing to work with us, we were worth investing in. Sony made us credible — even at an incredible cost. A partnership with Amazon, in Reed's view, could do the same thing.

I was dying to find out what had happened over the weekend. How many new Sony customers had ripped open their new players, noted down their product serial numbers, and headed to Netflix to redeem their offers? I knew Reed was equally curious. Maybe he thought we would have new numbers to go over at the end of the day. I made a note to myself to make sure I had up-to-date reports before he came back. But for now, there were plenty of other things to worry about. Like the morning monitors.

It was nearly six when Reed finally swept in. I was writing copy, but I could hear his progress through the office, from the front to the back. First, I heard the beach chair creaking in front of Eric's desk as Reed pulled it around to Eric's side so he could point something out on the screen. Then, a few minutes later, I heard him asking our controller, Greg Julien, for an update on cash. Soon he made his way back to my office.

"Got a minute," he said, with no upward inflection, like it wasn't a question, like he almost hoped I didn't.

Reed looked serious. And he was dressed the part, in the formal (for him) outfit he wore only for important meetings: black linen pants and a gray turtleneck, with black dress shoes. I pointed to his neck and tried to make a joke of it — "Reed, it's almost ninety outside" — but he didn't seem to hear me.

"We need to talk," he said. He was carrying his notebook computer open in his hand, holding it by the corner of the screen with the keyboard hanging below. I could see that it was open to a PowerPoint slideshow, and I could just make out the first slide. ACCOMPLISHMENTS, it read, in bold 36-point type.

Reed stepped into the room, grabbed the chair in front of my desk, and in one motion swung it around to my side, with the seat facing out. He straddled it, leaning his chest across the back, then spun the laptop so I could see the screen. It was exactly what he did when he wanted to show Eric how badly he'd bungled a piece of code.

Where is this going, I thought.

"Marc," Reed started slowly, "I've been thinking a lot about the future. And I'm worried."

He paused, trying to read my face. Then he pursed his lips, looking down at the screen like it was a set of cue cards, and continued. "I'm worried about us. Actually, I'm worried about you. About your judgment."

"What?" My mouth, I'm sure, dropped open.

Reed directed my attention to the screen, then hit the space bar. One by one, "accomplishments" animated their way onto the screen.

- Hired original team.
- Established coherent culture.
- Launched site.

It was like a slideshow at a funeral. I could tell it wasn't going to get better from here.

"What the fuck, Reed," I finally managed to blurt out. "You're concerned about where we're going, and you're going to lay it out for me in fucking PowerPoint?"

My voice had started to rise, but then, noticing my office door was still open, I dropped it to a whisper.

"This is bullshit," I hissed, pointing at the laptop. "There is no way I'm sitting here while you pitch me on why I suck."

Reed blinked and sat still. I could tell he hadn't expected this reaction. He pursed his lips again. I knew he was analyzing pros and cons, evaluating his next steps, his mind whirring just like the cooling fan in the Dell in front of us, still displaying its list of my accomplishments. After about ten seconds he nodded, then reached over and shut the computer.

"Okay," he said. "This isn't about how you suck, though."

"Good," I stammered. "Okay." I could feel my anger subsiding, replaced now by a sense of dread. I stood up and closed the office door.

"Marc," Reed started in as I settled back into my seat, "you've done some amazing things here."

He paused.

"But I'm losing faith in your ability to lead the company alone. Your strategic sense is erratic — sometimes right on, and sometime *way* off. I've seen issues with judgment, hiring, financial instincts. And I'm concerned that I'm seeing these kinds of issues at our small size. Next year's problems and the year after's will be much harder, and the consequences for missteps much more severe. Things are only going to get worse as the company grows."

There's a speaking tactic in business, useful for breaking bad news. It's called a *shit sandwich*. You open up with a string of compliments, praise for work well done. That's your first piece of bread. Once that's done, you pile on the shit: the bad news, the less than glowing report, the things your audience doesn't particularly enjoy hearing. You close with more bread: a blueprint for moving forward, a plan for dealing with all the shit.

I'm quite familiar with the shit sandwich. Hell, I'd *taught* Reed how to make one. So it was with a peculiar mix of bewilderment and a teacher's pride that I watched him serve one up to me on a silver platter.

"You don't think I'm a good CEO," I said, cutting him off.

"I don't think you're a *complete* CEO," Reed said. "A complete CEO wouldn't have to rely on the guidance of the board as much as you do."

He put his fingertips together and touched them to his chin, as though praying that he could get through what he was trying to say to me. "I think we both know that IVP was only willing to invest in us because I promised that I would be actively involved as chairman. That's a problem. And it's not just fund-raising. One of the reasons I've been so active is because I'm scared about what would happen to the business if I weren't. I don't mind the time, but the results to date have not been sufficient. No one can add enough value from the outside. Especially as the pace picks up."

For the next five minutes, Reed laid out a meticulous argument for why the company was in trouble, if I were to continue leading it alone. He put forth a clear-eyed assessment of my first year in charge, my accomplishments and my failures. It was like watching a computer play chess, ruthlessly and quickly. His analysis was both detailed and general — it veered from individual hires I'd made to errors in accounting to corporate communications. It all went by in a blur, but one thing he said really stuck out.

"You don't appear tough and candid enough to hold strong people's respect," he said. "On the good side, no one good has quit, and your people like you."

I had to smile at that. Forget radical honesty. This was brutal honesty. Ruthless honesty.

"Gee, thanks," I said. "Put that one on my tombstone: *He may have run his business into the ground, but no one good quit, and his people liked him.*"

Reed didn't react to this bit of gallows humor at all. He just kept going, like he was reciting something he'd memorized. I'd taken away his slides, but this was a speech he'd definitely rehearsed. He was nervous about delivering it.

"Marc," Reed said, "we're headed for trouble, and I want you to recognize as a shareholder that there is enough smoke at this small business size that fire at a larger size is likely. Ours is an execution play. We have to move fast and almost flawlessly. The competition will be direct and strong. Yahoo! went from a grad school project to a six-billion-dollar company on awesome execution. We have to do the same thing. I'm not sure we can if you're the only one in charge."

He paused, then looked down, as if trying to gain the strength to do something difficult. He looked up again, right at me. I remember thinking: *He's looking me in the eye.*

"So I think the best possible outcome would be if I joined the company full-time and we ran it together. Me as CEO, you as president."

He waited again. Seeing no reaction, he plunged on. "I don't think I'm overreacting. I think this is a thoughtful solution to an unhappy reality. And I think the CEO/president arrangement would give the company the leadership team it deserves. We could make history we are proud of for the rest of our lives."

Finally, mercifully, he stopped, rocked back slightly in the chair, and took a deep breath.

I sat there not speaking, just slowly nodding. That's what happens when a piano falls out of the sky on your head.

I'm sure Reed wondered why I didn't see the situation with the same clarity and logic as he did. I knew that Reed didn't — couldn't — understand what was going through my head. Thank God for that, because the words going through my head weren't polite.

I knew that a lot of what he was saying was true. But I also thought that we were talking about *my* company. It had been *my* idea. *My* dream. And now it was my business. While Reed had been off at Stanford and at TechNet, I'd been pouring my entire life into building the company. Was it realistic to expect anyone to get *every* decision right? Shouldn't I be allowed to work my way through mistakes?

He wasn't wrong about those, either. He had a point about some of our missteps, and our future going forward. But my initial reaction to what Reed was saying that day in the office was that it had more to do with him than me. I kept thinking: *He's realized that he made a life mistake.* Hadn't he been bored at Stanford, and dropped out? Hadn't he been disappointed by his work in education reform at TechNet? He'd skipped the early days of Netflix because he wanted to change the world, revolutionize education — and most of the teachers and administrators he'd encountered just wanted their pay grade to go up with seniority. And now that he saw that the little crazy idea we'd tested together had real potential, he suddenly found problems with my leadership? Was I not fit to run the company alone, or did he just want back in, without the ego hit of being my employee?

I was furious and hurt. But also, even in the moment, I knew that Reed had a point.

What this complex mix of emotions looked like, only Reed knows. But it must have looked pretty remarkable, because even he noticed that he needed to say something nice — to put the top bun on the shit sandwich.

"Don't be upset," he finally blurted out. "I have tremendous respect and affection for you. It pains me to be so harsh. There are a million good things about your character, maturity, and skill that I admire greatly. I would call you partner proudly."

Reed paused again. I could tell there was more coming. How could there possibly be more to say? My head was spinning.

"I need some time to process this, Reed," I said. "Look, you can't just come in here and propose taking over the company and expect me to say: *Oh, how logical, of course!*"

My voice was getting high again, so I stopped talking.

"I'm not proposing that I take over the company," he said. "I'm proposing that we run it together. As a team."

There was a pause, a long one.

"Look, I'm your friend no matter how this works out," Reed finally said, standing up. "But if this is something that you are dead set against, I'm not going to force it down your throat, even though in my position as a shareholder I could. I respect you too much to do that. If you don't believe that this is in the best interest of the company, and don't want to go forward this way, I'm fine with that. We'll just sell the company, pay back the investors, split the money, and go home."

When he left my office he shut the door quietly behind him, like someone leaving a hospital room. The sun was setting, but I didn't get up to turn on the light. I sat in the dark until almost everyone had left — everyone but Kho, who ambled in sometime after nine, whistling and drumming his fingers on a grease-stained pizza box.

Radical honesty is great, until it's aimed at you.

I'm not going to lie to you, or to myself. What Reed said to me that day in mid-September hurt. It really hurt. Not because Reed was being unkind — he wasn't — but because he was being honest. Brutally, astringently, *rip-the-bandage-off* honest.

This was radical honesty, the same type that we'd practiced from the beginning, back in my Volvo on Highway 17. Reed didn't have an ax to grind, or any ulterior motive. He was driven by what was best for the business, and he respected me too much to do anything else but tell the complete, unvarnished truth. He was just doing what we'd always done with each other.

And the more I thought about it, the more the PowerPoint touched me. Was it clumsy? Yes. Was it totally like Reed to try to frame a delicate, emotionally volatile conversation within the safe confines of a series of animated slides — a presentation of a type that I had taught him to deliver? Also yes.

But insulting? No. I could see, now that he was out of the room and I was sitting in the dark, that Reed had been so nervous about giving me honest feedback that he'd needed a prompt, a set of written reminders, something to make him feel like he was on solid ground. He'd wanted to make sure that he did it right. He wanted to make sure he said the things that needed to be said.

They were hard to hear. But it was even harder to admit to myself that Reed was right. I *was* having problems. Our IVP investment *had* almost fallen apart because of me — because our new partners knew that without some bold stroke born of dramatic, intuitive, and confident leadership, this company was never going to make it. They had never said it out loud, but it was probably obvious to everyone else in that room that the bold stroke, the dramatic and confident and intuitive leadership, was not going to come from me.

The more I thought about it, the more I realized that my dream had evolved. It had originally been a single dream: a new company, with me at the helm. But sitting in my office, hearing Reed articulate where I was falling short, and listening to him make the case for why the company needed both of us, together, at the helm, I realized that there were really *two* dreams, and that I might need to sacrifice one of them to ensure that the other come true.

The company was one dream. Me at the helm was another. And if the company was going to succeed, I needed to honestly confront my own limitations. I needed to acknowledge that I was a builder, someone creative and freewheeling enough to assemble a team, to create a culture, to *launch* an idea from the back of an envelope into a company, an office, a product that existed in the world. But we were exiting that initial stage. Now we were going to have to grow, and rapidly, and that took a different skill set entirely.

I have a pretty good sense of my skill as an entrepreneur. I don't think I'm tooting my own horn to say that I'm in the 98th percentile. I knew, even then, that I *could* lead the company as it grew.

But I also knew, even then, that Reed was in the 99.9th percentile. He's one of the all-time greats. And he was better at this stage of things than I was. More confident. More focused. Bolder.

It was totally obvious to me that when it came to our most pressing and urgent need — money — Reed was better. He'd almost single-handedly founded a company and had brought it through an IPO as CEO. He was a known quantity. Investors were far more likely to bet on him than me. We'd already seen that to be the case.

I had to ask myself: How important was it to see my dream come true? And was it even *my* dream anymore? We now had forty employees, each of whom was as emotionally committed as I was to making Netflix a success. They stayed late, worked weekends, missed commitments to friends and family, all in service to something that had begun as *my* dream — but which, God bless them, they had adopted as their own. Didn't I owe it to them to do everything I could to ensure that we survived, even if it meant that my role would no longer be the one I'd imagined for myself?

What was more important, my title or their jobs?

I stood up from my desk and walked to the window. I could see the nearly empty parking lot, the flower beds at its perimeter in full bloom, illuminated by the orange light of streetlamps. Tomorrow, by six in the morning, that lot would be filling up with Toyotas, Subarus, and VWs belonging to the people who worked for me. Many of those cars had payments attached to them, and insurance policies. Bills. And in a way, I was responsible for those.

When your dream becomes a reality, it doesn't just belong to you. It belongs to the people who helped you — your family, your friends, your co-workers. It belongs to the world.

Looking at those cars in the parking lot, I really knew that Reed was right. That the CEO/president arrangement *would* give the company the leadership it deserved. *Would* greatly increase our odds of success. *Would* create a company that we could be proud of for the rest of our lives.

And in retrospect, of course, Reed was right. Netflix might have survived with me continuing on as sole CEO. But you don't write a book about a company that *survives*. There is no doubt in my mind that without him assuming more of a leadership role, Netflix would not have become the company it is today. Paradoxically, if I hadn't relinquished the title of CEO to Reed in 1999, I wouldn't be writing this book.

The company needed us to run it. *Together.*

When I'm feeling down, and need to remember moments of courage from my past, I don't immediately think back to some faraway mountain peak, a dangerous climb, or a treacherous river crossing. I don't even think back to those mornings in Reed's car, or the first meetings in Hobee's, when I was trying to convince talented (and reluctant) people to quit their jobs for a crazy and illogical venture. I don't think of the original leap of faith, the running start, the hundreds of failed tests with no indication that any of them would ever work.

I think of leaving the office that night. I think of driving slowly home through the empty streets of Scotts Valley, ready to tell my wife that I'd decided I should no longer be sole CEO of the company I'd founded. And knowing that I was doing the right thing.

By now you know that chapters in the Netflix story rarely end neatly, all wrapped up in a tidy red-and-black ribbon. And this chapter is no different. I did make that lonely drive home, and I did sit on the porch with Lorraine for a few hours that night, a bottle of wine between us, as we went through the logic — and emotion — of my decision. And we did ultimately decide that Reed's proposal was the right thing to do — that I owed it to my employees, my investors, and myself to ensure that the company would continue to be successful, even if it meant stepping down as sole CEO.

But as I finished turning off the lights, and Lorraine carefully loaded our wineglasses into the dishwasher, I sat down at the kitchen table to do a last check of email. Flashing at the top of the in-box was an email from Reed. Time: 11:20 PM. SUBJ: Honesty.

The email summarized and reiterated the afternoon's conversation. I was sure it was essentially a transcription of the PowerPoint slides. There were bullet points dealing with my strategic sense, hiring, financial controls, people management, and ability to raise capital. Now that I'd had time to think about what Reed had said, it was easier to see it in writing. My eyes scanned to the end: "I sincerely wish things were different, Marc, for both of our sakes, but in my heart of hearts I believe everything I said today to be true."

Then there was something new.

But in a similar vein it is my best sense that the right thing to do to reflect the change is to re-split our stock options. IVP invested on the promise that we could execute as Chairman/CEO; it is not right to go back to them and say it didn't work, that we need another 2m options for me.

I couldn't believe what I was reading. In the sentences that followed, Reed was saying that in order to come in as CEO he needed more options. And worse, he was saying that a big slug of those shares should come from *me*. That I should give up some of my equity in the company, since we would now be splitting the responsibilities.

"That's bullshit!" Lorraine shouted, once I had explained to her what Reed was asking for. "You guys started out fifty-fifty even though you were doing all the work, pulling sixty-hour weeks as CEO and he was sitting on his ass as chairman. Now that he actually has to come to the office, suddenly the fifty-fifty isn't good enough?"

Lorraine was furious, shaking her head so hard I thought she might hurt her neck. I tried to calm her down, but it was a lost cause. "It's bullshit," she kept saying. "Bullshit. That's all."

After she stomped upstairs to the bedroom, I sat quietly at the kitchen table and carefully closed the lid of my laptop. I knew it would take me a while to get to sleep. There were a thousand things going through my mind — how we'd break the news to the rest of the company, what I was going to say to Reed the next day about the options. How my role would change in the coming months, and how I'd deal with the transition.

The future of the company stretched before me, daunting and open, and although I couldn't say, that night, that I was at peace with my decision, I knew that I would be, someday soon. I was starting to see how Reed and I could work together to make the company a success. I could practically hear the engine of our collaboration start to hum.

13.

Over the Hill

(spring 1999: one year after launch)

We moved the company to Los Gatos in March of 1999. The new office was just over the hill on 17, as close to Santa Cruz as you could get and still be in the Valley. It was fourteen minutes from my house. A far cry from the five-minute drive I'd grown accustomed to, that first year. But long enough to get three, or sometimes four, run-throughs of Sweet Adeline, or Down Our Way, or whatever barbershop quartet song I was working on at the time.

Let me explain. A few years before Netflix, in the mid-nineties, Lorraine was worried that I was burning myself out. She suggested I get a hobby that had nothing to do with work. "You always sing in the car," she said. "Why don't you join a choir?"

I not only joined a choir, I joined the Society for the Preservation and Encouragement of Barber Shop Quartet Singing in America. SPEBSQSA, for short. No women allowed. (They had their own group: the Sweet Adelines.)

The society had chapters all over the world, and the closest one was in Santa Cruz. Every Tuesday night, there was a group sing in the community room of the Felton Bible Church. Anyone who was a member of SPEBSQSA could drop in, and because of the standard repertoire, there wasn't any confusion, once you knew the songs and your part in them. Every sing started with "The Old Songs," the official theme of SPEBSQSA. After that, the director would call out different songs, sometimes relying on member requests. And after two hours or so, sometimes we'd go out for a beer.

There are four voice ranges in barbershop singing. Tenor is the highest, followed by lead, baritone, and bass. Since there are only men singing, there are no alto or soprano parts, and the ranges are much closer together. That leads to really tight harmonies — singers used to the wider ranges of mixed choirs often have a difficult time adjusting to the tricky parts that barbershop demands. Singing in a big mixed choir feels like being in an orchestra, with the timpani and double basses in the back and the flutes and violins in the front. But barbershop feels more like a guitar, one person playing chords made up of strings tuned pretty close together, in timbre and pitch.

I loved singing barbershop. I loved feeling like part of an instrument, feeling a chord come into being. I rarely sang the lead melody — instead, I was often tasked with intricate close harmony, just off the main line. I was a supporting voice, completely necessary but not the first thing you heard. Barbershop's like that — it's a truly collaborative form. Take out any of the parts, and the song doesn't sound right.

I never performed in public with SPEBSQSA. That wasn't the point. The point was those Tuesday nights. I attended them religiously. They were like AA meetings for me, except instead of sad stories and burnt coffee, there was joyful, old-timey music. Those nights kept me sane.

They almost drove my family nuts, though. To practice, I sang along to barbershop tapes in the car — special tapes that isolated my part. On the A-side would be just your part, and the B-side would be all the others, with your part dropped out. The idea was, you could play the A-side ten times in a row to really nail down your harmony part, and then flip the tape to practice singing it with the rest of the ensemble.

This is a useful technology, but it's *exceedingly* annoying for any passenger not enamored of barbershop quartets. Like my son.

"Stop singing!" Logan used to yell, strapped into his car seat, with his hands over his ears. "No more singing!"

I'd stop. But when I was alone, driving to and from work, I really let it rip.

It strikes me now that those morning singing sessions were useful preparation for the work I was doing in the office in late 1998 and early 1999. Every day, I was redefining my role. I wasn't always the lead voice anymore. I wasn't always in front of the ensemble. But I was part of a group, and we were making a big, beautiful noise together. I was learning how to sing a tight, close harmony with Reed.

Officially that spring, my title was "president." Day-to-day, little about my job had changed. I was still in charge of the aspects of Netflix that I loved (and was good at): customer relations, marketing, PR, web design, all the movie content, and our ongoing relationships with DVD player manufacturers. Reed took over the back end: finances, operations, and engineering. As far as I was concerned, the job titles were irrelevant. But titles mattered to VCs, and I wasn't stupid: I knew that when it came to raising money for a rapidly growing (and still not profitable) startup, having Reed as CEO was one of our best assets. Reed's presence calmed the board and reassured potential investors. That spring, I was more than happy to take a backseat pitching our company. I did what I did best: helping Reed soften his edges with both investors and employees.

Another person tasked with smoothing things over where Reed was involved was Patty McCord. Reed had brought her into the fold to run HR soon after we announced that we'd be running the company together. She'd been director of HR at Pure Atria, and she'd long been Reed's right-hand point person. She was a sort of Reed-whisperer. She understood him like few people did and, more importantly, knew how to nudge him into social niceties. Reed can be…blunt. Patty can be, too. But she's blunt in a charming, Texan way — she understands social graces. Patty knew that Reed didn't always notice when he'd ruffled someone's feathers, and that he was often oblivious to other people's hurt feelings — especially people who didn't know him well, like I did. If there was a contentious meeting, Patty knew how and when to take Reed aside and gently suggest that maybe he should apologize for calling somebody's idea "totally unsupported by reason."

Once, I overheard her telling Reed that our executive meeting had been very productive, before asking him who'd done most of the talking.

"Marc and I did," he said.

"Do you think other people in a meeting should talk, too?"

Reed stared at her for a second, and I wondered if he'd answer.

He nodded. "Point taken."

Patty's role went far beyond merely Reed, however. It's hard to overstate how enormous an impact she made on Netflix, as director of HR. Frankly, it's hard to overstate the impact she made on the entire field of human resources. She completely redefined it.

I've written in this book about how Netflix's culture, at least originally, wasn't the result of careful planning — of aspirational principles or cultural manifestos. How it was a reflection of the shared values and behaviors of the founders. How we trusted each other, worked hard, and had zero patience for traditional corporate bullshit.

All of that is true. But what happens when the team grows?

When a company is small, trust and efficiency go hand in hand. If you've got the right people on your team, you don't need to tell them exactly how you want them to do things — in fact, you often don't even need to tell them what you want them to do. You simply need to be clear about what you want to accomplish and why it's important. If you hired the right people — smart, capable, trustworthy — they'll figure out what needs to be done, and they'll go ahead and do it. They'll solve problems on their own before you even know the problems exist.

And if you didn't hire the right person? It'll be apparent, really quickly.

Our early culture at Netflix was born completely out of how Reed and I treated each other. We didn't give each other a list of tasks we expected the other to be doing and then "check in" frequently to make sure everything got done. We just made sure that each of us understood the company's objectives, and which aspects each of us were responsible for. It was up to us to figure out what needed to be done to accomplish those objectives. And it was up to us to be honest with each other — radically honest.

I've written about what that looked like — or, more accurately, what it *sounded* like. Raised voices, argumentative meetings, blunt statements about how an idea was stupid or wouldn't work. Sometimes it was hard for people to understand that Reed and I really *liked* each other — that we'd found that we were most productive when we dropped all the bullshit and just said what we meant. Reed and I had been doing this since those early days in the car on 17, and we'd never stopped. Whether it was just the two of us or a twenty-person departmental meeting, we felt that we owed it to the company (and each other) to make sure that we'd teased out the proper solution — or, more accurately, beat it out of each other with 4-irons and billy clubs. Sometimes the discussions would become so boisterous that Reed and I would lose ourselves totally in academic gymnastics, finally stopping only when we realized that one or the other of our ideas — or, more usually, some combination of the two — was obviously the solution, and that it was time to move on. It was not unusual for Reed and I to look up after a particularly loud session to see the quiet, stunned faces of our colleagues around the table, with expressions that seemed to ask, "Why are Mommy and Daddy fighting?"

But they got used to it.

Radical honesty. Freedom and Responsibility. These are phenomenal ideals, but for our first couple of years, they weren't really written down. We approached things on an ad hoc basis.

Here's an example.

At some point in 1999, one of our engineering managers came to me with a peculiar request. His girlfriend had moved to San Diego and he was trying to keep their relationship on stable footing. "How would you feel," he asked, "if I left work early on Fridays to fly down to San Diego?"

He explained that he would work from there on Monday, fly back home Monday night, and be in the office Tuesday morning.

My answer probably surprised him. "I don't care where you work, or what hours you work. Work from Mars, for all I care. If all you're asking me is about when you work and where you do it, that's an easy answer: it makes no difference to me.

"But," I continued, "if what you're really asking me is whether I'm willing to lower my expectations for you and your group so that you can spend time with your girlfriend? Well, that's an easy answer, too. No."

He looked at me uncertainly. I could see his dreams of San Diego weekends fading away.

"Look, where and when you work is entirely up to you. If you can run your group effectively on three and a half days a week in the office, all power to you. Go ahead — I'm envious. Wish I was smart enough to do that. Just remember: You're a manager. Part of your job is making sure that your team knows what you want them to accomplish and why it's important. Do you think you can do that without being around?"

Needless to say, his girlfriend was a free agent shortly thereafter.

I gave that engineer freedom to make a choice, but also reminded him of his responsibility to the team. I was radically honest with him — I doubted that he'd be able to keep up his end of the deal if he took off early for San Diego every week — but ultimately I left it up to him.

The manager felt empowered, free to make a choice about his own lifestyle, and the company ended up benefiting from his renewed focus. Everyone won.

Well, almost everyone. The girlfriend in San Diego probably didn't see it the way I did.

Freedom and Responsibility weren't just for managers, either. Take our receptionist, for example. When he started the job, there wasn't a seven-page list of all the things he could do or not do all day — *Keep the desk clean. Don't eat at the desk.* Instead, his job description was a single sentence: *Put the best face forward for the company.*

We gave our receptionist a clear responsibility and near-total freedom to figure out how to accomplish it. It was entirely up to him what hours during the day someone needed to be there; up to him to figure out how to cover when he was away, or sick, or needed a day off. It was up to him to figure out which behaviors *didn't* put the best face forward for the company (like eating lunch at his desk), and which helped. (I have a strong suspicion that he bought the popcorn machine.)

And you know what? We had a damn good receptionist as a result.

A culture of freedom and responsibility, coupled with radical honesty, worked like a charm. Not only did we get great results, but employees loved it. People who have the judgment to make decisions responsibly *love* having the freedom to do so.

They love being trusted.

But that just makes sense, right? If you fill your company with people who lack good judgment, then you have to build all kinds of guardrails to keep them in line. You have to define everything for them: how much they can spend on office supplies, how many vacation days they take, when they are expected to be at their desk.

Most companies end up building a system to protect themselves from people who lack judgment. And that only ends up frustrating the people who have it. Remember the engineers in the hot tub? If you treat people like children, it doesn't matter how many beanbag chairs and beer parties you throw at them. They will resent you.

In 2000, we were growing fast. And we were still hiring people with good judgment. But even people with good judgment had questions about culture and rules — and they shouldn't always have to find me or Reed to ask them.

We started to ask ourselves: What if you could build a process that was meant for people who had great judgment? What if you could free them from all the petty restrictions that drive the top performers crazy? How can we scale up this set of ideals that came so naturally to us, so that a growing company can benefit from them?

How do you codify culture?

That's where Patty McCord came in. She was brilliant at pushing the boundary of rules and freedom. She identified that what was special at Netflix was our particular combination of freedom and responsibility. And then she endeavored to put structure in place not to limit freedom — but to encourage and preserve it.

How far can you take freedom? How do you ensure shared responsibility?

Patty came down on the side of common sense. For example: If you were traveling for work, common sense said there had to be some mechanism for expense reimbursement. But none of us wanted lengthy, time-consuming, and ultimately pointless approval processes for it. If we were trusting them to make decisions on the company's behalf that could make or lose millions of dollars, we could certainly trust them to make decisions about what type of plane tickets they should book for themselves.

Same with vacation days. We hadn't kept track of them before because we didn't need to. The attitude was: *If you need to take a day off, just take it. I don't need to know about your root canal, or your kid's school schedule. Just get your work done, and cover for yourself when you're gone.*

But when a company has fifty employees, things get more complicated. People want to know what they can and can't do. Patty could have just replicated the standards of the time: fourteen days per year paid time off. Instead, she was curious. If we wanted our employees to take time off when they needed it, why couldn't we also let them decide how much time to take and when to take it? What if we didn't have a set number of vacation days? What if we just trusted our employees to get things done?

Unlimited vacation days and hassle-free expense reimbursement are almost clichés now. But they were groundbreaking at the time. In Netflix, Patty saw an opportunity to redefine the role of HR departments. No longer was HR just a lonely cubicle filled with employee handbooks, sexual harassment claims, and benefits summaries. Instead, she envisioned the department as a proactive agent for culture.

She saw an opening, and she drove a truck through it. She dismantled all the systems we had in place that limited the amount of freedom we granted our employees, and designed systems that were almost totally on the side of employee freedom. She fought hard to ensure that we didn't inadvertently create new paradigms that collared our workers, while also implementing structures that made it clear what we expected from them. Part of why she was so successful is because she held everyone, including senior leadership, accountable. It didn't matter who you were — Patty would call you on your bullshit. She was never afraid to speak truth to power.

She knew how to do something rare: scale up culture.

A good example: Remember new employee dress-up days? I'd long assumed that they would fall by the wayside as we got bigger. Asking someone to make a costume and endure a fake interview is easy when you're only hiring one person a week. But once we had five, six, or a dozen new hires every week, it wasn't all that practical.

But Patty saw the value in a quirky, film-oriented ritual. So she made it easier and more efficient: she filled an entire room in the new office with dozens and dozens of film-related costumes — Batman outfits, Wonder Woman capes, cowboy hats and fake six-shooters fit for a Western. New hires still had to dress up, but everybody had the same pool of outfits to wear. The pressure was off. It was just fun.

Patty also smoothed over some of our rougher edges. She tried to, anyway. For example, one of the only pieces of decoration in my office was an *Austin Powers: International Man of Mystery* promotional poster that a movie studio had sent me. It depicted the entire text of Dr. Evil's soliloquy to his therapist, halfway through the film, in which he recounts in baroque language his bizarre childhood, describes in detail his comically insane father, and rhapsodizes about the "breathtaking" feeling of "a shorn scrotum."

I knew it wasn't the most HR-friendly wall hanging. But I couldn't help it: I loved that movie. And that scene made me snort with laughter. It became an inside joke between Patty and me: Every time she popped her head into my office and saw my poster, she'd stifle a laugh and order me to take it down. And I would — at least until her back was turned. Then I'd put it right back up.

Just because Netflix was growing and had an honest-to-God HR person didn't mean that we couldn't have a little fun in the offices. Case in point: a little game we called Coins in the Fountain.

I don't remember who came up with it. All I remember is that the male employees of Netflix played it constantly. The rules were simple: You put a coin in the bottom of the urinal. The next person to use the facilities would see it and either ignore it, or reach into the bowl and take it. It was a sort of sociological experiment: How much money would it take for someone to do something disgusting and unsanitary, and reach into the bowl?

The game only worked, of course, if not everyone knew they were playing. But whoever seeded the urinal would usually tip me off. We learned a lot of interesting things about human nature, playing that game. For instance: a quarter would disappear much more quickly than three dimes. No one would touch paper money, unless the denomination was over five dollars. The highest cash value ever achieved was when someone threw in a twenty-dollar bill. It languished in the urinal all day, and was still there when I left at six for dinner with my family. But when I came back to the office later, at eight or nine, it was gone.

I still have my suspicions.

Another game we liked to play involved the kitchen. It was a typical mid-90s setup, the sort of thing you might recognize from *Dilbert* cartoons or *The Office:* refrigerator stocked with forgotten Tupperware, microwave stained by dozens of exploding popcorn bags. This was years before nitro-cold-brew taps dominated the kitchen spaces of American startups. We were decidedly more old-school. No on-site chef for us. Most of us brought our lunches to work.

This game was also a kind of willpower test, but in reverse — and with snacks. It arose from a common problem with shared kitchens and communal food. Anytime anyone brought a snack to share among the whole office — a dozen donuts from the shop down the street, or a bowl full of leftover Halloween candy — it would vanish within minutes. That's what long hours and stress will do to you. Crumpled fun-size Milky Way wrappers and powdered sugar littered the tabletops mere seconds after a batch of snacks had been dropped off.

Eventually, we made a game out of it. Was it possible to bring a snack that would last more than a few minutes in the kitchen? Could you bring something that would get eaten...but only over the course of an entire day?

The challenge wasn't to bring a food item so disgusting that no one would touch it. That would have been too easy. Just bring rocks. The point was to bring something just strange or unpalatable enough that it would eventually disappear, but would take an entire workday to do so. You had to walk a tightrope between delicious and unsavory, familiar and strange.

Here's an example:

One day, I brought in a huge bag of dried shrimp and seaweed from the Asian market in Sunnyvale. Delicious, if you like that kind of thing. But pungent, strange-looking, and most definitely not for everybody. I opened the bag and filled one of our popcorn bowls with the stuff, then camped out at a table with a good view of the kitchen. Within seconds, Boris had sidled up to the bowl and, his mind elsewhere, working on some coding problem in his head, reached in for a handful. The look on his face when he realized that he wasn't eating popcorn or M&M's was priceless.

I cackled inwardly. For the next three hours I watched as Te, Christina, and the rest of the office ambled up, tasted a bit of the sea, and left after one bite. The only person who showed absolutely no reaction to the shrimp was one of the engineers. He took a little bowl of them back to his desk and snacked away happily.

They lasted until five.

Another time, I brought in a dozen Balut. You might have heard of them? They're a delicacy in Laos and Cambodia: fertilized duck eggs that have been incubated for seventeen days, then boiled. There are embryos inside, tiny little ducklings. For obvious reasons, they're off-putting to most people. As a result of their preservation and curing, their yolks are a deep, dark green. The whites are dark brown. They look — and smell — like dinosaur eggs.

I neatly sliced a few, arrayed them on a paper plate, set out forks, and even made a sign: *Duck Eggs! Try one!*

Surprisingly, they only lasted two hours.

The new offices were at the northern edge of Los Gatos, and bordered Vasona Lake Park. They were big. Two stories, open floor-plan. This was no converted bank. It was a Silicon Valley office building, built to house a company. It was big enough to grow in. Whenever you hired somebody new, all you had to do was fit a few cubicle walls together.

I was on the south side, upstairs, with all the front-end web people, content producers, analytics, and marketing. Reed was on the other side of the building, hunkered down with the finance team and back-end developers. If we both stood up at the same time, we could see each other across the cavernous space.

We'd come to a détente on the issue of the shares. In the end, I'd agreed that a third of the shares Reed wanted, if he was to come in as CEO, would come from me. The other two-thirds he was going to have to ask the board for. Which he did — and which he got.

That spring, soon after the move, Reed had brought in two major hires who made a huge impact on the business. Barry McCarthy was the first one. A seasoned executive and former investment banker, he'd been working as the CFO of Music Choice, which piped music into homes through a set-top cable box. He had an MBA from Wharton and decades of experience as a consultant and investment banker. He was unlike anyone in the office — a hard-edged, East Coast preppy with a diploma from Williams College. In the shorts and sandals world of Los Gatos, his Brooks Brothers blazers stuck out like a sore thumb. Which is, I suspect, exactly why Reed liked him.

I liked him because he was smart, no-nonsense, and efficient. Also, he called me "Mr. Founder," even after I told him to say "Marc."

Barry's arrival spelled the end of Jim Cook's time at Netflix. Jim had always, from the start, wanted to be the CFO, and once Barry came in, it was clear that it would never happen. His departure wasn't dramatic — these things rarely are. But it underscored what was happening, that spring and summer: the startup team was starting to peel off, and the next phase was replacing them.

This is one of the facts of startup life: change. When you're building something from nothing, you rely on talented, passionate generalists: people who can do a little bit of everything, who buy into the mission, and whom you trust with your time, money, and ideas. But once you've gone from 0 to 1, and the seed you've planted is starting to grow, some shuffling happens. Often the person who was right for the job at the beginning is not right for the middle. Sometimes bringing in people with decades of experience and institutional know-how is the necessary thing to do.

That was definitely the case with Tom Dillon, whom we brought in as head of Operations after Jim left, in early 1999. Tom was semi-retired, in his mid-fifties, and had spent his entire life managing global distribution for massive companies, most recently as Chief Information Officer at Seagate and Candescent. These were huge businesses. Seagate in particular was massive and complex. They had twenty-four factories all over the world, staffed by more than 100,000 employees. It's hard to fathom what it takes to be in charge of tech for a company of that size and scale. Even more amazing, Tom presided over a time when Seagate decided to automate all its factories — which allowed the company to cut the number of factories (and employees) in half.

I don't know where Patty McCord found him, but I think Tom was one of the most important hires that Netflix ever made. I'm still kind of astounded that we got him. We were doing two thousand movies a week, all shipped within the United States, and this was a guy who had overseen companies doing *millions* of shipments, all over the world. Frankly, he was way beyond our pay grade — literally. We could only pay him about twenty percent of what he was probably used to.

But Tom Dillon's a different kind of cat. He's a total type B personality — surprising, for someone charged with the extreme detail-work his job required. A tall, somewhat shambling fellow, he had a big beard and a shock of receding white hair. He favored loose clothes and laid-back jokes. I never saw him stressed. He was like a real-life embodiment of Jeff Bridges as "The Dude" in *The Big Lebowski* — everyone's favorite stoner grandpa. Tom Dillon *abided*.

He saw our little company as a kind of retirement hobby. I think he liked the challenge. I mean, we had one warehouse and were still sorting everything by hand on card tables. It was like hiring Miles Davis to play your kid's bar mitzvah.

*　　*　　*

We had a new office, filled with new faces. But we had the same old problem: No one wanted to rent DVDs from us.

Sounds insane, doesn't it? Within a year, Netflix would be almost synonymous with rental. But from '98 to '99, the only way we could convince people to rent DVDs from us was to do it for free. We were a year and a half in, and we'd tried everything we could think of: rent-one-get-one-free, give-a-ways, bundles, promotions. We'd tried every single possible home page design we could think of. But we were coming up short. We still hadn't developed a way of obtaining customers — and then a way of getting them to come back — that made more money than it cost to acquire them in the first place.

Not exactly a stellar business plan.

But Amazon, as we'd always known they would, had started selling DVDs the previous November. And after a few months of directing our customers to Amazon when they wanted to buy, Reed had quietly shelved the initiative. We'd invested hundreds of hours adding Amazon links to our site, all designed to send our customers to Amazon to buy their DVDs. We fully expected them to make the same efforts pushing their customers back to us to rent — but the returns had been paltry. Amazon's links back to us were lackluster and hard to find. We were sending them tens of thousands of customers — they were sending us hundreds.

When the deal collapsed, Reed informed us that it had never been that important. Everyone was crestfallen, especially Christina. From the beginning, she had opposed the deal, but as always, she'd been a complete team player — and had worked hard on the Netflix end. A lot of conversations with Reed (and with Patty) were needed to get him to realize how demoralizing it could be, when you made something a priority, asked people to break their backs doing something they didn't agree with — and then didn't honor the work they put in.

Also demoralizing was the fact that without new renters from Amazon, and now without DVD sales to keep us afloat, we were hemorrhaging money. Reed and I put on a good face in front of our teams, spinning our depressing results as a kind of blessing. If we were ever going to figure out a way to make Netflix work, we pointed out, the company had to focus on one thing. And that thing was rental.

By the summer of '99, things had reached a breaking point. I was spending most of my lunch breaks jogging through the park next to our offices, hoping that at some point during my sweaty peregrinations on the Los Gatos Creek Trail, I'd land on a solution that would keep people renting from us.

There was one idea I couldn't shake. On one of my last trips to our warehouse in San Jose, I noticed that we had thousands — no, *tens* of thousands — of discs just sitting unused and unwatched on the warehouse shelves. When I came back to the office and shared my observation with Reed, it sparked another interesting Reed and Marc conversation: Why were we storing all those DVDs in a warehouse? Maybe we could figure out a way to let our customers store the discs. At their houses. On their shelves. Just keep the DVDs as long as they wanted.

What if we did away with late fees?

The more we thought about this idea, the more we liked it. We knew that one of the biggest problems with our current rental program was that it relied on a somewhat organized, prepared renter. Someone who thought several days in advance about what they might want to watch.

In other words, pretty much nobody that any of us knew. Most people (and loath as I was to admit it, I included myself in this category) figured out what movie they wanted to watch right around the time they pulled into the parking spot in front of Blockbuster. And in my world, that would have been considered prepared. Most people made the decision what to rent about ten seconds after they spotted it on the new-release rack.

But if they could keep the disc as long as they wanted? That changed things. Now they could let that disc sit on top of the TV as long as needed. And when the mood struck that it was time to watch a movie, it would be instantaneous. Even faster than driving to a Blockbuster. And if you had a bunch of movies sitting there, you could choose what to watch based on your mood. Was *The Thin Blue Line* a little bit too intense after a hard day at the office? Fine, let it languish. Luckily *Groundhog Day* was happy to step into the breach and lift your mood.

In a single stroke, this would completely turn our biggest weaknesses into our greatest strength.

And when they were done with a disc? Here we weren't sure what should happen. Well — what if users simply mailed the discs to the next renter, a peer-to-peer approach?

In other words, we were basically pulling things out of our asses. But by mid-summer, after weeks of debate and about a hundred miles of running, we'd come up with three ideas that we didn't think were total trash. They were:

1. **The Home Rental Library**. When we sent out an informal e-mail survey about the possibility of eliminating late fees, we'd gotten a warm response, so we'd designed a format that allowed users to rent four DVDs at a time, for $15.99 a month, and keep them as long as they wanted. As soon as they had returned one of the DVDs, they could come back to the site and rent another.

2. **Serialized Delivery**. We suspected that we might have problems with the "come back to the site and rent another" part. People were busy. Once a watched DVD was in the mailbox, it would be out of sight, out of mind. So maybe, we could have each customer create a list of DVDs they wanted. That way, when they returned a DVD to us, we could automatically (Te

used the term "auto-magically") send them the next movie on their list. I suggested we call our list the "Queue." I knew that queue meant line, but I also loved the idea that I could call the help section for this feature "Queue Tips."

3. **Subscription.** Having people hold on to our discs for as long as they wanted seemed good for customers — but we weren't sure what the business model should be. Do you pay a rental fee each time you swap? What if you never send one back? We decided that we should test a monthly fee — that we charged you every month you used the service.

Our plan was to test each of these initiatives separately, to see what worked and what didn't. We'd done this from the beginning, at Netflix. We'd designed our site so that the impact of even the slightest change could be measured and quantified. We'd learned, before launch, how to test efficiently. It didn't matter, in the end, how great a test looked — there could be broken links, missing pictures, misspelled words, you name it. What mattered was the idea. If it was a bad idea, even more attention to detail in our test wasn't going to make it a good one. And if it was a good idea, people would immediately fight to take advantage of it, despite obstacles or sloppiness on our end. Faced with a problem on our website, they would try again and again to make it work. They would reboot the site. Try to find a way to work around the problem. Call us up to place their orders (and we had an unlisted number!).

If people want what you have, they will break down your door, leap over broken links, and beg you for more. If they don't want what you've got, changing the color palette won't make a damn bit of difference.

So, by mid-1999, we were old pros at testing. We could do it quickly. But even quickly, each test would take about two weeks. When I ran this by Reed, he looked at me like I was crazy.

"That makes no sense," he said. "We don't have the time for that."

"Listen," I told him. "We've got to do something. We can't retain anyone, and no one's renting, and — "

"Exactly. That's why you should just test everything at once," Reed said, cutting me off.

I started to argue, but then I remembered the previous year of tests. It wasn't a bad idea. And it fit in with our ethos of faster, more frequent testing. We were always trying to avoid one of the number one pitfalls of startup entrepreneurship: building imaginary castles in your mind, meticulously designed, complete with turrets, drawbridges, moats. Overplanning and overdesigning is often just overthinking — or just plain old procrastination. When it comes to ideas, it's more efficient to test ten bad ones than spend days trying to come up with something perfect.

What the hell, I thought. I told Christina and Eric to combine all three tests into one offer. At this point, we had a pretty good flow of customers coming to our site to redeem their Free-Rental coupons, so it wouldn't take long to get some results. We set it up so that every tenth customer clicking the redeem button on the site would be directed to a custom page, offering them the opportunity to try — for free — a monthly subscription to the Netflix Marquee program: *no due dates, no late fees*. We would send them four DVDS, and when they sent one DVD back, we would send them another one. As many times as they wanted. And at the end of the month — if they didn't cancel — we would automatically (and here it was me describing it as "automagically") hit them up for only $15.99 a month, payable by any major credit card.

Home Rental Library × Serialized Delivery × Subscription. Just the last three halfway decent ideas we'd had, thrown into one pot.

"This probably won't work," I told Christina. "But, hey, at least we'll know."

14.

Nobody Knows Anything

(fall 1999: a year and a half after launch)

IT WORKED.

People didn't just *like* no late fees, a flat monthly rate, plus serialized delivery with a queue.

They *loved* it.

The first day of the test, 90 *percent* of the people who clicked on the banner ad gave us their credit card information. That's insane. I'd expected something closer to 20 percent — that's usually what happens when you ask someone for sixteen digits, even if they're getting a month free and can cancel before any charges. And it wasn't a fluke — day after day, the sign-up rates were that high. Visitors to the website were signing up for subscriptions at four or five times the rate they had chosen our à la carte rentals.

If people saw this new offer, they were taking the bait. Hook, line, and sinker.

We scrambled to build a service that could actually do what we were promising. There were a lot of things to figure out — how to run a rolling serialized delivery system alongside our normal operations, how to do automatic subscription billing, how to build a serviceable queue system. But within a week, the results were so positive that we knew we had a winner.

Several times a day, I'd pop over to Suresh's desk. Suresh extracted all the important data from the river of information we created each day and put it into a form that we could all digest and play with. I'm sure he grew to dread my caffeinated approach to his desk, my jittery requests for numbers. But I wanted to know — Were there more than yesterday? Fewer? How many were signing up for the plan? How many saw it and ignored it? Where in the process were they dropping off?

We'd know for sure after a month, when people who had signed up for their free trial (and given us their credit card information) could cancel their subscriptions. But things were looking up. It had taken hundreds of failed experiments, thousands of hours of work, and many millions of dollars, but it appeared that we had finally come up with a workable model for DVD rental by mail.

No one was more surprised than me. Not only had I fought against taking the risk of testing all three of our ideas simultaneously, but this was perhaps the least likely solution I could ever have imagined. If you had asked me on launch day to describe what Netflix would eventually look like, I never would have come up with a monthly subscription service. Even if you had tried to make it easy for me and put it in the form of a three-part multiple-choice question, I still would have had a one-in-three shot at picking the right answer.

A few days after we launched the test, Lorraine brought the kids over to Los Gatos for lunch. No more jogging for now. Instead, we ordered a pizza and had a picnic in the park. Afterward, Logan, Morgan, and I climbed up into the steam-powered train that ran along the park's periphery. Lorraine slid into the row behind us, holding a grunting Hunter. As we circled the lake in the middle of the park and I talked through our exciting new idea with Lorraine, I thought of my father, setting up his steam-powered train in the basement and calling me down to watch the wheels turn.

"Guess I was wrong, huh," Lorraine said when I told her about the initial numbers. "This thing is gonna take off, isn't it?"

"I really think so," I said. "But don't feel bad. It wasn't that good of an idea a few years ago. And besides, nobody knows anything."

Lorraine laughed. She knew I was quoting William Goldman, whose book *Adventures in the Screen Trade* we'd both just finished. You might not have heard of Goldman. He writes screenplays, so he largely labors behind the scenes and out of the headlines. People of my generation can thank him for writing *Butch Cassidy and the Sundance Kid*. Those a bit younger may have enjoyed the script he wrote for *The Princess Bride*. He also did *Misery, Heat, Magic, Marathon Man, The General's Daughter*...and over twenty-five more. He's won two Academy Awards for screenwriting.

But William Goldman is most famous for writing three words:

Nobody. Knows. Anything.

According to Goldman, those three words are the key to understanding everything about Hollywood. Nobody really knows how well a movie is going to do...until after it's already done it.

For instance, how is it possible that you can have a film directed by an Academy Award–winning director (Michael Cimino), starring a best-actor Academy Award winner (Christopher Walken), with a can't-miss script and a $50 million budget...and end up with *Heaven's Gate*, one of the biggest Hollywood flops of all time?

On the other hand, how can you have a film with a first-time director, a handful of amateur actors, no script at all, a budget under $50,000...and end up with *The Blair Witch Project*, which, after grossing more than $250 million, is one of the most successful independent films of all time?

There's a simple explanation.

It's because Nobody Knows Anything. And it's not just in Hollywood. It's true in Silicon Valley, too.

"Nobody Knows Anything" isn't an indictment. It's a reminder. An encouragement.

Because if Nobody Knows Anything — if it's truly impossible to know in advance which ideas are the good ones and which aren't, if it's impossible to know who is going to succeed and who isn't — then any idea could be the one to succeed. If Nobody Knows Anything, then you have to trust yourself. You have to test yourself. And you have to be willing to fail.

Silicon Valley brainstorming sessions often begin with someone saying, "There are no bad ideas." I've always disagreed. There *are* bad ideas. But you don't know an idea is bad until you've tried it.

And, as Netflix shows, sometimes bad ideas have a way of becoming good ones.

Not only had all the people who told me that Netflix would never work (including my wife) gotten it wrong, but so had I. We all had. We'd all known that the idea *could* work, but in the end nobody knew anything about *how* — until it did.

We had conceived of Netflix as an online version of Mitch's Video Droid: a video store. Informally, we even called it that — we never called Netflix.com a website, or a rental service. It was still always The Store.

But now we had a new model, one we never could have brainstormed into existence. The most revolutionary structure in e-commerce was the result of years of work, thousands of hours of brainstorms, dire finances, and an impatient CEO. The subscription model saved Netflix and quickly came to define it. But it wasn't something that we thought our way toward — it wasn't something anyone could have predicted ahead of time. It took a lot of hard work, a lot of hard thought.

It also took a lot of cards falling just right.

Other people call that luck. I call it nobody knowing anything.

A subscription model had the potential to solve a lot of our problems. But it also provided a number of new ones.

The first was our existing promotions. I had finally convinced the

DVD manufacturers to include our coupons in their boxes — after they'd said no countless times. I had promised them that we could be counted on to fulfill our promises. And now, as a result, there were hundreds of thousands of coupons promising "3 Free DVD Rentals!" in circulation. And due to the lags in the DVD manufacturers' supply chains, they would be coming out of the woodwork for years. We knew that the best way to jump-start our subscription program would be to substitute every request for free DVD rentals with a free month of unlimited rentals fulfilled through Marquee. But would customers accept that? Or would they consider it a bait-and-switch? We were also worried about the manufacturers themselves, who would have every right to insist that we fulfill the terms of the coupons to the letter.

The second issue was our "first month free" promotion, in which we gave each customer a free month to evaluate the program for themselves before having to decide to continue paying for it. We liked the free month plan — it had brought thousands of new users to our service — but we couldn't quite agree on what was going to happen after that first month. How could we convert users taking advantage of a promotion into paying customers? You could always just ask them if they wanted to continue. But I felt strongly that we should utilize a "negative option" — that is, not even ask. Instead, we would automatically roll customers into their next month of membership — and bill their credit card — unless they proactively canceled. You see this all the time now — Amazon Prime and virtually every subscription plan does it. But at the time it seemed like an overly aggressive money grab — verging on sleazy. Reed hated it.

The third issue was our à la carte DVD rental service. While it had never reached the point of being able to support the company on its own, quite a few people liked being able to rent DVDs one at a time, with no long-term commitment. But just as almost exactly twelve months earlier we had been confronted with the complexity of doing rentals and sales at the same time — and realized that our best chances of success were to focus on one — we now had to make a similar decision. Should we focus all our effort and resources on the program that might save us, or try to offer both models simultaneously?

The first problem was easier to solve than I expected. Turns out it's easier to negotiate with an enormous consumer electronics company when you've been working with them for a year *and* your new initiative is proving to be a massive success with users. What was obvious to us was obvious to the Sonys and Toshibas of the world, too — a subscription model was a game changer. It's hard to imagine that, now that tech startups offer subscriptions for everything from socks to sex toys. But in 1999, we were doing something that no one had done before: we were convincing people to pay for potential. By saying that they would be paying the same amount, no matter how many movies they watched, we were, in effect, daring them to use our service as much as possible. And by eliminating the penalties for keeping discs for days or weeks at a time, we were providing a viable alternative to the video stores for the heavy renters — traditionally the stores' most valuable customers.

We were operating from a position of confidence, in other words. So when I approached Mike Fidler and Steve Nickerson at Sony and Toshiba, I didn't *ask* if we could change the terms of our promotion. I explained the shift in our business model and gave them some numbers about the popularity of the program. Customers would still get their DVDs — and for free. But they'd be signing up for a subscription to do it. It took all my persuasive powers to craft a perfectly pitched argument, but in the end, it worked — nobody jumped ship.

The issue of the negative option was a little thornier.

"You can't just charge people's cards without asking them," Reed said. "It's totally unethical."

"It's totally the norm, Reed," I told him. "Haven't you ever subscribed to a magazine?"

"I don't like it."

"They have a chance to get something for free," I said. "We have a chance to get them hooked. That's the trade-off. They know it when they start."

"Maybe they forgot."

"Listen, if they liked the offer enough at the beginning to hand over credit card information, chances are they'll like us enough to let us keep it."

Reed frowned. He didn't agree. But in the end, I won: After all, we were sending them a hundred dollars' worth of DVDs. Customers had to input their credit cards to take advantage of the trial. That didn't feel funny to them.

"Let's just start from the assumption that everyone is going to like it," I argued. "If that's the case, they'll be happy to have their subscription automatically continued and their credit cards automatically charged."

Despite my optimism, I'm not completely crazy. Four weeks after we launched the free trial, I was half-prepared for a rash of cancelations. All day, I shuffled back and forth between my desk and Suresh's, checking on the numbers. By five o'clock he was starting to shout them at me before I'd gotten to him. All day, the message was essentially the same.

"They're doing it!" he said. "They're letting us charge them!"

The thorniest problem by far was the issue of à la carte rental. Some renters loved it, especially low-volume renters who didn't watch a ton of movies but liked the convenience of online ordering.

But a *lot* of renters loved the subscription service. In the first three months of its existence, Marquee drove up our site traffic by 300 percent.

The question we had to ask ourselves was: Was it worth trying to offer both models? Or did it make more sense to focus on subscription, jettisoning some of our earliest users?

To answer that question, I'd like to tell you about something I called the Canada Principle.

Netflix, for its first twelve years, limited its services to the United States. When we were just starting out, we didn't have the infrastructure or the money to serve the international market. We had a couple of guys in a bank safe hand-stuffing envelopes, and our entire business model was based on U.S. postage rates. Nonetheless, we thought frequently about expanding into Canada. It was close, the regulations were easy, and the postage and transport costs were low. When we ran the numbers, we saw that we could probably get an instant revenue bump of about 10 percent.

But we didn't do it.

Why? Two reasons.

First, we knew that it was inevitably going to be more complicated than it looked. Because French is the main language spoken in some parts of Canada, we would have translation headaches. Canadians use a different currency, which would have complicated our pricing — and the fact that Canada also calls that currency a "dollar" threatened to be a communications nightmare. Postage was different, too, so we would have had to use different envelopes. In other words, even something seemingly simple was bound to be a pain in the ass.

But the bigger reason for staying out was even simpler.

If we took the amount of effort, manpower, and *mind*-power Canadian expansion would require and applied it to other aspects of the business, we'd eventually get a far greater return than 10 percent. Expanding to Canada would have been a short-term move, with short-term benefits. It would have diluted our focus.

When Reed started advocating for dropping à la carte rental, I was initially against it. Even though the numbers were good, I was nervous about the financial hit of jettisoning that part of our customer base. Why couldn't we do both for a little while longer, easing the transition for our users and our bottom line?

But once I realized that the decision was similar to the one we had faced six months earlier, when we'd decided to drop DVD sales — once I realized, in effect, that we were facing an opportunity to apply the Canada Principle — I was on board. Reed was right — if we knew that the subscription model was the future, there was no point in continuing to work on the à la carte past. À la carte users only made up a small percentage of our users. We were only diverting energy, money, and talent to a model we had outgrown. Plus, as with DVD sales, we were confusing customers, giving them too many options.

By February of 2000, we'd dropped à la carte rentals and switched entirely to the subscription service, which now cost $19.99 a month. Now Netflix was Marquee and Marquee was Netflix.

Focus. It's an entrepreneur's secret weapon. Again and again in the Netflix story — dropping DVD sales, dropping à la carte rentals, and eventually dropping many members of the original Netflix team — we had to be willing to abandon parts of the past in service of the future. Sometimes, focus this intense looks like ruthlessness — and it is, a little bit. But it's more than that. It's something akin to courage.

Moving the business entirely to Marquee almost immediately took one of our biggest liabilities — delivery time — and in one fell swoop turned it into one of our biggest advantages. Now we weren't several days slower than going to a Blockbuster — we were many times faster! If you wanted to watch a movie, no more driving to the store. There was already a stack of movies waiting for you, right on top of your TV. It was as close to "movies on demand" as we could get.

We imagined a user with a rotating, constantly refreshed library of DVDs. Watch a movie at night, drop it into the mailbox on the way to work the next morning, and by afternoon get an email that the next DVD was on the way.

Not *quite* instant gratification, but close.

We didn't know what this meant for our shipping methods. Tom Dillon had already restructured all the picking, packing, and shipping systems we'd been using for the previous year, to make them more efficient and user-friendly. He'd also figured out that it was much cheaper — and more efficient — to ship all DVDs separately and as they became available, even if a user had ordered more than one. (I'm reminded of this every time I go to a hip new small-plates place with Lorraine and they inform me that they'll be bringing each dish out as soon as it's been cooked. Sounds like a chill dining philosophy, but really it's just easier for the kitchen that way.)

But although Marquee didn't necessarily *require* faster shipping — since our customers already had movies they could watch sitting on top of their TV — we thought it would be pretty cool if subscribers could get a new movie the day after returning one. It would be like magic. And after all, who wanted to wait a week for a DVD?

Some of our local customers were already enjoying next-day delivery. By virtue of proximity, Netflix users in San Jose, where our warehouse was, tended to get their DVDs within a day of ordering them, while users in Florida often waited six or seven. But when we looked at the numbers, we didn't see any correlation between delivery time and customer retention. After a few months, the customer retention levels in the Bay Area and in Florida were roughly equal.

"What gives?" I asked Reed one afternoon, bouncing a tennis ball off the side of a cubicle. "You'd think those people in Florida would say, 'Screw it, this ain't worth the fifteen dollars.'"

"They're probably just used to it," he said. "They know we're across the country and probably just assume things will take longer for them. We might be dodging a bullet here. If we don't have to build warehouses all over the country to facilitate overnight shipping, we'll save a lot of money."

"It just doesn't make sense," I said. "Next-day delivery *should* move the needle. There has to be something we're not seeing."

I tossed the ball slightly too hard, and it bounced past me to Reed's desk.

"I have an idea," I said. "We've never *turned on* next-day delivery for a city, offering it from the beginning. If we do that, we can measure the impact on all our variables, see if it matters."

Reed shrugged.

I'll never forget the look in Tom Dillon's eye when I told him we needed to test next-day delivery in another market, just to make sure. I wasn't quite certain how to do it — obviously, we couldn't just build an entirely new distribution center to test the service in one city. Right?

"Just do it in Sacramento," he said, chuckling. "Don't build a warehouse. Just drive everything up from here every night for a month, and drop it off at the Sacramento post office."

"Are you volunteering?"

"Hell, no," he said. "It was your idea."

Which is how Dan Jepson found himself driving a panel van two hours up I-80, all the windows down, the edges of thousands of Netflix mailers fluttering gently behind him in the breeze.

For the next few months, Dan drove to Sacramento every morning to pick up the mail and bring it back to Los Gatos, and then a few hours later, he did the entire trip a second time to drop it back off in Sacramento again. For months, we measured the results. What we found was incredibly surprising. Next-day delivery didn't really change our cancelation rates. Where it mattered was in new customer sign-ups.

"This makes no sense," I said, standing next to Christina's desk with a printout of new sign-ups in my hand. "We're not telling them *ahead of time* that they'll be getting their movies the next day — we're just doing it! Do they just...intuit that they'll be getting things quickly?"

Christina rolled her eyes. "Marc, no. You're missing the forest for the trees."

I waited.

"They're telling their friends. It's word-of-mouth advertising."

Christina was right. The longer we ran the test, the more apparent it was that next-day delivery was a real game changer — just not in the ways we thought. It didn't affect retention — it affected *sign-ups*. Next-day delivery inspired real dedication, the kind that makes you tell all your friends about this new service you're using. Over time, we noticed that our penetration into the Sacramento market was approaching Silicon Valley levels. Silicon Valley! Where all the early adopters of DVD technology lived!

The whole saga had provided a valuable lesson: trust your gut, but also test it. Before you do anything concrete, the data has to agree. We'd suspected that next-day delivery was important, but we'd been myopic in our analysis of our tests, so we hadn't understood why. It took an additional test, with a truly outside-the-box execution, to understand what we'd already intuited to be true. And once we understood it, we could refine the idea and maximize its potential — which was huge. Next-day delivery was like magic. We knew it *had* to be part of our plans going forward. Now we just needed to figure out a way to make it work without driving the DVDs ourselves or building enormous warehouses all over the country.

"I'm on it," Tom Dillon said.

Whenever anyone asks me what my favorite movie is, I never tell the truth.

The public answer — the convenient lie — is *Pulp Fiction*. All the cinephiles and tough guys in the audience nod their head with approval when I mention it. And it's true — I love that movie. I love the writing, I love the cinematography, I love the performances by Samuel L. Jackson and John Travolta and Uma Thurman. I've probably seen *Pulp Fiction* more than any movie but *The Wizard of Oz*.

But it's not my favorite movie. My real favorite movie is *Doc Hollywood*, a 1991 comedy you've probably forgotten about, if you saw it at all.

In *Doc Hollywood*, a young Michael J. Fox plays an arrogant plastic surgeon in Washington, D.C. Driving across the country in his

Porsche, he gets into a wreck in small-town South Carolina. He's mowed down some fences, and as community service, he's ordered to work shifts at the local hospital.

Complications ensue. It's essentially a fish-out-of-water story — he's a big-city surgeon in a small town with small-town values, and he eventually realizes that being a small-town doctor is what he really loves.

Doc Hollywood is no one's idea of a masterpiece. But it speaks to me — I'm not sure why. Maybe it's simply because it taps into some deep desire to live an uncomplicated life with a real connection to people, family, and place. In many ways, *Doc Hollywood* is my fantasy. It makes me yearn for the simple life, for a place where everyone knows and cares for each other. Where you go to work, you come home, sit on the porch, and then get asked to judge a barbecue cook-off.

Doc Hollywood is not the first movie I'd name if you asked me for the greatest films of the twentieth century, or even the 1990s, or even 1991. But if I see my copy lying around the house, I'll slide it into the DVD player more times than not. It's not the *best* movie, or a classic, or a hot new release — it's just my *favorite*.

Helping people find their favorite movies, movies they'd *love*, was our real goal at Netflix. From the beginning, we'd known that our company couldn't be tied to a shipping service or a mere product — because if it was, we'd be obsolete the second the technology changed. If we wanted any chance of surviving long-term, we had to convince customers that we were giving them something better than an online library and quick shipping. Neither the technology nor the delivery method mattered. What counted was seamlessly connecting our users with movies we knew they'd love. That would be relevant regardless of what direction future technologies took us.

Easier said than done, of course.

One disadvantage of being an online store was that it made browsing difficult. If you knew what you were looking for, you could just search for it. But if not, finding movies was surprisingly difficult. You could only view one page at a time, and there was a limited number of movies you could fit on a page. You had to make a snap judgment based on the cover art or a synopsis. This was a problem in brick-and-mortars, too, of course. According to Mitch, most people walked into video stores completely unsure of what they were looking for, and simply drifted from section to section. But in a brick-and-mortar, you could ask a clerk for help. Or, at the very least, you could wander the aisles, and hope that you'd serendipitously stumble across something that looked promising.

We wanted to make browsing easier, and we also wanted to connect users with recommendations and reviews. So Christina, the editorial content team, and I designed content-rich landing pages for a variety of genres. If you were looking for a thriller, we had an entire page dedicated to them, replete with top-ten lists, reviews of recent and classic thrillers, and highlighted selections from our inventory. If you liked Tom Cruise movies — same deal. The idea was to provide gentle suggestions and guidance, something akin to what a sympathetic (and knowledgeable) video store clerk could offer.

We wanted to offer a personalized touch. The problem was, it was enormously expensive — not to mention time-consuming — to do it all manually. When we had 900 titles, it was somewhat feasible to create content to match. But by late 1999, we had almost 5,000 movies to work with. It was hard to keep up, and even harder to browse.

Reed, in typical Reed fashion, pushed for automation.

"Forget the landing pages," he said. "We're redesigning the site anyway. Instead of hard-coding pages, how about we just do it like this: Create a frame on the home page that has slots to display four movies at a time. Each slot can show the cover of the movie, run time, date of release, a little capsule synopsis — the data we already have. Then just make a list of fifty movies you might want to have appear there, and have the site randomly pick which four to display. Or better yet, just define how to build the list — maybe call the list 'thrillers' and let the system randomly pick from *any* movie we have that is tagged as a thriller."

If I recall correctly, I reacted with horror to this suggestion. I hated it. It seemed cold, computerized, random — all the things we *weren't* trying to be.

But have you used Netflix lately? Reed's slot structure survives — with alterations. The most crucial of which is that the films in the slots aren't randomly chosen. They're the product of a complex algorithmic matching service, one that's calibrated to both your taste and Netflix's needs.

That algorithmic matching service can be traced directly back to 2000 and Reed's slots. Because he was right, of course — users needed a more efficient, easier way to find movies they would like, something even more intuitive than an editorially curated landing page. Putting DVDs into slots was a start. Now we just needed to figure out some way to arrange them that wasn't random.

In talks all that fall, we discussed ways to build a service that would give users movies they'd love while also making our life as a distributor easier (and more profitable). When users sat down to decide which movies to order next, we wanted them to see a list of films that had been customized to their taste — and optimized for our inventory. If we could show customers what *they* wanted to watch, they'd be happier with the service. And if we could also show them what *we* wanted them to watch? Win-win.

Put simply: Even if we were ordering twenty times more new releases than any Blockbuster (an enormously expensive gambit), we wouldn't be able to satisfy *all* demand, *all* the time. And new releases were expensive. To keep our customers happy and our costs reasonable, we needed to direct users to less in-demand movies that we knew they'd like — and probably like even better than new releases.

For example: Say I rented (and loved) *Pleasantville,* one of the best movies of 1998 and a clever dark comedy about what happens when two teenagers from the nineties (Tobey Maguire and Reese Witherspoon) are sucked into a black-and-white television show set in 1950s small-town America. The ideal recommendation engine would be able to steer me away from more current new releases and toward other movies, like *Pleasantville* — movies like *Doc Hollywood*.

That was a tall order. The thing about taste is that it's subjective. And the number of factors in play, when trying to establish similarities between films, is almost endless. Do you group films by actor, by director, by genre? Release year, award nominations, screenwriter? How does one quantify a thing like mood?

I worked with Reed and the engineers for months on a solution. The problem was coming up with an algorithm that actually spat out movies that made sense together. Since it could only use the data available to it — things like genre, actors, location, release year, language, and so forth — the algorithm often made suggestions that made sense to a computer but didn't really take into account any kind of real-world similarity. Or, it would give unhelpful suggestions: "You like *Top Gun*? Here's another movie that came out in 1986!"

In the end, we realized that the best way to give users what they wanted was to crowdsource data from them. At first, we did what Amazon did. Using a process called "collaborative filtering," Amazon would suggest products to you based on common buying patterns. They still do this. Essentially, if you buy a wrench from Amazon, it groups you with other users who have bought a wrench, and then suggests that you buy other things that they've bought.

Here's how it worked with rentals: Let's say Reed and I each rented three movies from Netflix. I rented *Armageddon*, *The Bridges of Madison County*, and *Casablanca*. And Reed rented *Armageddon*, *The Bridges of Madison County*, and *The Mighty Ducks*. Collaborative filtering would say that since we'd both rented two of the same movies, we would probably each enjoy the third movie that the other person rented. Therefore, the site would recommend that I rent *The Mighty Ducks* and that Reed rent *Casablanca*.

The problem with this method, of course, is that filtering for rental history doesn't really tell you whether I liked *Casablanca,* or if Reed liked *The Mighty Ducks*. It just tells us that we both *rented* those movies. We could have hated them. We could have rented them for our kids (or our wives).

If we were going to use collaborative filtering to group customers and recommend films, we needed to know what customers enjoyed rather than just what they rented. We needed a reviews system: a movie rating system. Grouping customers by ratings — by "clustering" users according to overlapping positive or negative reviews — meant that we could efficiently recommend films to users based not on what they'd rented but what they *liked*. Ultimately, the algorithm would become much more complex than that. But for it to work at all, we needed users to review movies — lots of them.

Ultimately, we decided that we would ask our customers to rate movies by assigning each movie from one to five stars. Five stars for a movie they loved. One star for a complete time waster.

It sounds simple enough, but that stupid star rating system was the source of hundreds of hours of argument. More battles about fewer pixels have never been waged. Could you give something zero stars? Should we offer a half-star option? When you *gave* a rating it was whole stars, but when we *predicted* a rating, should it be in whole stars or in tenths? When should a user be prompted to review a film? Where should the widget go?

In the end, we asked Netflix users to review films early and often. We would ask them to rate films whenever they visited the site, whenever they returned a movie, and whenever they rearranged their queue. The great thing about movie rentals is that you don't have to rent a movie to have already seen it — unlike buying a wrench, a review didn't have to be tied to a sale. Theoretically, a user could review every movie he or she had ever seen — even if he or she had never rented a single movie from us. And it turns out that people *love* to be asked for their opinion. Everyone's a critic.

It was remarkably easy to amass enough reviews to build a collaborative filtering function that could actually predict — with reasonable accuracy — what someone might *like*. After that, Reed's team went to work integrating these taste predictions into a broader algorithm that made movie recommendations after weighing a number of factors — keyword, number of copies, number of copies in stock, cost per disc.

The result — which launched in February of 2000 as Cinematch — was a seemingly more intuitive recommendation engine, one that outsourced qualitative assessment to users while also optimizing things on the back end. In many ways, it was the best of both worlds: an automated system that nonetheless *felt* human, like a video store clerk asking you what you'd seen lately and then recommending something he knew you'd like — and that he had in stock.

Actually, it felt better than human. It felt invisible.

If it sounds like two of the most innovative and influential developments in the history of Netflix happened quickly, hot on the heels of Reed and I deciding to run the company together — well, if it sounds that way, that's because it's true.

Reed and I came to our CEO/president agreement in September of 1998. Within a year, the subscription plan was live. Within a year and a half, it was the only way to rent from Netflix — and a redesigned site was connecting with customers using an innovative algorithm that gave them exactly what we knew they'd want...and what we wanted them to have.

Those two key innovations would be enough to prove to almost anyone that we'd made the right choice when it came to running the company. We were really singing together. The team I'd built was bursting with creative ideas to connect with our users, and Reed's had a singular focus in streamlining our vision. Reed's laser focus helped us concentrate on the future. My goal was to make sure that however quickly we moved, however efficient we got, we were always fundamentally seeking to connect with our users.

Past and future, heart and brain, Lennon and McCartney — Reed and I were a perfect pair.

15.

Drowning in Our
Own Success

(September 2000: two and a half years after launch)

ALISAL RANCH MIGHT NOT be at the end of the earth — but you can see it from there.

If you want to see for yourself, head to Santa Barbara. Then drive thirty miles north, up the 101. Veer east when you reach the town of Solvang and its rows of faux-Danish storefronts. Leave the quaint markers of civilization behind, and continue on a single-lane secondary road, through brown bunchgrass meadows dotted with California oaks. Kick up clouds of dust for what seems like hours. And just when you think you're really and truly lost, you'll find yourself coming around a sharp bend and there it will be: the Alisal Guest Ranch. Ten thousand acres of rolling California foothills in the middle of nowhere.

I don't know what we were thinking — or even who was thinking it — but the Alisal Ranch is where, in September of 2000, right as the last bit of air was streaming out of the dot-com balloon, we decided to have our first corporate retreat.

There was plenty for us to retreat and talk about that September. Earlier, in the spring, we'd raised another $50 million in financing — our Series E — bringing the total amount of money invested in Netflix to more than $100 million. The share price for the Series E had come in at nearly $10 per share. And since I still owned a shitload of shares, I was now worth an absolutely obscene amount of money…at least on paper. Since I couldn't sell any of my stock, it was just imaginary — funny money. Still, it reduced the frequency with which Lorraine brought up the idea of selling the house and moving to Montana.

Netflix now had more than 350 employees, and we had long since passed the point where I knew everybody. We'd continued on our streak of making major talent hires — the most recent being Leslie Kilgore, whom Reed had convinced to leave Amazon to head our marketing efforts as CMO, and Ted Sarandos, who now managed our content acquisition.

Since walking away from à la carte rentals, our no-due-dates, no-late-fees program had steadily built up steam. Users loved Cinematch, our recommendation engine. We did, too. It kept our subscribers' queues full — and nothing, we found, correlated more to retention than a queue with lots of movies in it. We were now approaching nearly 200,000 paying subscribers. Our other metrics were looking pretty impressive as well. We now carried 5,800 different DVD titles and shipped more than 800,000 discs a month, and our warehouse was packed with more than a million discs. Tom Dillon was making headway on a method to ensure that users could get access to those discs within a day of ordering them.

Earlier in the year, at the height of the dot-com boom, we'd seen the bankers circling us like vultures with briefcases, and had even flirted with going public. More than flirted, really. We'd chosen Deutsche Bank to manage the offering, had hired accountants to go over our books, and had drawn up an S-1 (also known as a registration statement), the document laying out to the Securities and Exchange Commission a summary of our business: what we did, how we did it, and what our risk factors were.

We'd even started changing Netflix's identity to appeal to risk-averse banks and their customers. The big trend, in the late 1990s and early 2000s, was for internet companies to be *portals* — entry points on the internet for a specific niche. The popular wisdom at the time was that if you wanted to be a successful website, you had to be all things to all people — if you wanted to chase money, you had to chase traffic first. That meant that Netflix couldn't just be a rental service aimed at helping people find the DVDs they'd love — it had to be a place for *movie* lovers of all stripes.

The VCs on our board had told us that if we wanted to go public, we needed to think big: Movie showtimes. Movie reviews. A monthly column by Leonard Maltin, king of the video guides. Etc. We'd done all of it, but I'd been unable to shake the suspicion that we were getting distracted, salivating over dollar signs and eyeing possible valuations.

Then the bubble had burst. From its high in March, the Nasdaq stock exchange — which is where most technology companies are listed — had entered a period of steady decline, punctuated by a terrifying 25 percent drop the week of April 14. That was the exact week that we filed our S-1 with the SEC, asking permission to go public. Over the following months, as the market continued to slump, Deutsche Bank had continued to project false enthusiasm, offering steadily weakening reassurances that we would be okay.

By the fall, though, it had become obvious to everyone that the numbers we'd been excitedly bandying back and forth as the solution to all our problems — $75 million? $80 million? — had evaporated into thin air. I'd gotten the call that Deutsche Bank was pulling the offering one rainy Saturday morning in September, while I was shopping with Lorraine in Carmel. Needless to say, we didn't buy anything.

At the time, not going public had felt like a major blow. But in retrospect, it was possibly one of the best things that ever happened to us. If we'd gone public in the fall of 2000, we would have been tied to the portal idea and to the unrealistic financial expectations that we had built around it — and that would have been a disaster. We never would have been able to make any money as an *all things to all people* site. Becoming a "movie portal" was the complete opposite of the Canada Principle. It didn't allow for the rigorous focus that set us apart — and which ultimately provided us with the business model to succeed on our own terms.

We quietly started abandoning most of our portal-oriented efforts. If the people who wanted movie showtimes and in-depth critics' reviews and top-ten lists were just the banks and their customers, and the bank didn't want to take us public, then why keep them?

So by September, we were back to where we started. We didn't have $75 million in our pockets, and we were losing money — lots of money. Up until now, with Reed at the helm, we'd been able to find funding fairly easily, and we had long reassured ourselves that as long as we could continue to use Silicon Valley money to support our growth, we would be okay. But in a post-bubble era, getting it from our usual VC sources would be hard. Really hard.

I worried about how the bursting of the dot-com bubble would affect Netflix's finances. But I have to confess that I wasn't sad to see some sort of adjustment coming down the pike. All of the dot-com hype had seemed crazy to me. Watching the Super Bowl with Lorraine back in January, I'd kept a running tally: No fewer than *sixteen* companies with dot-com in their names had advertised during the game, spending upward of $2 million for each spot. That was more money out the door *per spot* than Netflix had spent its entire first *year*.

At the height of the dot-com boom, the prevailing attitude at many companies had been *spend now, worry later*. It had become routine for companies to spend lavishly on parties, promotions, and facilities. No one put it better than Stephan Paternot, CEO of TheGlobe.com. After his 1998 IPO, he famously said, "Got the girl. Got the money. Now I'm ready to live a disgusting, frivolous life."

That wasn't us. Netflix had long since outgrown its card tables and beach chairs, but we were still pretty frugal — when we moved to Los Gatos, we'd bought used cubicles and secondhand furniture. The only nod to lavish decoration was a popcorn machine in the main atrium, and even that didn't work most of the time. I'd never understood what companies were thinking when they spent tens of thousands of dollars on carpeting or bought thousand-dollar Aeron chairs for every employee. Frankly, I don't understand it even now.

It had been an age of decadence, in other words. And like all decadent eras, it hadn't lasted. By the time we were headed to Alisal Ranch, there wasn't much decadence left. Boo.com, the online clothing e-tailer, had filed for bankruptcy after spending more than $175 million in only six months. The rumor mill had Pets.com on the verge of collapse after the company spent more than $150 million in the first half of the year. Webvan's stock would fall from $30 per share to 6 *cents* per share after the online grocer spent nearly a billion dollars on expansion. Drkoop.com, the online portal founded by 82-year-old retired surgeon general C. Everett Koop — which had managed to go public with not a single penny in revenue — was losing tens of millions of dollars every quarter.

Reed and I viewed these failures with — I have to admit it — a little bit of schadenfreude. One of our pastimes that year was scrolling through entries on Fucked Company, the cynical website of record for troubled and failing dot-coms, thinking *that could have been us*, even when reading about obviously mismanaged and doomed-from-the-start entries.

But we were especially concerned to read about the troubles of Kozmo.com, an urban delivery service that had launched in 1999 promising to deliver a huge range of products — including DVDs — to customers' homes within an hour. In 1999, we'd worried that Kozmo would enter the rental market and use its one-hour delivery to crush our slower service. But as Kozmo floundered through 2000, first squandering the $280 million it had raised from investors (including a $60 million investment from Amazon!), and then canceling its planned IPO, we found ourselves wondering if the company's prominent failure would doom everyone else in their category — no matter how tangentially.

Fortunately, unlike Dr. Koop, Boo.com, or Webvan, we actually had a business model that made sense. A subscription to Netflix cost a user $19.99 per month — on average, $4 more than it cost us to actually provide the service. We made money on every transaction. Basic economics.

We had a different problem than the Dr. Koops or Webvans of the world: we were successful, and success is expensive.

In fact, we were drowning in our own success. The faster new customers poured in, the faster money poured out. Our business model was hard to explain to potential customers, but we knew that if people tried our service, they'd be hooked. That's why everyone who wanted to try Netflix got their first month free. That was expensive.

What's more, we were a subscription service. Rather than charging our customers an annual fee when they signed up, we charged them a smaller amount each month. So when you added it up, we were in a perpetual cash crunch: we had to pay the full cost of every free trial all at once, up front. But the money we could use to pay it all back dribbled in slowly, month after month. The faster we gained customers, the more these up-front payments outweighed the much smaller amount we collected in monthly charges.

Basic economics again. And unfortunately, not so favorable to us. Our company was successful, but it had a voracious appetite for cash in an environment where cash was hard to come by. After the dot-com bubble burst, venture capital — which had once been comically easy to acquire, if you had a ".com" in your name — had become not just hard to get but almost completely unavailable.

It was time to *seek strategic alternatives*.

Sound like jargon? That's because it is. Silicon Valley is full of nonsense phrases just like it. For instance, when someone says that he's *leaving to spend more time with his family*, what that really means is *my ass got fired*. When someone says *this marketing copy just needs some wordsmithing*, what they really mean is *this sucks and needs to be completely rewritten*. When someone says *we decided to pivot*, what they really mean is *we fucked up, royally*.

And when a company decides to *seek strategic alternatives*, what they're saying is: *We've got to sell this sucker. And fast.*

We'd come a long way since declining Amazon's hazy low-eight-figure offer. The company had totally revamped its business model, undergone enormous growth, and become synonymous with online rental of DVDs. So the obvious strategic alternative this time wasn't Amazon but our biggest brick-and-mortar competitor: Blockbuster.

Blockbuster had been the brainchild of Wayne Huizenga, who in the late 1980s saw an opportunity to "roll up" the still mostly mom-and-pop video stores that dotted the country. Rapid expansion in the 1990s — at one point, the company was opening one new store every day — had given them a near monopoly on video rental and had made them one of the most ubiquitous brands in the country. They were king of the world in 2000, but we had no idea if they even knew who we were. Or if they cared.

As big a deal as we were online, we did a fraction of the business they did. We were on track to do $5 million in revenue in 2000 — Blockbuster was aiming for $6 *billion*. We had 350 employees — they had 60,000. We had a two-story HQ in an office park in Los Gatos — they had 9,000 stores.

They were Goliath. We were David.

But we knew that e-commerce was the future. If Blockbuster wanted to survive, it needed to develop an alternative to brick-and-mortar stores. If they recognized that, they might want to do what larger companies always did when faced with an upstart competitor — buy it.

Eliminate the competition and save money on development, all in one fell swoop.

Reed had asked Barry McCarthy to reach out to his contacts at Blockbuster to try to get a meeting. We'd asked our VCs to tap into their networks. We'd done whatever we could to try to get Blockbuster's attention. But as of the corporate retreat that September, we'd heard nothing. Not even crickets. Silence. It looked like we would have to get out of this on our own.

It's common knowledge that things in Silicon Valley are pretty casual. There's not a lot of room for suits, ties, that sort of thing. People have come to understand that it's a sign of great respect if I shave for a meeting.

I think the reason the Valley is so casual is because, unlike most industries, tech is about as close to a true meritocracy as you can get. In many disciplines, being a smooth talker or a snappy dresser can grease your ascent to the executive suite. But in Silicon Valley the only thing that really matters is the quality of your work. It's a programmer's world, with a programmer's ethos. Every programmer is accustomed to having their code subjected to peer review, in which fellow coders evaluate its brevity, elegance, cleverness, simplicity, and ultimate effectiveness. It's all there in black and white. It matters not at all what you look or dress like; what you talk or smell like. You don't need to speak English. If your code is good, you're in. If your code sucks, it's immediately apparent to everybody.

In a place where you're evaluated solely on the quality of your work, no one really cares about your appearance. That carries over, too. Even those of us who wouldn't know a line of code if it wrapped itself around our necks and sang the national anthem still get to take advantage of the fact that some fraction of the company shows up each day in shorts, Birkenstocks, and stained *Star Wars* T-shirts.

If things are that relaxed during the regular workweek, you have to really work at it when you go on a retreat. Here's what I packed for three days and two nights at Alisal:

- Two pairs of shorts
- One Grateful Dead tank top
- One tie-dyed T-shirt
- One pair of flip-flops
- One Life Is Good baseball hat, to be worn ironically (I hate that brand)
- One pair of Oakley sunglasses
- Three Harley Davidson rub-on tattoos: one Harley logo, one flaming hog, and one buxom bikini babe

In case you're wondering why I bought Harley Davidson rub-on tattoos, the answer is simple: I thought it would be funny. (That's the ruling criterion for a lot of my behavior.) Despite the casual dress code of the normal workweek, employees at Netflix were required to wear shirts in the office. So no one, up to this point, knew whether or not I was sporting ink under the corporate-branded swag I usually wore. I was pretty sure no one suspected that the forty-five-year-old dad would be inked up, even if he was from Santa Cruz. So how better to lighten the atmosphere than to peel off my Built to Last tank top at the pool and let the gossip fly?

What can I say? I'm easily amused.

When I think back to our 2000 retreat, I don't remember any of the business that we conducted. I don't remember discussions about apportionment of investment, realignment of priorities, departmental initiatives, or any of the other corporate bullshit we might have felt honor-bound to spend some time on.

What I remember are the things that built culture.

Alisal offered the usual activities that I'm sure most companies would have engaged in — horseback rides, trust falls, tennis — but at Netflix we were wired a little bit differently. Inspired by our employee onboarding, the highlight of our retreat was to be a skit throw-down between the Netflix departments, each of which would enact a scene from a recently released DVD.

As luck would have it, one of the biggest DVD releases of that summer was the Kirsten Dunst vehicle *Bring It On*. Remember that movie? If not, here's the synopsis we used on the website:

> *Torrance Shipman's cheerleading squad at Rancho Carne High School in San Diego has got spirit, spunk, sass, and a killer routine that's sure to land them the national championship trophy for the sixth year in a row. But the road to total cheer glory takes a shady turn when they discover that their perfectly choreographed routines were in fact stolen from the Clovers, a hip-hop squad from East Compton.*

Sounds like my kind of thing, right?

The only option, clearly, was for the entire executive team at Netflix to dress in cheerleading outfits and do a team cheer. Imagine us all chanting *Brrr...*, *it's cold in here! / There must be some Netflix in the AT-mosphere!* Imagine Reed Hastings in a cheerleader outfit, pom-poms in each hand. And me and Ted Sarandos, representing the squad from East Compton, in do-rags, oversize jerseys, baggy shorts, and a lot of gold chains, letting loose a rousing rendition of that summer's mega-smash by the Baha Men, "Who Let the Dogs Out."

Did I mention that alcohol was involved?

Later that night, we had a full banquet, with hundreds of us squeezed together at long wooden tables covered in red-and-white checkered tablecloths, eating heaping plates of ribs. Our invitation had specified "Ranch Formal" dress, without any details about what "Ranch Formal" actually was. Interpretation ranged from my lederhosen (don't ask) to Reed's tuxedo (nattily paired with a straw hat) to product manager Kate Arnold's vintage red gingham dress.

It was hot, it was loud, and the group was quickly feeling the effects of the open bar, which served cocktails in quart-sized mason jars. Boris had somehow convinced one of the bartenders to give him a bottle of ice-cold vodka, a tray, and dozens of shot glasses, and he was drunkenly wandering around the mess hall, solemnly asking everyone he encountered the same question: "Are you *een?*" This was remarkable in and of itself, because Boris rarely spoke. I'm sure most of the office didn't know what his voice sounded like, or that he had a strong accent, until that night.

"Are you *een?*" he'd say, holding the tray on his shoulder like a waiter, a solemn expression on his face.

Many people, I'm sure, had no idea what he was talking about. Many people, I'm sure, got vodka shots that night just because they looked confused and didn't say no. Boris, at any rate, took shots regardless of what your answer was. (For a while, anyway. I faintly recall seeing him asleep on a picnic table before dinner was even over.)

Just as things were starting to get wonderfully out of hand, I decided that I would bring the whole group together in song. Pulling several folded pages out of my pocket, I clambered up onto one of the long benches and, wobbling slightly, banged a spoon on the regrettably empty mason jar that had once held my gin and tonic. The crowd quieted.

Using the melody from "God Rest You Merry, Gentlemen," I began:

Come join me friends and raise a glass to toast our newfound luck.
Each week from every member we now extract a buck.
It seems Marquee was just the key
To prove that we don't suck!
And we soon will be rolling in dough . . .

At this point, I held off, waiting for the lackluster call-and-response. A few in the group, sober enough to realize what I was looking for, weakly responded:

Rolling in dough, and we soooon will be rolling in dough.

I continued:

Our engineers built Cinematch and boy it's doing great.
Our customers all love how many movies they can rate.
I doubt they'll even notice
that we launched it two months late!
Or that porn's always getting five stars.
(Getting five stars! Or that porn's always getting five stars.)

(That's a true story, by the way. Although Reed had made a decision pretty early on not to ship the really hard-core stuff — Clinton DVD fiasco aside — we were still renting out soft-core pornography in 2000. And the reviews were typically...enthusiastic.)

The crowd was waking up a bit, singing along.

Now marketing they're geniuses, they get the world to see
How life will be so wonderful once we all use Marquee.
If that won't sell
Then what the hell —
Just give 'em twenty free.

Things were loud now, and I picked up speed.

The finance folks, they try so hard, but still they will not learn
That Wall Street could care less about the rate our members churn.
But they'll drop trou'

Once we show how
A profit we can turn.
And we stop losing bundles of cash.

At this point, people couldn't wait to blast out the response, amplified with alcohol-fueled enthusiasm. The next stanza was largely about Reed and Barry, and as I began to sing it, I looked over to try to catch their eye. Reed's seat was empty, though. And just across the table, Barry sat with his head down, his right hand cupping his phone to his head, the index finger of the other pushed into his ear to block out the noise.

As I leaned into one of the last stanzas (*They fix each tweak, but then next week, Reed makes us change it back!*), I could see a commotion starting at the far end of the hall. I could just barely make out who it was. Was that Kate? In her red gingham dress? I could barely see her through the crowd, which was now hooting and hollering, facing away from me.

I was losing them. The group was even more distracted as the red gingham dress got closer to the middle of the room. And then I saw it — what everyone was yelling about. It wasn't Kate in the red dress. It was Reed! Wearing that gingham like it had been made for him. And behind him, there was Kate, decked out in Reed's black tuxedo.

I could barely breathe, I was laughing so hard. Reed doesn't really drink — back then, he would get drunk exactly once per year — but when he does, he makes it count. I was just on my way to see if he'd bat his eyes at me when Barry grabbed me by the arm and pulled me into the hallway, away from the noise. He wasn't laughing at all. He didn't say anything until the doors to the mess hall had closed behind us, giving us a bit of protection from the mayhem inside.

"That was Ed Stead on the phone," he said, referring to Blockbuster's general counsel. "They want to see us. Tomorrow morning. In Dallas."

Barry turned and looked back through the doorway. Reed was now standing on one of the benches, flouncing the ruffles of his dress and curtseying. He was yelling something, too, but we couldn't hear him over the rapturous noise of the crowd.

"This is gonna be some red-eye," Barry said, shaking his head. "I hope he has something to change into before the flight."

16.

Crash

(September 2000)

BARRY SLOWED HIS BMW to a crawl as he made the turn into Santa Barbara Airport. In the distance, a faint glow on the horizon was teasing us that it was close to dawn, but in front of us, the road was almost invisible, dark and shaded by the overhanging oak trees that lined the driveway. I almost expected one of them to go full Wizard of Oz on us and start pelting us with acorns.

I'd been to the Santa Barbara Airport dozens of times, but I'd never been *here*.

Barry leaned forward and squinted, trying to make out the faint lettering on a sign. "That way," pointed Reed from the front passenger seat, stretching a finger toward an even darker driveway cutting off the main road. As Barry turned and steered the car slowly onto the gravel, I could just make out the sign: General Aviation.

Within a minute or two, we pulled into a parking lot in front of a low wooden building. Flower boxes were in the windows. The roof was shingled. It looked residential, vaguely New England — less like an airport facility than a forgotten cottage. Just beyond it was an ornate wrought-iron fence, about eight feet tall. Through the bars I could see the blinking wing lights of a small plane, parked on the runway.

Barry pulled up to a gate in the fence. Even in the pre-TSA era, it was clear that this was one of those entrances you needed some kind of authority to enter — and that in this case, "authority" translated to "money." Luckily, we'd wired it earlier that morning.

Barry rolled down his window and pushed a small red button on the call box mounted next to the gate.

"Tail number?" a scratchy voice croaked.

"What's a tail number?" I whispered to Reed, leaning forward into the gap between the two front seats. Reed turned his head and gave me a look, the same one I often found myself giving my kids at any restaurant fancier than McDonald's. The look that meant: *I can't take you anywhere.*

The password given, the gate started to glide silently open. Barry rolled up his window and crept the car forward. As we passed through onto the tarmac and drove slowly toward the plane, I looked back and saw the gate sliding noiselessly back into place behind us.

"No going back now," I thought to myself.

Less than twelve hours earlier, as soon as the commotion over Reed's grand-in-gingham entrance had subsided, Barry, Reed, and I had retreated to a picnic table near one of the Alisal swimming pools.

"Not just tomorrow," Barry was complaining. "That would have been bad enough. But *eleven thirty* tomorrow? They want us there at eleven thirty in the goddamn morning? Impossible."

Barry picked up his mechanical pencil with one hand and used the fist of the other to scrub a clean spot on the wood of the picnic table. "First," he said, scribbling a number right into the wood grain, "Dallas is on Central Time, so that means nine thirty our time. Then it's a three-and-a-half-hour flight from San Francisco — so probably about the same from Santa Barbara. Plus, if you add on enough time to get to the airport…" He paused, adding some figures onto the table. "You would have to leave here by five a.m. And I don't even need to check to know there isn't a nonstop from Santa Barbara at five in the morning. We're screwed."

Barry slumped back, retracted the lead of his pencil, and somewhat guiltily tried to erase the figures from the table.

"So we fly private," Reed said, opening up his palm to the two of us as if it were self-evident. "We take off at five, land at ten thirty, have a car waiting. We'll be there right on time. Probably even have enough time for Marc and me to grab an espresso."

Barry didn't react, as if trying to figure out what was more absurd: the fact that Reed was proposing spending money on a private jet or the fact that he was doing so while wearing a dress.

Reed, for his part, seemed to have forgotten all about his new attire.

"Reed," Barry finally blurted out, "that's gotta be at least twenty thousand round-trip."

He moved to write something again, then thought better of it.

"And I don't need to tell *you* that we don't have that type of money."

"Barry," Reed said, "we've waited months to get this meeting. We're on track to lose at least fifty million dollars this year. Whether we pull this off or not, another twenty grand won't make a difference."

"Yeah, Barry," I piped up. "Twenty grand. Isn't that what you finance guys call a 'rounding error'?"

"You guys are a piece of work," Barry muttered to no one in particular.

From behind the plane an orange-vested worker appeared, holding an illuminated torch, and waved Barry's car to a position just off the wing. As our headlights swept the area, I saw that a red carpet had been rolled out from the base of the plane's stairs. A uniformed pilot appeared in the hatch, stepped down, and walked over to us.

"I'm Rob," he said, smiling and extending his hand. He gestured toward the trunk of the car. "Can I grab your bags?"

Reed and I looked at each other and laughed. Reed opened his briefcase and pulled out a folded white T-shirt. "This is it."

Luckily for me, we were only on day two of the retreat, so some of my clothing was still clean. Dressing in the dark that morning, I had put on my one remaining clean item: my tie-dyed T-shirt. I'd opted to leave the lederhosen behind (as well as the Harley Davidson tattoos) and had instead substituted an almost-new pair of shorts, accented with black flip-flops.

Reed grabbed hold of the cable handrail and bounded up the stairs, then ducked through the doorway and vanished into the plane. I followed him up, not quite sure what to expect from a private jet. Gold-plated bathroom fixtures? A giant king-size bed? A stand-up bar? (This latter amenity was actually the last thing in the world I wanted to see, since I was still struggling with the aftereffects of the previous night's mason jars.)

The interior of the jet was surprisingly businesslike — if you consider a huge platter of breakfast pastries and sliced fruit, a thermos of coffee, and a pitcher of freshly squeezed orange juice perched on the counter of a jet "businesslike." Bottles of water and soda were visible through the glass door of a half-size refrigerator. A wicker basket overflowed with granola bars.

The plane, a Learjet 35A, was smaller than I had imagined — but much nicer. Every surface seemed to be either leather or rosewood. It looked like someone had taken Steve Kahn's living room and folded it around the inside surface of an airplane fuselage. As I started down the single narrow aisle, I noticed I could stand up straight, but barely. Immediately to my right, facing to the front of the plane, was a single leather captain's chair, nicer than any piece of furniture I owned. Directly behind it was a group of four chairs facing each other — two forward and two back, with enough legroom that you could fit a dining room table between them. In fact, as I found out later, there *was* a dining room table, neatly folded into the windowsills between the seats.

Reed was already settled in the front-right rear-facing seat, his long legs stretched lazily into the open space. I later learned that private jet aficionados, like home theater aficionados, have a "money seat" — although in a jet, you're looking for the safest, smoothest, and most comfortable ride, not acoustics — and that Reed, accustomed to private plane rides, knew enough to snag it immediately.

Reed stretched out an arm, gesturing toward a seat facing him, and as I struggled to figure out the four-point harness, Barry casually settled in across the aisle from me, balancing a plate of fruit on top of his laptop. Despite my efforts to play it cool, Barry knew that I was getting a kick out of all of this.

"Like it?" he said, neatly spearing a piece of fruit. "I was talking to Rob outside. This jet belongs to Vanna White. She charters it out when she's not using it. I guess flipping letters for a living pays better than I thought."

He took a bite of pineapple. "Pretty cool, huh?" Then, flashing me a quick smile, he lowered his voice to a stage whisper. "Don't get used to it."

We landed well past rush hour in Dallas, but you wouldn't have known it from the traffic. All the time we had saved by hiring a car to meet us at the foot of the plane's stairs was wasted as we crawled through downtown.

"That's it right there," said our driver, pulling the car to the curb. He leaned his head forward, looked up through the windshield, and gestured at the office building across the street. "That's the Renaissance Tower. Tallest building in Dallas. Probably the most expensive one, too."

The building rose straight up out of the sidewalk, without setbacks, spires, or features of any kind; it was an unbroken cube of steel and glass. Its only gesture toward decoration was a giant X of slightly darker windows, diagonal lines stretching across the entire height and width of the building. The building's immensity and lack of adornment made it seem serious: it was clear that this was not a building to be trifled with. There was no playfulness here. No joy. This was where business was done.

As the elevator opened onto the 23rd floor, I was relieved to see that things looked a bit more familiar and less intimidating. The walls of Blockbuster's lobby were covered with framed movie posters, and even though I recognized many of the same ones that we had back at the office, I couldn't help but notice that Blockbuster's were all framed considerably more tastefully, each movie in its own gleaming stainless-steel frame, encircled by a ring of lightbulbs like the marquee posters you see in theater lobbies. "Do you know what those things cost?" I couldn't help but mutter to Reed, as we were ushered into the conference room.

I was happy to see that their conference room was almost like ours — if ours had been about fifty times bigger. And with a view across the entirety of Dallas, rather than the Dumpsters between us and the park. And with a thirty-foot-conference table made from an endangered hardwood with hidden power outlets and audiovisual plugs, rather than an eight-foot folding table with an extension cord and surge protector.

So, you know, pretty much the same.

I was already feeling a little like a country mouse in the big city — and in my shorts and T-shirt, a little chilly in the arctic blast of Texan AC — when the Blockbuster boys came in and introduced themselves.

Blockbuster CEO John Antioco came in first. He was dressed casually but expensively. No suit, but his loafers probably cost more than my car. He seemed relaxed and confident — and with good reason, too. Antioco had come to Blockbuster after nearly ten years as a turnaround specialist, known for parachuting into struggling companies — Circle K, Taco Bell, and Pearle Vision among them — figuring out which core aspects of the business showed promise, restoring company morale, and coaxing the balance sheets back into profitability.

Blockbuster had needed him. After explosive growth and massive

profits in the eighties and half of the nineties, the company had floundered at the turn of the millennium. A string of poor decisions — like
selling music and clothing in the stores — had largely backfired, and
the company had been slow — extremely slow — to adapt to new technology like the DVD, and to the internet.

Although he had no experience in entertainment, Antioco had recognized in Blockbuster the characteristics he was intimately familiar
with: a struggling chain with thousands of stores, tens of thousands of
demoralized employees, and the opportunity to bring things back to
profitability.

Antioco's methods had shown promise almost immediately. Renters
were returning to the stores, revenue was up, and the stock price of
Blockbuster's parent company, Viacom, had doubled, in no small part
because of Blockbuster's success.

So as Antioco strode into the conference room that morning in September of 2000, I'm sure he was feeling self-assured. He had taken
Blockbuster through an IPO just a year earlier, raising more than $450
million in cash, and he was now the CEO of a publicly traded company. He was ready to hear us out, but what we said had better be good.

As we shook hands with Antioco and his general counsel, Ed Stead,
it was hard not to feel a bit intimidated. It was partly the loafers. Anti-
oco was wearing beautiful Italian shoes and I was in shorts, a tie-dyed
T-shirt, and flip-flops. Reed's T-shirt was crisp, but it was still a T-shirt.
And Barry, always the best dressed of the group...well, at least his
Hawaiian shirt had buttons.

Really, though, we were intimidated because Blockbuster was in
a much stronger position than us. Flush with cash from their recent
IPO, they weren't dependent on the good graces of VCs to keep them
afloat. They weren't struggling with the scarlet letters ".com." And
worst of all, they knew it.

There's nothing like going into a negotiation knowing that the other
side holds almost all the cards.

Notice that I wrote "almost." There were, in fact, a few points in our favor. To start, everyone hated Blockbuster. This, after all, was a company that had "managed dissatisfaction" as a central pillar of their business model. They knew that most customers didn't enjoy the experience of renting from them, so their goal as a company wasn't so much to make the customer happy as it was to not piss them off so royally that they'd never come back. And there was a lot to piss them off: late fees, crappy selection, dirty stores, poor service...the list went on and on.

And it wasn't just customers who hated them: the movie industry did, too. The studios felt burned by the hard bargains that Ed Stead had negotiated on Blockbuster's behalf as the chain had gained market share. They also resented Blockbuster's insistence that it was Blockbuster itself that was creating demand for their movies rather than just fulfilling the demand that the studios felt they had created.

But the most important point in our favor was the inexorable march of progress. The world was going online. No one knew exactly how it would happen, or how long it would take, but it was inevitable that increasing numbers of Blockbuster's customers would want — no, *insist on* — transacting their business online. And not only was Blockbuster ill-positioned to take advantage of that trend, they didn't even seem to see that it was coming. The way we saw things, they could use our help.

We just hoped they could see it that way, too.

Reed had carefully worked on his pitch, just as he had worked on the PowerPoint to me the year before, and as he leaned over the conference table and started building the shit sandwich, I couldn't help but smile. It was a thing of beauty. A real triple-decker.

"Blockbuster has some tremendous attributes," he started in, laying down that first thick slice of bread. "A network of company-owned and franchised stores in thousands of locations, tens of thousands of dedicated employees, and a passionate user base consisting of nearly twenty million active members." (He tactfully left out the part about how many of those users actually hated the service. That could come later.)

Picking up speed, and readying himself to start stacking the meat, Reed continued. "But there are certainly areas where Blockbuster could use the expertise and market position that Netflix has obtained to position itself more strongly."

He laid out the proposal that we had all agreed was the strongest. "We should join forces," he started, joining his hands together for emphasis. "We will run the online part of the combined business. You will focus on the stores. We will find the synergies that come from the combination, and it will truly be a case of the whole being greater than the sum of its parts."

Reed was doing well — he was concise, to the point, but not arrogant or overconfident. He belonged in that room, and he knew it. As he continued to point out the perceived advantages of a union, Barry and I nodded at all the right beats, occasionally interjecting a supporting comment. It was all I could do to hold back from spontaneously shouting, "Amen, brother. Hallelujah!"

"Blockbuster," Reed pointed out, "will be able to use us to greatly accelerate its entry into DVD, and do so at a much lower cost. With us focusing on back-catalogue items, you'll be able to concentrate your inventory on the new releases which are at the heart of your business, improving availability and increasing customer satisfaction.

"Netflix will also benefit," Reed continued, "by taking advantage of Blockbuster promotions, both in the store as well as to the user base." He paused. "And even if we don't combine forces, just working together as independent companies could be of tremendous benefit to both of us."

Reed stopped. He looked from Antioco to Stead, and then back again as he settled into his chair. He knew he had made the sandwich perfectly. All that mattered now is if they would take a bite.

*   *   *

The objections were just what we had anticipated. "The dot-com hysteria is completely overblown," Antioco said. Stead informed us that the business models of most online ventures, Netflix included, just weren't sustainable. They would burn cash forever.

Finally, after Barry and I parried back and forth with them over the major objections, Ed Stead raised his hand and waited for everyone to be quiet.

"If we were to buy you," he started, pausing for emphasis, "what are you thinking? I mean, a number. What are we talking about here?"

We had rehearsed this. Or at least we had rehearsed it about as well as three people can at 5:00 a.m. on a plane after a night of drinking at a dude ranch.

"We've taken a look at recent comparables," Barry began, "and we've also tried to consider what the ROI might be were Netflix to be rolled out to the Blockbuster user base. We've also considered how to make this accretive rather than..."

Out of the corner of my eye, I could see Reed fidgeting. I had seen this before. It was just a matter of time before he lost all patience. Hold...hold...

"Fifty million," Reed finally interrupted.

Barry stopped. He looked at Reed, his hands falling into his lap, then smiled at Antioco and Stead. He shrugged. What more was there to say?

We waited.

Through Reed's pitch and Barry's windup, I had been watching Antioco. I knew his reputation as a gifted empath, a great listener — someone who could make anyone feel that they were important and had something to say worth hearing. During the pitch, I had seen him use all the tricks that I'd also learned over the years: Lean in, make eye contact, nod slowly when the speaker turns in your direction. Frame questions in a way that makes it clear you're listening.

But now that Reed had named a number, I saw something new, something I didn't recognize. A different expression in his body, a slight tension in his face. His earnest expression slightly unbalanced by a turning up at the corner of his mouth.

It was tiny, involuntary, and vanished almost immediately. But as soon as I saw it, I knew what was happening.

John Antioco was struggling not to laugh.

The meeting went downhill pretty quickly after that, and it was a long, quiet ride back to the airport. We didn't have a lot to say to each other on the plane, either. We left the tray of sandwiches and cookies on the counter by the door, untouched. The champagne in the refrigerator — provided by Vanna, and available for purchase — went unpopped.

Each of us was lost in his own thoughts. Reed, I'm sure, had put the meeting behind him, and was already puzzling through some new business problem before we hit cruising altitude.

Barry, I could tell, was running numbers in his head, trying to figure out how long our existing cash would last, how he could slow the rate at which we were burning through it, what clever financing rabbit he might be able to pull from his hat to buy us a few extra months.

But I was on a different wavelength. We'd been in trouble before, but the dot-com crash was different. The springs were drying up, and we couldn't count on unlimited venture capital anymore. Selling had seemed to be our only way out. And Goliath didn't want to buy us — he wanted to stomp us into the ground.

As long a shot as Blockbuster had been, I had genuinely held out hope that they could be the deus ex machina that would save us. That in one bold stroke we'd be out of the mountains and safely on the trail back to camp.

Now it was clear that if we were going to get out of the crash alive, it was entirely on us. We would have to be ruthless in our focus on the future. We would have to look within. As my father used to tell me, sometimes the only way out is *through*.

As Vanna White's plane swept us quietly and quickly back to Santa Barbara, and as we all sat lost in our own thoughts, I grabbed an empty champagne flute and tapped it with a plastic spoon from the fruit tray. Reed looked up sleepily, and Barry paused the number-crunching long enough to look me in the eye.

"Well," I said, pantomiming a toast. "Shit."

I paused, taking in the absurd particulars of the scene: the Lear's leather interior, Barry's billowing Hawaiian shirt, the tray of fruit big enough for a family of five. I smiled, feeling resolve flood my chest.

"Blockbuster doesn't want us," I said. "So it's obvious what we have to do now."

I smiled. Couldn't help it.

"It looks like now we're going to have to kick their ass."

17.

The Belt Tightens

(2000–2001)

AMONG CLIMBERS, IT'S A matter of dogma that if you haven't reached the summit by early afternoon, it's time to think seriously about turning around. As noted Everest climbing guide Ed Viesturs tells his clients, "Getting to the top is optional. Getting down is mandatory." When you're thousands of feet in the air and miles from camp, you have to leave yourself plenty of daylight — otherwise, you can get stuck just where you don't want to be.

That's what happened to Netflix, metaphorically speaking, in the fall of 2000. After Blockbuster refused to buy us, Netflix was in a no-man's-land: we were no longer in grave danger, but neither were we entirely out of the woods.

Unlike many companies our size (and larger), we'd survived the dot-com crash. Our business model was good: no-due-dates, no-late-fees was *working*. People loved Cinematch. We were on track to acquire 500,000 users by the end of 2001.

But our subscription model was fundamentally expensive. We were still hemorrhaging money, and the landscape we found ourselves in was a far different one than we'd encountered a year before. Burning cash at the rates that had been normal the year before now looked irresponsible. We needed to speed things up. We didn't have to become

254

profitable, necessarily. But if we ever wanted to go public, banks (and the investors they recommended our stock to) would have to see a *path* to profitability. If we were still in the cycle of raising $40 million every year, and then posting $45 million in losses, we wouldn't look like a very good bet.

We knew that if we wanted any chance of surviving in a post-bubble world, we had to be ruthless in our dedication to the Canada Principle. Over the course of late 2000 and throughout 2001, we streamlined our processes. The ".com" suffix that had been a ticket to free money in 1999 was now an albatross — so we cut it from our name. The "portal" ethos that had ruled the world (and the boardroom) a year before had crashed and burned alongside Dr. Koop — so we shelved it.

We called this ruthless streamlining *scraping barnacles off the hull*.

Companies are like boats: sometimes you have to put them in dry dock to remove the barnacles that have accreted on the hull, slowing down forward progress. In the wake of the Blockbuster fiasco and the crash of the dot-com market, we took time to self-assess, then mercilessly pruned back all programs, tests, additions, and enhancements that weren't contributing anymore.

We'd always done this. And it hadn't always been easy. Sometimes, what looks like a barnacle to you is someone else's favorite feature. For instance — when we were determining the price point for Marquee, we had tested dozens of prices and DVD quantities. We'd had some customers getting four discs at a time for $9.95, others $19.99, and still others $24.95. We'd allowed people to keep two discs at a time, eight, and every number in between. And while the standard plan was to swap as often as you liked, some customers were limited to just a handful of swaps. We were eventually sued over one of our more interesting experiments, in which we expedited service to some customers to see if that encouraged the light renters ("birds," in Netflix parlance) and artificially slowed down service to discourage heavier users (internally — and secretly — called "pigs").

All of this testing was undeniably useful. Because of it, we didn't have to argue about whether higher prices slowed down sign-up rates, increased churn, or encouraged higher usage. We had proved whether it did each of these things and knew exactly by how much. But once we'd learned what we needed to learn, the usefulness of the test fell to zero for us.

Unfortunately, the cost stayed the same. And each new feature we added on to the service had to then work flawlessly with the old ones, so as to accommodate all our customers, no matter which plan they were on. Doing so meant that design got complicated. Testing got harder. And everything slowed down.

An outdated feature was a barnacle. The drag it imposed might be tiny — but multiplied by a thousand? It slowed us down and cost us money.

So we scraped. Every meeting, before we could launch into any discussion of what we planned to do going forward, we had to start by looking backward, coming up with a list of what we could decide to *stop* doing. It wasn't easy. Most times, deciding what *not* to do is harder than deciding what to do. Yes, the customers who were on the $24.95 plan were delighted to have their test terminated and get switched onto the $19.95 group. Not so much the lucky few paying $9.95 for the same service. Or getting eight discs at a time.

After a while, we got pretty callous about it. *Let 'em scream,* we would rationalize. *We're okay with upsetting a thousand if it means we get it right for ten thousand.*

As 2000 slid into 2001, with the Blockbuster opportunity steadily receding in the rearview mirror and the idea of an IPO shelved for the foreseeable future, Barry was furiously scraping barnacles from every aspect of the business, desperate to make our boat go faster.

At first, the items on the cut list were easy to tackle. If we weren't going to go forward as a portal, we didn't need to develop technology to serve up advertising on our pages. Christina and her team could drop their efforts to develop a showtimes feature, and the content team no longer needed to assemble data for every movie on the planet — we could just focus on the DVD catalogue.

But we didn't need Barry's spreadsheets to tell us what was becoming increasingly obvious to everyone who sat around our E-Staff table every Monday: we had more people than we needed.

Under ordinary circumstances, being a little heavy would have been okay. At the rate we were growing, we could have easily absorbed extra employees by waiting a quarter or two, until the added volume and complexity of the business both warranted and economically supported having more staff. But things were different now. As Barry worked through the numbers and confronted the new post-crash landscape, it was clear that we had to be not just a lighter company — we needed to be a different one.

In a post-bubble landscape, we couldn't look like a money pit. There had to be a point where not only were we making money from each customer each month, but there were enough customers to cover the fixed costs of running the business. In the past, we had mostly focused on only one side of the equation: getting more customers. Now, it was becoming increasingly obvious that we had to focus on the other side of the equation: spending less money running the business.

There were only so many costs we could cut by eliminating big things. And we were running out of barnacles to scrape. We had a clean hull and the destination was clearly defined, but the boat was still too heavy. If we were going to make it to shore, we'd need to lighten the ship.

Our usual Tuesday E-Staff meetings always began with the same agenda item: *Who fucked up?* That wasn't the official name for it, of course — but that's what I called it. In the interest of transparency and radical honesty, each of us would go around the room and say something that wasn't working. We didn't need to know what was going well — things that were working didn't need any attention from the rest of us. Instead, we wanted to know what *wasn't* working. *Who*, in my elevated parlance, was *fucking up*.

It's a maxim of startup life: You're going to get things wrong. You just don't want to get the same things wrong twice.

At one meeting in the summer of 2001, just after the morning's ritual flogging was complete, Reed gestured to Barry that it was time for new business. Barry stood up from his seat and walked to the whiteboard, grabbed a green marker, and wrote in large letters: *2,000,000*.

"That's the number," Barry announced, turning toward us. "At our current overhead levels, that's how many subscribers we'll need to get to profitability."

He leaned down and squinted at his laptop.

"But that's seventy-three weeks away. And every month between now and then, we're burning money. We'll run out long before we'll get there. And I don't need to remind anyone that people aren't exactly lining up to throw money at our feet."

Barry paused, then squinted down at his laptop again. "We have to cut our expenses. And deep. We have to be lean enough to make it to profitability on the money we already have. And the only way we do that is by lowering our costs so that we can be profitable on a smaller subscriber base."

He picked up the green marker and turned back to the board. With the edge of his palm he erased the 2 at the head of the number and replaced it with a 1.

"We'll only survive if we can be profitable on one million subscribers. And this?" he said, opening a manila folder and sliding a stapled set of papers around to each of us. "This is how we're going to do it."

Layoffs. That was Barry's plan.

After his dramatic reveal, Reed, Patty, Barry, and I met for lunch every day, chewing through dozens of scenarios. Which departments should we cut to the bone? Which should survive unscathed? Should we cut highly paid (but more valuable) employees or make it up in volume, by drastically reducing the ranks of customer service agents?

These were complicated questions. We needed to cut expenses dramatically, but we had to do it in a way that wouldn't damage our ability to grow our business.

After a particularly grueling session, I swung by Joel Mier's desk and tapped him on the shoulder. Joel was my director of research and analytics. In his role he had to straddle art and science, data and intuition, and his appearance supported that. At 6′4″, he was a powerful presence, but he held himself in a gentle way that made him approachable. In an office full of shorts and unwashed T-shirts, Joel dressed like a university professor: button-down shirts, cardigans, corduroy pants, and black oxfords. He was extremely measured in his speech and chose his words carefully. He was an even more thoughtful listener, nodding slowly and considerately at even the stupidest utterances, as if the failure to find some genius in them must lie with him.

But his professorial manner hid a sharp wit and a hooligan-in-the-back-row sense of humor. Joel loved a good practical joke — he was a consummate player of Coins in the Fountain and loved nothing more than to stock the Netflix kitchen with half-edible delicacies. He'd once put out a bowl of freeze-dried garbanzo beans that had prompted an enraged Mitch Lowe to scream: "You almost broke my tooth, motherfucker!" I still laugh when I think about it.

Joel's combination of data-driven intelligence and sophomoric humor had made us fast friends from day one. It didn't happen often, but whenever we could, Joel and I liked nothing better than to sneak away at lunch to a booth at the Black Watch, the sole dive bar in Los Gatos, to carefully dissect our colleagues, our heads collapsing helplessly in laughter onto the beer-stained tables.

"How's it hangin', boss?" Joel murmured now, barely looking up from his screen.

"Up and to the right," I said, giving the ritual response to our usual greeting. I flipped my head toward the stairs. "Let's go for a walk."

Earlier that week, Reed, Barry, and I had brought all the Netflix directors into the cone of silence and shared our intentions with them. Since the majority of the employees in the company directly reported to this group, they had the best idea of who was actually getting things done, who was irreplaceable, and who could be easily done without. I had gotten in the habit of taking daily walks with most of them, making lazy circles around the building as we talked out loud about each person in the department. I needed their help, because deciding whom to let go was complicated. Talent and indispensability turned out to be the easiest dimensions to figure out. It was the other stuff that got us tangled. How much weight should be put on personal situations? What if an employee were the sole breadwinner in her family, with a new baby? Should she stay on rather than someone young and single (but more talented)? And what about the handful of married couples working at Netflix? Would it be just too cruel to fire both of them at the same time?

Joel was pulling on his jacket as he pushed open the building's front door with his hip and joined me on the sidewalk. Without saying anything we turned and began the loop, circling clockwise around the building.

"I've been thinking, boss," Joel began, as soon as we were safely out of earshot of an employee getting out of his car.

"That's always dangerous," I replied.

Joel smiled and continued.

"I know we have talked about doing this LIFO, but I'm not feeling it."

LIFO stood for last in, first out, meaning that the last people hired, having the least tenure, would be the first ones to be let go. We'd borrowed the term, which usually applied to inventory. Although LIFO, for our purposes, didn't necessarily correlate to talent, it did correspond to experience on the job, and to some degree it made people feel like there was a rational basis to a process that could often feel pretty random.

"It's Kyle that I'm worried about," Joel finally blurted out. "He's definitely not next in line to go when you use seniority. But his attitude..." Joel left the thought hanging.

I knew exactly what he meant. In one of the analytics meetings that we periodically held, where we brought together people from different disciplines in the company to wrestle with particularly challenging analytical problems, Kyle was consistently proving himself to be...how shall I put this...*difficult.*

At Netflix, there was nothing wrong with disagreement. In fact, disagreement was a critical component of our culture of radical honesty. We *expected* disagreement, because we encouraged vigorous debate. In Netflix meetings, there was no seniority, and no one's opinion was more valuable because of their title, age, or salary. Everyone was expected to fight for their point of view until a consensus had been reached.

Still, no matter how passionate the argument, there was a shared expectation at Netflix that, once the self-evidently correct conclusion had been reached, it was time to fall in and implement it. Disagreement was collaborative, not ego-driven. It didn't matter *who* was right — all that mattered was that *we* got it right.

And that was where Kyle was falling short. He just couldn't get over it when things didn't go his way, and his bad attitude was infecting everyone.

"I get it. He's out of here. We'll keep Markowitz," I said to Joel, referring to one of Joel's direct reports.

"Good," he said flatly, without looking up at me.

I'd known Joel long enough to understand that there was something on his mind. As we turned the corner and passed the picnic tables that sat in a small courtyard to the side of the building, I finally figured it out.

"By the way," I said quietly, "if I haven't already made it clear... you're safe."

The look of relief on Joel's face was immediate. He nodded and with a big smile said, "Up and to the right, boss. Up and to the right."

Barely a week later, we were once more gathered around the table in the conference room, but the crowd had swelled to include the entire management team. It was a Monday night, just a few minutes before 8:00, and people were still shuffling in from dinner, looking for places to sit or stand. Outside the room, the rest of the office was deserted, the clusters of empty chairs and cubicles a somber premonition of what would be happening in less than twenty-four hours.

I caught Joel's eye from across the room and he gave me a curt nod. Patty sat at the front of the room, two white binders open on the table in front of her. Reed hovered over her left shoulder, looking down intently and gesturing at something. Patty whispered something back, and with her pen drew a line through a row of type halfway down the page.

One major player was already gone: Eric Meyer. He'd been nudged out the day before, his talents — although prodigious — no longer right for the challenges ahead of us.

As for everyone else? After two final marathon sessions over the weekend, we had come to our final list. Now it was time to act.

Patty looked up from her notebooks, pushed up her sleeve to check her watch, and loudly pushed back her chair. "Okay, boys and girls. Here's how this is gonna work."

The email came out right on schedule, at 10:45 on Tuesday morning. It was short and to the point: there would be an important announcement at 11:00 in front of the building.

The company had long since swelled past the point where we could fit everyone in a single room. Not even the lobby could hold us. Now, when we needed to assemble the entire company, we had to rent the 100-year-old Los Gatos Theater on Santa Cruz Avenue or just gather like a mob outside, in the picnic area by our front entrance. Today, it was the courtyard. There was no sense renting a theater to tell 40 percent of your company that they were losing their jobs. That would just be cruel.

As I walked through the rows of cubicles on my way to the stairwell, I instinctively stepped into the conference room at the head of the stairs. This would be where my departments would be doing their layoffs, and I thought I should do one last check to ensure that, at the very least, there were two chairs in there. Getting fired was bad enough, I thought — you should at least get a chair to sit in.

But it was okay. Two chairs. An empty table, a clean whiteboard. Nothing to indicate that there wouldn't be a regular meeting there.

Outside, there was already a big crowd gathered in the courtyard. People stood in small groups, nervously talking. I found Joel and stood stoically next to him. A few minutes after 11:00, Reed climbed up onto one of the picnic tables. The crowd quieted.

"For more than three years, we have all worked tremendously hard to get Netflix where it is today, work we should all be very proud of. But we've all known that there would be days that we had to make hard decisions. I'm afraid that today is one of those days."

Reed paused and looked around. There wasn't a sound. From across the park beyond the fence I could just hear the steam whistle from the park railroad, and the scream of excited children. Somewhere, at least, somebody was having fun.

"It should be clear to everyone," Reed continued, "that the funding environment has changed dramatically over the last twelve months. Not just for us, but for every company in the Valley. We can no longer count on venture money to carry us along. We need to become self-sufficient. We need to control our own destiny. To do so, we have to reduce our expenses such that we can achieve profitability with a smaller subscriber number, and we have to reduce our spending levels to ensure that we have enough money to last us to that point."

Across the crowd, I could see Joel's employee, Markowitz, visibly shaken. Face pale, upper lip sweating, he was tearing a napkin to shreds in his hands. I nudged Joel.

"You should probably reassure him," I said. "Guy looks like he's about to pass out."

Joel nodded and weaved his way through the crowd. I saw him take Markowitz by the shoulder, whisper something in his ear.

Instantly, Markowitz's expression changed. He looked enormously relieved.

Reed, on the other hand, appeared to be wavering. Perched atop the picnic table, above a now visibly restless crowd, he looked like a revolutionary starting to realize that he was failing to inspire the mob. He glanced down at Patty for reassurance. She was looking up at him and slowly nodding.

"There are going to be layoffs today," he said, gathering his strength. "Some of our friends and colleagues will be leaving us. But this is not because they have done anything wrong — it's purely because this is what must be done to make the company stronger. Go back inside, and wait for your manager to give you instructions about your particular situation."

The crowd dispersed noiselessly, and I let myself be swept along toward the entrance and up the main stairs. Something about being surrounded by my scared employees made me see the situation from their perspective: *How had it come to this? We were there! We figured it out. No due dates, no late fees. We focused relentlessly on what was important. We got Cinematch off the ground. We figured out next-day shipping. We figured out how to get new customers efficiently. Why retreat now?*

As I turned at the top of the stairs, I noticed out of the corner of my eye that there was something different about the conference room I'd checked out not more than twenty minutes earlier. There was now something on the table: a powder-blue box of Kleenex, perched in the exact center, one tissue puffed artfully out of the top.

We even figured out how to do a layoff, I thought, not without some bitterness.

It was all over by 11:30. People stood in small groups, some crying, some relieved, some just shell-shocked. The office was almost empty.

When it started, everyone had been on edge as managers had moved silently through the office, summoning employees to their respective conference rooms. If you were called early in the process, it was pretty clear what was going on. For the rest of the group, each person called away that wasn't you was one more dodged bullet — until finally a manager would emerge from their conference room and give a relieved "all clear" to their department.

For the people doing the firing, there was no avoiding the discomfort. We had all been through hell together. These were friends. They were colleagues. Some — like Vita, who got the ax that day — had been there from the beginning. And now I was telling them it was time to leave. I cried with all of them.

When it was all over, I just lay there on my couch, emotionally drained, tossing a soccer ball up in the air over and over again, replaying in my mind what I'd done.

My last layoff had been Jennifer Morgan, one of our newer analysts. When I approached her cube, she sat with her back to me, engrossed in her screen, even then able to concentrate on the problem in front of her. I touched her shoulder, and as she slowly turned to me, I saw that there were tears in her eyes. "I knew it," was all she said, as she gathered up her purse and prepared to follow me to the conference room. "I just knew it."

*   *   *

Shortly after we were finished, I gathered the remainder of my departments together. I gave them a short talk about moving forward, and the solemn responsibility we had to demonstrate — to ourselves and everyone else — that this layoff had not been done capriciously or cruelly but with the sole focus of ensuring that Netflix survived. We owed it to everyone to make sure that happened.

Later, after everyone dispersed — some for lunch, some for home, some just to do slow laps through the building to see who was still left — Joel came to join me in my corner. We didn't talk much. There wasn't much to say. The future could start tomorrow. We just sat there, tossing the soccer ball back and forth, until I noticed a lone figure at the periphery of my vision. Just from the tennis shoes I knew it was an engineer. When I looked up, I saw someone I had hired myself, many years ago: a hard worker, a skilled coder, a nice guy.

He just hadn't made the cut.

"Sorry, Marc," he started. "I don't want to interrupt you, but I wanted to come back and make sure you were okay. This must have been really tough on you."

I held the soccer ball and cocked my head. I didn't know how to answer. It didn't make sense. He'd just been laid off, and he was wondering if *I* was okay?

"Well, anyway," he awkwardly continued after a few seconds. "Thanks for everything."

He turned and started to walk away. But then, just before he passed the end of the row of cubes, he stopped, as if he had suddenly remembered something.

"Hey," he shouted back, a smile on his face. "Crush Blockbuster, okay?"

And with that he was gone.

18.

Going Public

(May 2002: 49 months post-launch)

IN THE WEEKS AND months following September's painful layoffs, we started to notice something.

We were *better*.

We were more efficient. More creative. More decisive.

Winnowing our staff made us leaner and more focused. We no longer had time to waste, so we didn't waste it. And while we certainly had to lay off some very talented individuals, we'd been left only with superstar players. With superstar players doing all of the work, it was no wonder that our quality of work was very high.

You see this often in successful startups. The business gets off the ground because of the focus, dedication, and creativity of a small group of dedicated people. It hires, grows bigger — and then contracts itself. It rededicates itself to its mission — and often, accomplishes it through the renewed focus and energy of its most valuable members.

Hiring and keeping star players is about much more than just quality of work, however. It's a culture thing. When you retain *only* star players, you create a culture of competitive excellence. It's more fun to come to work when you know you're part of the handpicked elite. Plus, it's much easier to attract other elite talent to your team when you've established a reputation for superstar talent.

*   *   *

In some ways, Netflix in late 2001 was like June 1998 all over again: a handpicked team of extremely capable people, working very hard on a singular goal: one million subscribers. And just like 1998, we hit it — this time, months in advance. By Christmas.

We reached the finish line early in large part because Tom Dillon had found a way to guarantee quick shipping — next-day shipping — to users all over the country. In many ways, it was an extension of our Sacramento tests — and our old idea about users mailing DVDs to each other. Turns out you didn't need to build huge, expensive warehouses all across the country to ship DVDs if 90 percent of the DVDs people wanted *were already in circulation*. Tom had applied to shipping a principle we all understood intuitively: when it came to movies, people were lemmings. They wanted to watch what everyone else was watching. If you'd finished *Apollo 13* yesterday, then it was highly likely that somebody else wanted it today. Conversely, if the next movie in your queue was *Boogie Nights*, it was just as likely somebody else was returning it that day. Tom's brilliant idea was to recognize that when a user mailed a DVD back to us, it didn't need to go to a warehouse the size of a Costco. It didn't even need to go back on a shelf. It could go right back out the door to someone else! And we could run *that* business from a shoebox.

Tom analyzed hundreds of thousands of data points to figure out where to place small Netflix shipping "hubs," basically storefronts the size of your neighborhood Greek restaurant. His data showed that you could service 95 percent of the country with next-day delivery if you judiciously placed about sixty of these hubs all across the country. They weren't warehouses; they were "reflection points." Nothing was really stored there. DVDs coming in would almost immediately "bounce" right back out to other customers.

Here's how Tom's reflection-point method worked: Customers

mailed their watched DVDs to the post office closest to that region's reflection point. At 9:00 each morning, a local employee would pick up the mail, and for the next three hours, that employee (and four or five others) would use a slitter to open the mailers, remove the discs, and scan each DVD into a Netflix inventory program. The DVDs would temporarily go into neat piles on the table. The employees would transmit all that data to headquarters in Los Gatos, and while they took their lunch breaks, our servers would match up all the DVDs that had come in with all the movies those customers wanted next. After lunch, the employees would scan each disc again, but this time, the system would spit out a mailing label bearing the address of the customer who wanted the disc next.

The process worked obscenely well. Out of every hundred discs that arrived each day, ninety of them had a customer in that region who wanted them, so out the door they would go. Another seven or eight of the hundred DVDs would be new releases or high-demand items that no one wanted that day but which we were pretty sure somebody would want within a day or two. These discs were stored in the reflection point's tiny shoebox library. Of the hundred DVDs coming in, there were usually only two or three for which we didn't have an immediate customer — or anticipate there being one soon. These — and only these — were sent back to the mothership warehouse in San Jose.

This might sound like hyperbole, but Tom's method was one of the greatest innovations in the history of shipping. It was efficient, fast, and cheap. It meant that we didn't have to waste money on big warehouses. Since we didn't have movies sitting on shelves — even overnight — our utilization of inventory was exceptionally high. All we needed were a few dozen cheap storefronts, a couple hundred remote employees, and a bunch of shoeboxes and — bingo: next-day delivery to almost every mailbox in America.

*   *   *

We'd survived. We were hitting our goals. But things were different. So many parts of the original founding team were gone. Jim was working for an Amazon affiliate called WineShopper. Te was working for Zone Labs, an internet security startup. Vita had been laid off in September, and so had Eric. Christina had taken time off for a health issue in 1999 and had never been able to return full-time.

The original crew of skilled generalists had been replaced with superstar specialists. I was glad to be working alongside some of the most brilliant minds in Silicon Valley. But as one of the last links to the original team, I was starting to wonder about my future role in the company. Where did I fit? More importantly — where did I *want* to fit?

By early 2002, I was spending most of my time in product development. To me, that's where the energy really was. We were, even then, looking toward a day that didn't include DVDs. The growth of broadband DSL technology in the early 2000s was making it newly feasible to stream content online. We knew it was only a matter of time before streaming began to compete with physical media, and we wanted to position ourselves to take advantage of technological shifts. It was kind of funny, really — we'd finally figured out a way to make our original idea of DVDs by mail work, and here we were, looking ahead to a future without either DVDs or mail.

We knew digital delivery was the future. But how soon would that future arrive? And what form would it take? Would people download their movies, or stream them? Would they lean forward and watch on their computer or lean back and watch on their television? What kind of infrastructure would have to exist before the technology could be widely adopted? And what about the content? Did you start by focusing on a single genre, and if so, which one? And how did you convince the studios that their movies — once in digital form and so easily copied and shared — were safe in your hands?

To answer these questions, I talked to movie studios, television networks, software companies, and hardware manufacturers. A few things were clear:

The first was that the studios and networks were terrified of being "Napster-ed." They'd watched the music industry fall victim to widespread piracy and cratered sales, so they weren't very keen to give up digital rights. No matter how many assurances I gave them, they didn't trust the digital future. The way they saw it, once TV shows and movies were digitized, they'd lose all control of their product — along with any ability to make money off it.

The second was that hardware and software companies were going full speed ahead, digital rights be damned. Apple, Microsoft, and pretty much every other major computer company were working overtime to take advantage of the jumps in bandwidth speed, and were designing products that could conceivably deliver very large files — movie-sized files — directly into viewers' homes.

Everyone was competing for the same prize: Who would own the portal that would deliver entertainment directly into viewers' living rooms? Would it be the producers of the content, like movie and television studios? Would it be the developers of the hardware and software necessary to view it in the home? Or would it be the cable companies — which were already delivering content to millions of homes?

I spent a lot of time that fall and winter spitballing with Neil Hunt, who had joined Netflix in 1999 and was now in charge of our programmers. Tall and rail-thin, Neil rarely ventured out of his cube without a coffee cup in his hand — sometimes gliding into a conference room with a full French press, which he would punch down a few minutes later, ideally at the exact moment he was trying to make a point. Neil was soft-spoken, delicate, and somewhat reserved. Many times, when he knew he would soon need to do a code review for a colleague, I would watch from my window as he did laps through the parking lot, steeling himself to deliver the bad news. He was undeniably brilliant.

271

At a company where meetings usually hit decibel levels just short of a Stanley Cup Final, Neil didn't need to shout. As soon as he began to speak, people would lean in to listen.

Like me, Neil saw the national increase in internet bandwidth as a possibility: a way to use digital means to deliver Netflix movies directly to TV sets and further shrink the time between finishing one movie and getting the next one. Instantaneous streaming wasn't possible in 2002, and downloads would take hours — but we were betting that even so, passively downloading a movie while you were asleep or at work was still preferable to getting in the car and driving to Blockbuster. In our ideal, spitballing world, customers would always have a few downloaded movies ready to watch in a device on top of their TV, and an even bigger list of movies in their queue. They could choose a movie to watch, and when they were finished, they could just mark it as complete. Then their queue would automatically start downloading the next film on the list.

The next day? Boom, new movie to watch.

Still, it was tough sledding convincing the studios and tech companies that our idea was a good one, and even more difficult trying to convince them that we were the ones to pull it off. As far as they were concerned, we were just a content company that had figured out how to use the post office. Digital delivery? Leave it to the big boys.

I'll never forget driving out of Microsoft's headquarters with Neil after a particularly dispiriting meeting with some of their executives. We were in Redmond, a suburb of Seattle, and I couldn't help but think of my trip to Amazon with Reed three years before. But this time, instead of a shabby office building in a rough part of town, I was driving through a glittering corporate campus, shaded by towering redwoods and bordered by pristine artificial lakes. Instead of rough-looking men huddled outside a methadone clinic, there were Microsoft employees playing ultimate frisbee on manicured lawns.

Our meeting had been with two of the technical gurus working on their upcoming Xbox gaming station. They were only a few weeks away from launch, but Microsoft was already late to the party and was in a desperate scramble to catch up to Sony and Nintendo. In an effort to leapfrog these competitors, the Xbox would include two killer features: an ethernet port and a hard disc, which would allow the Xbox to connect to the internet and then store whatever it downloaded. Publicly, Microsoft was positioning these features as a way to enhance the gaming experience, but we knew that they were looking into using them for downloading television and movies — and we'd been eyeing a potential partnership. The way we saw it, Microsoft had the technology, and we had the content.

But the whole thing had fizzled. As usual, the answer was cloaked in politesse, but the message was the same: *Why do we need you?*

"What a waste of time," Neil was saying, slumped over in the passenger seat as I took the turns in the Microsoft roundabouts at high speed. "Travel all the way up here, rent a car, just to hear a polite 'no thanks.'"

"No doesn't always mean no," I said, and smiled.

Neil groaned and waved off what I'd said as a platitude, a lie to make him feel better. "Stop trying to cheer me up," he said.

But I wasn't kidding. Hadn't I seen it before? All of the consumer electronics companies saying "no thanks" to our "3-FREE-DVDs!" coupons. Alexandre Balkanski shaking his head wearily. Over and over in the Netflix story, I'd listened to people tell us no — and then watched as, slowly, they changed their minds. Or were proved wrong.

I knew that our idea was good. It might not happen now, but it would one day.

Here's what I've learned: when it comes to making your dream a reality, one of the most powerful weapons at your disposal is dogged, bullheaded insistence. It pays to be the person who won't take no for an answer, since in business, no doesn't always mean no.

An example:

My dream coming out of college was to land a job in advertising.

Quite a leap for someone who had graduated with a degree in geology, but I'm optimistic. And persistent.

The only job in advertising accessible to an undergraduate with my nonexistent qualifications had been a position as an account manager, the "suit" who was the interface between the client and the advertising agency's creative team. Although this was predominantly a job that went to MBA graduates, some agencies did extend their recruitment to undergraduates, so I jumped at the chance to interview when a representative of N. W. Ayer came to campus.

To my surprise, I made the first cut and was invited with a dozen other students to come down to New York City to interview. After a full day of meeting with representatives from almost every department, I again got the news that I had made the cut, the only one from my school to do so. I was now one of only five students from throughout the Northeast, all of us competing for a single job.

I didn't get it.

I bounce back quickly, so my disappointment in not having gotten this dream job quickly turned to confusion. What could I possibly be missing that some other candidate had? Ignorant of all the invisible criteria that were being applied to me (and that I would be especially aware of when it was later my turn to be on the hiring side of the table), I frankly couldn't conceive of what I was missing.

So I decided to ask.

I wrote a long letter to every single person who had interviewed me, taking the opportunity to recap for them all of my positive traits. I explained that while I had concluded that I must be missing something important, I was hoping they might be able to explain to me exactly what that was. "You see," I explained, "since there is a one hundred percent certainty that I will be applying for this job next year, I would like to take the time to work on whatever skills I am deficient in."

I'm cringing thinking about this now.

But it worked. Just four days later, I got a call. One of the senior partners in the agency wanted to meet with me. This was the guy who ran the whole business side of the agency. Several days later, as we sat in a plush corner office forty-two stories above Sixth Avenue, he offered me the job. It turned out that none of the candidates had actually been offered the job the first time around. N. W. Ayer knew that being an account executive was a selling job. A turning-a-no-into-a-yes type of job. So they had said no to all of us.

And I was the only one of the candidates who hadn't taken no for an answer.

Microsoft didn't agree to partner with us. But someone would.

In the meantime, I was quietly redefining my role at Netflix. I wasn't president anymore. Technically, I was an executive producer — even then, we were starting our transformation from geeky software startup to full-fledged entertainment company. (Now, if I could only remember which dry cleaner had my New Media Outfit...)

Reed had the reins. And he deserved them. Raising over $100 million in capital would *never* have been possible without him. His leadership had taken us through the dot-com bubble's age of irrational exuberance — and beyond it.

I was in a funny position. I'd founded Netflix. I had seen the coming internet wave and had paddled in at just the right moment. It had been, in the beginning, *my* company. But slowly, ever since that fateful PowerPoint from Reed, things had shifted. I was fine with that. Reed's emergence as the face of the company had saved our asses. But it had also left me somewhat marooned between the past and the future. And the future was something I was thinking a lot about in 2002.

I had family I adored: three young children and a beautiful marriage with my best friend. I wanted to make sure that the future was assured, for each of them. And though I'd earned enough at my previous start-ups to live comfortably, this was going to be a financial event of a totally different magnitude. Put simply: I didn't want all my assets to be tied up in one company's stock, no matter how much faith I had in it. I had seen too many people lose everything due to circumstances beyond their control, and I was smart enough to know that I didn't want that to be me. If we were going to go public in 2002 — and after we hit one million subscribers in December, and Barry started making the rounds again with banks and potential investors, that was looking likely — I wanted to be able to sell my stock.

The problem, of course, is that banks and investors don't usually view a high-ranking executive in the company selling off massive amounts of stock as a *good* thing. It looks bad — like he knows something they don't.

That wasn't the case for me. I had complete confidence that Netflix was going to succeed. I'd never been surer that the company we'd built was destined for long-term success. I just wanted the option to sell.

For that to happen, I needed to be way less visible to banks and investors. I couldn't be listed as "president" on our S-1. That meant two things needed to happen: First, I needed a title that didn't make it look like I was in charge. And second, I needed to give up my seat on the Netflix board.

The first was easy. I don't care about titles, and I never have. "Founder and Executive Producer" was fine with me.

Leaving the board was a little harder, though. I'd fought hard for that seat. And I'd already almost lost it once. Soon after assuming the role of CEO, Reed had asked me to give up my seat so that an investor could take it. I'd refused, adamantly, arguing that I'd give up my title as CEO, I'd even give up some shares — but I wouldn't give up my seat on the board of directors. That was one step too far. I wanted some control over the direction of the company, and I thought it was important that a founding member of the company was there to counterbalance the interests of the VCs.

"Everyone who's ever been on a board says that they're only interested in the success of the company," I'd told Reed. "But you and I both know that 'success' means a slightly different thing to VCs than it does to a company's founders."

This is true, by the way. It's something I tell startup founders all the time now. VCs will always say that they're aligned with your mission, that they want what's best for the company. But what they really want is what's best for their *investment* in the company. Which isn't always the same thing.

Everyone is aligned when the wind is blowing the right way. It's when a storm comes up that all of a sudden it becomes apparent that people have different goals and objectives.

Reed hadn't quite seen it that way. But Patty, the Reed-whisperer, had agreed with me.

"If things go bad," she'd asked him, "who do you want around the table? Who do you want there, so that when you need to ask a tough question, you know you'll get a straight answer?"

Reed later told me that the second Patty asked that question, he knew that keeping me on the board was the right thing to do — not just for me but for the company.

So giving up my seat in 2002, after I'd fought so hard to keep it, was a somewhat bitter pill to swallow. But it was a decision I had to make if I wanted the financial security of liquidating any material amount of my stock. It was clear by early in the year that no dot-com bubble was going to stop us this time. We were going to go public. And it was going to be a life-changing event.

Too bad I had no idea what that change was going to look like.

"Dad, what's a tail number?"

Logan strained against his seat belt in an attempt to see out over the dashboard. I rolled up my window as the metal gate slowly opened in front of our car. Ahead of us, a plane sat waiting for us on the runway, its wing lights blinking in the predawn sky. I drove out to meet it on the tarmac.

"I asked the same question last time I did this," I told him.

It was May 22, 2002 — the day before our IPO, and about five years after I'd first lobbed the idea of DVDs by mail across the car to Reed. I wasn't driving a Volvo anymore. Six months earlier, my economic confidence growing, I'd finally taken the plunge and bought a new car, an Audi allroad. It had four-wheel drive for driving through snow, adjustable height suspension for back-road approaches to my favorite surf spots, and, of course, space for two car seats in the back. It wasn't a luxury car, in most people's eyes — but it felt like one to me. I covered my embarrassment about such conspicuous consumption by never washing the exterior and always keeping a surfboard, a bicycle, or a wet suit stashed in the back.

The Audi wasn't the only upgrade in my life since our ill-fated trip to Blockbuster HQ in Dallas. The plane was a step up, too. We weren't flying in Vanna's Lear anymore. Instead, Reed had chartered a Gulfstream G450. Where the Learjet was small and delicate, like a toy plane, the Gulfstream was heavy, powerful, and menacing. The stairs leading up into it were solid and substantial, unlike the Lear's flimsy, dangling steps. Upholstered and plush, with huge leather club chairs, the interior felt like the lounge of a luxury hotel. Forget having to stoop — the ceiling was full height. The walls barely seemed to curve. Without the circular windows, it would be easy to forget that this lounge would soon be heading east at almost 700 miles per hour.

Logan could barely believe his eyes. Pushing past me as he came through the doorway, he excitedly yelled an inventory of all the plane's luxurious appointments. "Check it out!" he said, running down the aisle. "A couch! On an airplane!"

He launched himself onto it, stood back up, then jumped again to a new position a few cushions down. After a few moments he chose his own money seat, sat back comfortably, crossed his legs, and beamed. "This is my seat," he announced.

I stashed my backpack under the polished walnut table that sat between four of the club chairs and settled in. Turning to look out the window, I could just see Reed's gold Avalon pulling up to the plane. Walking briskly across the tarmac, he was clearly in business mode: black linen pants, the gray turtleneck, this one with a Netflix logo on the chest.

I'd made the appropriate gestures toward business attire myself. I was wearing my only clean pair of khakis and a gray blazer, the collar of my black polo haphazardly escaping from beneath it. I'd dug up a pair of black tasseled loafers and polished them the night before, and I'd worn my "dressy" glasses, a pair of tortoiseshell frames that — I thought — made me look like an economist. In a nod to sartorial elegance and techy flair, I'd made sure to clip to my belt my trusty StarTAC phone.

"Big day tomorrow," Reed said as he settled into the seat across from me. "Merrill is thinking we'll probably be in the thirteen- to fourteen-dollar range."

He leaned out into the aisle to wave to my son. "Hi, Logan." He added, "Lookin' sharp!"

Logan smiled and waved back. He did look good. Lorraine had spruced him up nicely. When we'd decided that he would accompany me to New York, we had quickly decided that his usual uniform of shorts and T-shirts probably wouldn't cut it, and Lorraine had made a trip to Mervyn's, the discount clothing store at the Capitola Mall. She'd returned with a blue blazer ("*Special! $39.99!*") and a sharp pair of $18.49 black loafers.

"I don't care how much money we're going to have after this," Lorraine explained to me as she expertly cut the tags off the new jacket. "He's ten. It just doesn't make sense to spend a lot of money on something he's just going to grow out of."

"Or spill something on," I added.

Lorraine had also picked up a red necktie for him, but once Logan learned that I wasn't planning on wearing one, he insisted on leaving his behind, substituting a shark-tooth necklace he hadn't taken off since his summer on the beach as a Junior Guard.

Just as I got up to show Logan how to fasten his seat belt, Barry stepped onto the plane, briefcase in hand. As usual, he looked better than all of us: banker's haircut, blue blazer, blindingly white shirt, and — unlike the rest of us — a beautiful silk tie.

"My name's Barry," he said, leaning over the top of his seat to shake Logan's hand. "Glad to see you'll be helping with the opening."

It was just like Barry to treat a ten-year-old-boy like he was an executive of the company — or at least like he one day could be. You never knew who might end up being useful to you.

"Jay's running late," he said to no one in particular, settling into a chair. He pulled a yellow pad out of his briefcase, then slid his case into the space next to his seat.

Jay was Jay Hoag, one of our VCs. It was no surprise that he'd wanted to come east with us — he was our biggest investor. Jay had co-founded a venture capital firm called TCV, short for Technology Crossover Ventures, with the mission of supporting companies with investments both before *and* after their IPOs. His support had been critical to our success. TCV had not only led our Series C funding in early 1999 with a $6 million investment, but more importantly, they had convinced LVMH, the French luxury goods conglomerate, to follow their lead. Based almost entirely on Jay's having vouched for us, the LVMH representative had flown to Silicon Valley, taken a single one-hour meeting with me and Reed, and then, just a few days later, wired over $25 million.

Best of all, on April 4, 2000 — just ten days before the dot-com bubble truly burst — TCV had gone all-in, with an additional $40 million. Considering the timing of that investment — and the Silicon Valley carnage that followed — Jay must have been pretty sure that he'd seen the last of his firm's money. It must have been especially pleasing for him now, two years later, to be flying toward a Netflix IPO — just one more passenger on the last leg of a wild ride.

* * *

Somewhere over Nebraska, as we descended for refueling, Barry pulled out his phone.

"Just want to see how the book is building," he told us, tucking the phone between his ear and his shoulder and opening his pad to a clean page. "Market's almost closed. They should have a pretty good idea of what's queued up for tomorrow."

"Building the book" is the final stage in the run-up to an IPO. The process had reached peak intensity just a few days before, when Reed and Barry had gone on the road to present the Netflix story to potential investors.

On the day you take a company public, only some of the stock is bought by individuals — "retail," in Wall Street terms. The majority of what gets sold on day one is institutional: large funds managed by sophisticated investors who are taking the long view. Think pension funds, university endowments, retirement funds, mutual funds — not to mention "ultra-high-net-worth individuals," people with so much money that they hire entire offices of investment professionals to manage it.

Since Merrill Lynch, the lead bank in the consortium that was taking us public, had committed to selling more than $70 million worth of stock on opening day, they weren't going to leave anything to chance. So in the two weeks leading up to the IPO, they had put together a tightly choreographed "road show" that covered all the major financial markets. Like a Broadway production of *Miss Saigon* opening in New Haven before hitting the Big Apple, the road show began far from Wall Street and ended in New York. Starting in San Francisco, in front of tech-friendly investors, the chartered jet had made stops in Los Angeles, Denver, Dallas, Chicago, and Boston before finally landing for two days in New York City. At each stop, Barry and Reed had been rushed from office to office, conference room to conference room, breakfast meeting to lunch presentation, cycling through all the reasons Netflix was a compelling investment.

It took them a while to hone their pitch — to figure what worked, what was confusing, what they should leave out. At one point, mid-tour, after a tough night with a crying child, I had come to the office at five in the morning to find Joel and Suresh already at their desks.

"You're here early," I'd said, feeling as groggy and disoriented as Joel and Suresh looked.

"We've been here all night, actually," Joel replied, explaining that Reed and Barry had been getting a lot of pushback about churn — the rate at which subscribers canceled their subscriptions.

"We've been looking at how different segments are behaving. But every time we send Reed the data he's looking for, he comes back with another question."

"Doesn't that man ever sleep?" Suresh asked, rubbing his eyes.

The answer to that question was: barely.

But even Reed gets tired. By the time he and Barry got to New York, the two of them were basically sleepwalking through the presentation. Luckily, they'd honed it to a fine, focused point. By the end of the tour, Barry told me later, they were finishing each other's sentences, anticipating investors' questions before the words were even out of their mouths.

Once Barry and Reed finished the tour, the baton was passed to Merrill and its fleet of salespeople, who followed in their footsteps, gathering in whatever demand Barry and Reed had created, and then funneling it to the main desk in New York, where it was tabulated in a detailed electronic register, still called — by tradition — "the book."

The book wasn't written in indelible ink, of course. All of the preliminary orders — excuse me, "expressions of interest" — had been made with only a rough idea of price. Some customers wanted Netflix regardless of what it was going to cost, while others had a clearer view of what price it would eventually trade at — and could then set strict upper limits. Below that price, they were in. Above it, and they were out.

The bank's challenge, the morning of our IPO, would be to figure out the ideal number to use as the opening price for individual shares. Set the price too high, and interested purchasers would drop out — and we would miss our $70 million target. Set it too low, and Netflix would leave millions on the table.

Another complicating factor? Given the choice, the bank didn't really mind a price that was too low. Part of the reason they'd fought so hard for a deal with us — above and beyond the big commission — was the opportunity to give their best customers an opportunity to buy low at the opening and sell high at the closing. Banks call that an opening day "bounce."

A bounce is not necessarily a bad thing. The quick jump in price can show the public that a company is "hot" and has "momentum." But if somebody was going to make a ton of money on day one, we wanted it to be us, not Merrill Lynch's customers. We wanted a healthy bounce — but we didn't want to feel like we were being launched off the trampoline.

"Dad!"

Logan paused mid-bite, a huge scoop of vanilla ice cream balanced on his spoon. "Barry's talking on the phone. On the plane. I thought we couldn't do that."

He looked at me quizzically, carefully spooning ice cream into his mouth, then looking down to gather up more of the brownie at the bottom of his sundae.

"Pretty cool, right?" I couldn't help but smile at his enthusiasm. "You want to make a call? Maybe call Mom?"

I hit speed dial for home and waited for Lorraine to pick up.

"Greetings from Omaha," I said when she answered. "I've got someone here who wants to talk to you."

Logan grabbed the phone and filled Lorraine in about the ride. He barely took a breath until he recounted the menu for lunch: Caesar salad, baked potato, and filet mignon, which he pronounced "min-yin."

"He sounds pretty excited," Lorraine said when I finally managed to get the phone back.

"A little wound-up. But very happy. You should have seen him when we got to cruising altitude. He was doing somersaults down the aisle. No joke. A forward roll between the seats."

"Well, I'm glad he's happy," Lorraine answered, and, imitating Barry, lowered her voice to a stage whisper. "Tell him not to get used to it."

I looked over to where Logan was scraping at his dish, trying to coax the last bits of chocolate sauce into his spoon. I wasn't any less excited than he was — I was just better at hiding it. Truth be told, I think that was true for all of us. If we were honest, we would have all been doing somersaults right along with him.

It was well after dark when the town car crunched to a stop under the portico of my parents' house in Chappaqua. Logan was fast asleep, slumped against my shoulder.

I was home again.

"Welcome back, Mr. New Media Executive," my mom said, holding open the door for me as I carried Logan up the front steps and into the kitchen. He blinked sleepily in the sudden light when I set him down.

"You can sleep in the den," my mother said to him. He nodded and shuffled up the stairs.

I slept that night in my childhood bedroom, surrounded by my books, my beer bottle collection, and my Little League trophies. In some ways, it felt like I'd never left. I was forty-four years old. I was married and had three kids of my own. I owned a big house and an Audi allroad. But inside, I still felt like I was in high school, excited about the next day's soccer match against Fox Lane.

How would I feel the next day, after it was over? Would I feel like more of an adult? And what about the money? Would that change me?

Lorraine and I would certainly worry less, I knew that. But I didn't think we would be any happier. If growing up in Chappaqua had taught me anything, it was that happiness existed on a totally different axis than money. I grew up around fabulously wealthy, fantastically miserable people. You could spot them a mile away — impeccable loafers, beautiful bespoke suits, and an empty half smile on their face.

I tossed and turned most of that night, my mind endlessly anticipating everything that could possibly go wrong. What if I woke up and the market had collapsed overnight? What if there were another terrorist attack? What if Reed were hit by a bus? What if, after all this work, I had to go back to square one?

The only thing that calmed me down was staring at the train on the dresser against the wall — one of my father's most elegant creations, completed sometime in the mid-seventies. The steam engine gleamed in the moonlight, so that the pistons almost seemed to be moving. It was the last thing I saw before I fell asleep.

In many ways, it was an anticlimax.

Like most tech companies, Netflix was going to be listed on the Nasdaq exchange, which is 100 percent electronic. There is no trading floor, no mass of hysterically shouting traders in flamboyant blazers, no balcony with a bell to ring. At the Nasdaq, every trade happens almost instantaneously — buyers matched with sellers — within an invisible, efficient, quiet, and orderly world of computer servers.

That iconic image of the happy entrepreneur, ringing a bell over a sea of people, covered with falling ticker tape? That was the New York Stock Exchange. Sorry, wrong address.

While total digitization might make for efficient markets, it's a bit of a letdown if you've been building toward an IPO for almost five years. If we wanted to celebrate the actual first trade taking place, we had two options: gather in a windowless, climate-controlled Nasdaq server room somewhere in Weehawken, New Jersey, or watch things go down from the Merrill Lynch trading floor. Which, I hate to break it to you, has just about the same amount of drama as the windowless server room. But at least it has vending machines — a long row of them lined up in an alcove opposite the elevator.

Logan found them immediately.

"Are those the ones Uncle Randolph was talking about?"

"Something like it," I replied. Logan's uncle, my brother, was a banker at Merrill Lynch. One evening at our house, Randolph had shared stories from the trading floor, with Logan listening wide-eyed.

"These are people who gamble for a living," Randolph had started off. "So they're always looking for something new to wager on. I mean *anything*. One time, the bet was whether a trader could finish one of every item from the vending machine in a single day. We all kicked in twenty bucks apiece and told him he could keep the pot if he finished, but it was the side bets that were insane. People were throwing around hundreds of dollars wagering whether he would make it or not — and if not, where he'd quit."

At this point, Logan's eyes were wide.

"For most of the morning he was making good progress. He made it through the Snickers, the Fritos, and the spearmint gum, which he chewed once and then swallowed. But by the time he got to the Doritos, he was visibly flagging. There were three rows of them. So one of my friends — who had a sizable side bet going that the guy was gonna finish — ran downstairs to the Duane Reed we had on the first floor of the building."

"Why?" Logan asked.

"To buy a blender," Randolph said, cracking up.

Now Logan was in front of the vending machines, eying the wares, doing calculations of his own.

"No way," he said. "There's just no way."

The trading floor may have been quiet, but it was huge: an unbroken stretch of desks that filled a room the size of a football field. Each desk supported three monitors, positioned at a slight angle to one another, so that the occupant of each station could see an unbroken stretch of screen from one side to the other. Some of the traders had a second row of three screens perched above the first. The screens were full, with colored lines tracking the seemingly random movements of various financial instruments. Each station had a special oversized keyboard containing the standard QWERTY, augmented by dozens of other keys — a crazy mix of letters and numbers that seemed almost nonsensical. The traders had no problem manipulating these bizarre keyboards, though — they played them like prodigies blasting their way through Chopin.

Each station had a giant phone console, all of its red buttons blinking crazily. When Logan and I arrived, Barry had one of the phones cradled between his shoulder and his ear, his jacket half off, animatedly talking to someone. Reed was calmly answering emails at the next desk. Jay Hoag was standing off to one side, relaxed as always in his wrinkled blue oxford shirt.

"Nothing happening yet," Jay reported. "The markets are about to open, but they're still working on finding a price. Could be another hour or so."

He pointed over to a corner of the trading floor, where four or five traders were frantically talking into their phones, some of them into two at once.

"Every time they try a new price, they have to call everybody back. This could take a while."

This presented a bit of a problem. We could wait all day — but back in Los Gatos, the mood was a little different. Since Los Gatos was three hours behind New York, the entire company had come in early for a 6:00 opening day breakfast. Everyone was assembled in one of our downstairs wings, eagerly awaiting the start of trading. I'd promised that I would call in periodically from the floor to report, but what was I going to say?

There was nothing happening.

At 9:15 a.m. Eastern Standard Time, fifteen minutes before the opening, I called the offices.

"Good morning, Los Gatos!" I announced, imagining my voice echoing from the big speakers that had been set up. I pictured everyone stopping their conversations and putting down their coffee. This, for them, was the moment. They didn't know the moment hadn't yet arrived.

"I'm here on the Merrill Lynch trading floor with Reed, Barry, and Jay," I continued. "It's about fifteen minutes before opening, and…" I paused, trying to figure out what to say. "Well, um, absolutely nothing is happening."

There's nothing like trying to describe the process of "price matching" to a roomful of people you can't see or hear. I felt like a baseball play-by-play announcer trying to fill airtime during a rain delay. Turns out, it takes a lot of skill to make a room full of desks sound interesting. I was boring myself — I can't imagine how bored my audience was.

Finally, mercifully, Patty picked up the line and suggested that maybe I should just call back when I had more information to share.

Amazingly enough, Logan wasn't the least bit bored by the delay. He was fascinated by everything. One of the traders showed him how to bring up market quotes. He learned to use the Bloomberg terminal and searched for news about Santa Cruz. He typed away, happy as a clam at high tide.

For me, though, the wait was unbearable. In between my random reports back to Los Gatos — *There's a guy talking on two phones at once. There's someone watering a plant.* — I paced the floor, biting my nails. I felt like I was in the hospital waiting for a loved one to come out of surgery. Imagining every possible outcome — most of them bad — made me nervous and jittery. I needed something to do. Eventually, remembering the disposable camera Lorraine had shoved in my jacket pocket, I occupied myself by taking photos. I got Barry on the phone, Reed staring pensively. The one I took of Logan — looking up from his desk chair, hands clasped in front of him, a serious look on his face, as if he were deeply concerned with the erratic futures pricing of the Krugerrand — is still one of my favorite photos of him.

When the moment finally came, there were no flashing lights. No clarion of trumpets. No announcement at all, really. Just Barry wandering over to where Jay, Reed, and I were huddled and announcing:

We've got a price.

Across a long screen on the wall and the top of most of the monitors in the room, there was a crawl of letters and numbers reflecting trades as they were happening. An experienced trader could watch the crawl and have an immediate and visceral understanding of what was happening: APPL — 16.94 _MSFT — 50.91 _CSCO — 15.78. We all turned our eyes to the screen, staring, trying not to blink and miss it. Even Logan knew something important was happening and turned his eyes up to see if he could figure out what everyone was looking at.

And there it was: NFLX — 16.19.

Finally, I had something to tell Patty.

"Put me on speaker," I said.

On the floor, it was a strangely emotional celebration. Reed and I hugged. Barry, Jay, and I shook hands. I bent down and gave Logan a long squeeze. The various Merrill execs who had been shepherding us through the process stopped by to give their congratulations. Someone opened a bottle of champagne. Even Logan had a few sips. He hated it.

Reed and Barry were going to stick around to speak to reporters, but my job as the play-by-play announcer was done the second I heard cheers erupt in Los Gatos. Logan and I could leave. Our flight didn't leave Teterboro — the general aviation terminal that handles private flights in and out of New York City — until five o'clock. In the meantime, we had the afternoon free.

I knew what I wanted to do. I wanted to see the *Intrepid*, the World War II aircraft carrier permanently docked at a pier on the Hudson. There was a museum there, too, and a submarine.

But first, there was a more important errand Logan and I had to take care of.

We descended to the street and as we pushed our way out through the revolving doors, I carefully peeled off our security name tags and tucked them in my backpack as a souvenir. I raised my hand, and a cab slowed to the curb. "Eleventh Street and Sixth Avenue," I told the driver as I climbed in after Logan.

"Where are we going?" Logan asked.

"You'll see," I said. "I know you're a California kid, but it's time you were baptized as a New Yorker."

As the cab pulled into the late-morning traffic, I settled back on the cracked seat and watched out the half-open window as the blocks spooled by. It was starting to dawn on me that my life had just irreversibly changed course. In the time it took for a ticker symbol to scroll across a screen, an entirely new path had opened up. For the first time in my adult life, I didn't need to work. And I never would have to, again.

The cab stopped for a red light, and I found myself gazing out the window at the people in the crosswalk in front of us. A man in a suit, frowning over a donut. A woman in a nurse's uniform, tired after a twelve-hour shift. A construction worker, his yellow hard hat in hand.

They all had to work. But I didn't. Just a few hours before, I'd been the same as them — but now, suddenly, things were different. I didn't know how I felt about the shift.

It wasn't a question of money. It was a question of usefulness, of the pleasure of utility. Working, for me, was never about getting rich — it was about the thrill of doing good work, the pleasure of solving problems. At Netflix, those problems had been incredibly complex, and the joy came from sitting around a table with brilliant people and trying like hell to solve them.

I didn't love Netflix because I thought it would make me rich. I loved Netflix for the Nerf guns. The water fights. The limericks. Coins in the fountain, epic argumentative battles in the conference room. I loved it for freewheeling brainstorming sessions in the passenger seat of a car, for meetings in a diner or a hotel conference room or a swimming pool. I loved building the company, watching it stumble, then rebuilding it again. I loved the arrivals and the departures, the triumphs and the losses — the raucous laughter at the offsite and the stunned silence on Vanna White's jet.

I loved it for Christina, Mitch, Te, Jim, Eric, Suresh, and all the hundreds of other people who had sacrificed their nights and weekends, worked holidays, canceled plans and moved appointments. All to help Reed and I make a dream come true.

It wasn't about the money. It was about what we did before we ever knew we'd get it.

So what happened now?

I wouldn't be getting the money right away. In the interest of preventing a flood of selling, the banks had required that all of us agree to hold our shares for six months. So in a way, nothing was really changing. In a few hours, I'd get on a plane and fly back to California, and I'd probably head straight back to the office to deal with email for a few hours before heading home.

After all, we still had a lot to do. Blockbuster was gunning for us. We were hearing disturbing whispers about Walmart entering online rental. We still had tons of things we wanted to test. And I was eager to get back to my research on streaming.

But a part of me knew that one phase of the journey had just ended. The dream was a reality. We'd done it — we'd turned an envelope and a Patsy Cline CD into a publicly traded company. It was the sort of success we'd all hoped for, the thing that we had promised the people who had invested their money in us. And had held out as a reward for those who had invested their time. The sort of success that, for most people, would call for caviar, champagne, and steaks the size of dinner plates. A long dinner at Le Bernardin, followed by a nightcap or three at the Ritz.

But that's not where my son and I were headed.

The cab stopped and I shoved a twenty through the partition. Outside, the banner of Famous Ray's Pizza shone dully in the daylight. Pies laden with pepperoni, sausage, and cheese rotated on spindles in the window. For a moment, before I opened the door, I savored that scene — on the day I'd dreamed about for years, minutes after the entire trajectory of my life changed, I was going to have a slice of genuine New York pizza with my oldest son.

I was just where I wanted to be.

"Are we there yet, Dad?" Logan asked, looking up from the printouts he'd smuggled from the trading floor, listing thousands of share prices.

"We sure are, Logan," I answered, and opened the door. "Come on. We made it."

EPILOGUE

Randolph's Rules for Success

When I was twenty-one years old, fresh out of college and about to start my first job, my father gave me a handwritten list of instructions. The whole thing took up less than half a page, in my father's neat engineer's handwriting. It read:

RANDOLPH'S RULES FOR SUCCESS

1. *Do at least 10% more than you are asked.*
2. *Never, ever, to anybody present as fact opinions on things you don't know. Takes great care and discipline.*
3. *Be courteous and considerate always—up and down.*
4. *Don't knock, don't complain—stick to constructive, serious criticism.*
5. *Don't be afraid to make decisions when you have the facts on which to make them.*
6. *Quantify where possible.*
7. *Be open-minded but skeptical.*
8. *Be prompt.*

That original list survives, framed and behind glass, hanging next to the mirror in my bathroom. I reread it every morning when I brush my teeth. I've given a copy to each of my kids. And I've tried, for my entire life, to live up to all eight rules.

Randolph's Rules for Success are wide-ranging, broad-minded, and idiosyncratically punctuated (my kids and I laugh about the missing comma in #2 all the time). They somehow manage to be both extremely general ("Be open-minded but skeptical") and charmingly precise (I love how the succinct "Be prompt" ends the list — it seems like the most minor rule, but its placement implies the opposite). The conduct they prescribe is one of openhearted, hardworking rationalism: an ideal my father — a curious, decent, and devoted man — exemplified in his own life.

Randolph's Rules helped me at school. They helped me in the outdoors. And they helped me — immeasurably — in my career. In them I see the basis for my practice of constant testing (#2, #6), my ethos of curiosity and creativity (#7), and my willingness to take risks in service of a goal (#5). I see the seeds for Netflix's culture of Radical Honesty in #4's admonition to *stick to constructive, serious criticism.* And of course there's a direct path from rule #1 — *Do at least 10% more than you are asked* — to all the espresso- and pizza-fueled late nights in the Netflix offices.

My father very rarely got to see the professional side of his son. Since my parents lived on the East Coast, they hadn't really gotten to encounter me in my professional element. Sure, I'd hit my mom up for money in the seed round for Netflix. And I told them all about my work: at Borland, at Integrity, at Netflix. By 1999, when I came to New York to give a speech to a bunch of DVD executives and invited them, they knew that Netflix was successful and growing. But they'd never quite seen it in person. At least not until that night.

I remember being nervous. Also proud — immensely proud — to look out at a full auditorium and see my parents in the back row.

Afterward, my dad and I sat in the empty auditorium. The stage was bare in front of us. He put his hand on my shoulder and congratulated me, said he was proud. Then he told me that his doctor had picked up something strange in a cranial X-ray and that he was going in for a brain biopsy at Mount Sinai the next day.

My breath caught in my throat. My mother had already told me that he'd been acting a little funny lately — hence the visit to the doctor in the first place — but this didn't sound good. I covered my anxiety the way I usually do: with a joke.

"You need that like you need a hole in the head," I told him.

He laughed.

We had the same sense of humor.

My father died of brain cancer in March of 2000. It was an intensely painful time for me, and it happened largely in the background of the story I've been telling. Throughout 1999 and early 2000, as we were testing various aspects of what would become Marquee and putting the finishing touches on Cinematch, I was flying back to New York at least once a month, as my dad underwent treatment. It was the most time we'd spent together in years.

My dad faced his diagnosis with the same attitude he faced most things in life. He was open-minded but skeptical when given positive feedback about his progress. He didn't complain. He was courteous and considerate to everyone he dealt with in the health-care system — doctors and surgeons, nurses, orderlies and assistants. And he was prompt to appointments and meetings.

When he died, I took about a week off to grieve with my mother in New York. Then I flew back to California.

But something was different from then on. My father's death put things in perspective for me. It led me to evaluate what truly mattered in my life — what fulfilled me as a father, a husband, an entrepreneur. As a person.

I started to realize that the pride I felt, that night in the auditorium in lower Manhattan, wasn't about the fact that the room was full, or that my parents could see how successful I'd become.

Well, it was partly about that.

But more importantly, the pride I felt came from the message I was giving that night: *how the media landscape is changing, and what you can learn from the companies that are changing it.*

My father died just days before the collapse of the internet bubble. As a value investor, he'd never understood the hype, never understood the frenzy. He would have been unspeakably delighted to have seen that he was right all along.

I wish he could have seen it. And I wish he could have seen us survive it. He never got to see us take the company public. He never heard my stories about taking a private plane to New York with my son in tow. He never got to hear me talk about the financial windfall of the IPO and all that it entailed for my family.

But you know what? It didn't matter. Because he got to see me onstage, talking about the thing I love: Solving problems. Team-building. Building a culture that works. How to refine your startup mentality.

He saw me doing what I loved. That's what really mattered.

As you get older, if you're at all self-aware, you learn two important things about yourself: what you like, and what you're good at. Anyone who gets to spend his day doing both of those things is a lucky man.

By the beginning of my seventh year at Netflix, the company had changed dramatically. My role had changed as well. I still ran the website — continually tweaking how we signed customers up, what we charged them, how they chose their movies, and in what order we shipped to them — but I had gradually transitioned many of the other aspects of the company to more capable executives.

We had long since passed the one-million-subscribers mark. We had moved headquarters twice, as a swelling workforce successively burst our figurative seams.

We had finally figured out a way to get next-day delivery to the majority of the country, and the positive word-of-mouth that this gen-erated accelerated our growth.

We'd gone public. With the money that provided — and our grow-ing reputation — we were able to attract amazing people to come work for us. People who were stars in their field. People who had run their own companies, or had done the logistics for multinational corpora-tions, or had built the infrastructure of the internet.

We were now deep in the throes of our battle with Blockbuster for rental supremacy. By then, Reed had started trotting out the familiar origin story for the company. Remember it? It went something like this: Reed came up with the idea for Netflix when he found an old rental copy of *Apollo 13* in his house, went to return it to Blockbuster, and saw a $40 late fee. Then he thought: *What if I never had to do this again?*

If this book has taught you anything, I hope it's shown you that the story behind Netflix was a little more complicated than that. And I *also* hope it's shown you how useful narrative can be. When you're trying to take down a juggernaut, the story of your company's founding can't be a 300-page book like this one. It has to be a paragraph. Reed's oft-repeated origin story is branding at its finest, and I don't begrudge him for it at all.

Is it a lie? No — it's a story. And it's a fantastic one.

The truth is, the patrimony of any innovation is complicated. There are always multiple people involved. They struggle, they push, they argue. They each contribute different backgrounds and inspirations: years in the mail-order business, a passion for algorithms, an enduring desire to do the right thing for the customer, an insight into the cost-effectiveness of first-class mail, a knowledge of the power of per-sonalization. Yes, maybe even a late fee on a movie. And through a process that might take days, might take weeks, or might even take years, this group of people comes up with something new and different and great. And as you've seen, in our case the result was Netflix.

But that story is messy.

And when you're talking to the press, to an investor, or to a business partner, people really don't want to hear it. They want a version that's neat and clean with a bow on it. Reed recognized that almost immediately, and so Reed came up with a story. It's a great one: simple, clear, and memorable. That story captures the essence of what Netflix is about, and it solved a big problem for us.

That story gave us a narrative.

By 2003, Netflix had been around long enough to write its own story: David versus Goliath. And it was looking like David might have a shot.

Netflix had grown up. But so, I realized, had I.

I still loved the company. I loved it with the passion only a parent would know. I righted wrongs, dispatched enemies, and was always pushing the company even harder to succeed. But as quarterly numbers mechanically came and went each successive year, I slowly realized that although I loved the company, I no longer loved working there.

It turns out that I did know what I like, and what I'm good at. And it wasn't a company as big as Netflix. It was small companies struggling to find their way. It was newly hatched dreams for which no one had yet discovered a repeatable scalable business model. It was wading into companies rife with crisis, to solve really complex problems with really smart people.

And I'll blow my own horn here for a minute: I'm pretty damn good at it. Every startup has hundreds of things going wrong at the same time, all clamoring for attention. I have a sense of which two or three issues are the critical ones, even if they are not the ones screaming the loudest. But they are the issues that, if you fix them, then all the rest will take care of itself.

I have an almost obsessive ability to focus on those singular things — single-mindedly attacking them at the expense of everything else until I have wrestled them to the ground.

I have the ability to inspire people to quit their jobs, take a pay cut, and help wage an improbable battle against an apparently implacable foe.

These are critical skills for running a startup. They're less applicable to running a company with hundreds of employees and millions of subscribers.

The time had come.

I think I knew that for a while, after the IPO. But it didn't become real until the spring of 2003, when I asked to work on developing a Netflix kiosk with Mitch Lowe.

We had often tried to figure out how to compete with Blockbuster's ability to provide immediate service to its users. Although Netflix customers had a ready supply of movies on top of their TVs, that was as close to instant gratification as we got. If a customer later decided they wanted something different, they were out of luck. But Blockbuster customers could just drive to one of their thousands of stores instead of waiting for the mail. It was our Achilles' heel. We were deathly afraid that Blockbuster would roll out a blended model, combining online with retail. We knew that would be compelling for customers.

Mitch Lowe had been a relentless advocate for a kiosk solution, in which Netflix subscribers could use small outposts of the service to rent and return DVDs. Well before joining Netflix, he'd dreamed of developing the technology as a facet of Video Droid. And now it was looking like Reed was amenable to testing the idea out.

"Mitch and I found a great site for the test in Las Vegas," I told Reed. "And I'm thinking I should be there with him. I need to focus on this. Maybe even exclusively."

"That's fine," Reed said. "We can move all of your front-end stuff over to Neil. Combining the project managers and the front-end engineers under a single person will probably work better for everyone."

"But if this *doesn't* work...," I said, watching Reed's face as we both came to the same realization. "I'm not sure it's fair to Neil for me to yank it all back six months from now."

Reed swallowed and cocked his head. "Well," he said, "I guess we'll have to talk about severance. Just in case."

There was an awkward pause, and then I couldn't help it — I laughed.

Reed smiled warily.

"I mean, we've talked about this," I said. "We both knew it was coming, sooner or later."

And it was true: Reed and I had spoken often about how I was feeling. He's too smart not to have noticed that my skills weren't the ones that Netflix would be needing in the years ahead, and too honest to hide that from me for very long.

Now, though, he looked relieved. Under this arrangement, he wouldn't have to have an uncomfortable conversation with me. He wouldn't have to draft up another PowerPoint, craft another shit sandwich — because the decision wasn't his.

I was working one last project. Then, if it didn't work, I was leaving — on my own terms.

Six months later, I was back in Los Gatos, wearing the New Media Outfit one last time. Or at least a version of it. I'd kept the iridescent blazer, but I'd swapped out the khakis for jeans. And the moiré shirt was gone, replaced by a T-shirt.

If I was going out, I was going out comfortable.

Netflix had rented out the historic Los Gatos Theatre for my going-away party. The little company that went months without an office, ran up epic tabs at Hobee's, and conducted our first meetings in a seedy motel conference room was now too big to assemble in any one place in the office. And to send off its original founder, another mass gathering at the picnic tables wouldn't do. Instead, I was getting the red-carpet treatment — or at least the red velvet seat treatment. The Los Gatos Theatre is the kind of place with velvet curtains on the walls and real velvet on the seats. Like the Netflix offices, it has a popcorn machine in the front. But this one is the real deal, made in the days when popcorn was the only thing you could buy at the concession stand.

In other words, it actually worked.

As I walked up to the front of the theater with Lorraine and the kids, I couldn't help but be struck by the sheer size of the company now. People were spilling out of the lobby and onto the street. I recognized most, but not all of them.

"Wow," Lorraine said. "I knew it was big, but part of me still imagines you going to work every day with ten other people, sitting on our old dining room chairs."

I laughed. But she was right. Things had really changed. The original team of eight now numbered in the hundreds. Our IPO had instantly netted the company nearly $80 million. Gone were the days of calling up Steve Kahn or my mother for $25,000. That initial investment from my mother had gone up nearly a hundredfold. She bought an apartment on the Upper East Side with it.

But gone, also, were the scrappy underdog days. I missed them. I missed the late nights and early mornings, the lawn chairs and card tables. I missed the feeling of all hands on deck, and the expectation that every day you'd be working on a problem that wasn't *strictly* tied to your job description.

I'd felt that again, in a way, with Mitch during our stay in Las Vegas. We'd had a blast. For three months, we'd lived together in a condo in Summerlin, a community west of Vegas, near Red Rock Canyon. We'd set up a prototype kiosk in a Smith's supermarket a few blocks from the condo, offering instantaneous rentals for Netflix subscribers. In true Netflix fashion, we hadn't actually built an electronic interface for customers to use. Instead, we'd just employed our usual validation hacking — we built a miniature store inside the supermarket, where Netflix subscribers could pick from a selection of DVDs and return movies from their queue. Mitch had used a shaper in Santa Cruz to build a NETFLIX EXPRESS sign made from a surfboard, and we'd hung it from the ceiling of our little store. We weren't testing whether or not a computer kiosk could work — we were testing how customers would use one. Would they pick movies up? Bring movies back? Just add to their queues?

We'd spent a lot of time in the supermarket that summer, usually at night. In the summer, that's when people in Vegas go grocery shopping. It's too hot during the day, and people work weird hours at the casinos. At one in the morning, we'd watch the cocktail waitresses, dealers, and strippers try to use our pseudo-kiosk. We'd wander the aisles with clipboards, asking questions about how they felt about being able to return and rent movies at the grocery store. If they weren't Netflix customers, we tried to convince them to sign up — and if they didn't want to, we listened to their reasons why.

We learned a lot. Most importantly, though, we learned that the kiosk idea was a winner. People loved it.

I was sad when the three months in Nevada were over. I'd grown accustomed to going mountain biking in the predawn hours, taking early evening hikes with Mitch, or just sitting around the deserted condo pool in the afternoon, talking about business and life. Mitch was excited to show our findings to Reed. He thought that the tests had proven that kiosks could be an intermediary solution to our immediacy problem — when one-day shipping wasn't fast enough, maybe a kiosk could bridge the gap.

But upon our return to California, Reed hadn't agreed.

"It's expensive," he'd said. "Once you go kiosk, you're in the hardware business, and you'll have to hire and manage a whole fleet of people all over the country to stock the kiosks. It's a good idea, but our focus is better spent on our core business."

"The Canada Principle," I said.

Reed nodded.

It's a great principle. But it left me out of a job. Kiosks were a no-go. That meant that I was drawing up my severance package.

Mitch, for his part, used the tests from our three months in Vegas to start another little company. You might have heard of it. It's called Redbox.

So there I was, sitting onstage at the Los Gatos Theatre, looking out over a sea of faces on my last day at the job. Lorraine was next to me. So was Logan, in his IPO blazer and loafers. Morgan was trying to keep Hunter — five years old now and much more mobile — from taking off his shoes and throwing them into the audience. She wasn't succeeding.

"It's sort of crazy, isn't it?" I said to Lorraine as Reed made his way up to the microphone. "I mean, this has kind of been our life for the last seven years."

"I hear the post office is hiring," Lorraine said with a smile. "They need a guy out near Missoula. You game?"

I stifled a laugh as Reed cleared his throat and started on his speech. It was, in true Reed fashion, concise. But it was also heartfelt and genuine. He gave a miniature history of the entire company, highlighting my role in the early days. He spoke eloquently about our working relationship, and how it had evolved over time. He ended it by thanking me and inviting several of my colleagues to the stage.

What followed was part of a grand Netflix tradition. You know how some people say they want their funerals to be celebrations? How instead of a wake, they want a parade? Well, that's how things were at Netflix. When someone left the company, the party wasn't a sad occasion. No dirges were played. Instead, it was more like a roast. There would be a succession of speeches — but the state of the art was to deliver your farewell as a limerick.

That evening, the limericks were long, inexpertly rhymed, and raunchy. I had to cover Logan's ears a couple of times. But I was crying laughing.

Eventually it was my turn. My speech that day was off-the-cuff, so I can't reproduce it here. But it was about how much the company and the team had meant to me — how fortunate I felt to be a part of something that was truly changing the world. I thanked my colleagues, thanked Reed — thanked everyone in that room who'd made Netflix what it was.

And then I ended with a poem of my own. It was the only part of my speech that I typed out. Unfolding the paper and clearing my throat, I began:

I'm a little surprised, if I may
By the tone of the rhymes here today
I expected some toasts
And instead I got roasts?
Well, two can play that game, I say.

I went on, roasting many of my colleagues, most of whom had already read poems about me.

Then I got to Reed.

And Reed, well, the guy can't be beat
Whether pitching to us or the Street
But that late-returned movie
Apollo 13? Fooey!
It was actually Teen Vixens in Heat.

Roars from the crowd. I looked at Reed, who was laughing and shaking his head.

I was winding up. Just one more stanza to go. I found Patty McCord in the audience and winked at her. Then I took a moment, surveying my audience of friends and colleagues for the last time, and smiled.

I read the last words on the page:

Lastly, Patty, who's mad 'nough to spit
Because of that last "iffy" bit.
I've been dying to roast her
Since the "shorn scrotum" poster
And hey, you can't fire me: I quit.

Wait — the story doesn't end there.

You're probably used to reading that by now. But it's true — because the Netflix story is far from over, of course.

Reed is still there, still CEO and chairman, still having the time of his life. Unlike me, Reed is not only a phenomenal early-stage CEO — he's as good (or better) as a late-stage CEO. He's taken the company to heights I could only dream of. We're still good friends. He tells me that occasionally he gets angry emails from people who've been cut off in traffic by someone with a NETFLIX vanity plate and assume that it could only be him.

After a few years off, Christina founded an exercise company called Poletential, which runs empowering pole dancing exercise classes for women in Redwood City. Can't say I saw that coming! But her dedication, organizational genius, and commitment to women's health has inspired thousands of people to nurture their bodies and minds.

Te went on to take the VP of marketing position at several companies, including MarkMonitor and Recurly. She still has her Boston accent.

After Netflix, Eric Meyer took a position as CTO at LowerMyBills, taking Vita (and eventually Boris) with him. Now he's VP of software at Align, a huge 3-D printing company.

Boris eventually became a CTO himself, first at ShoeDazzle and then at Carbon38. Vita lasted a few more years as a technologist before changing tracks entirely and getting a doctorate in psychology. Last I heard, she was a postdoctoral fellow at USC.

After Netflix, Jim Cook spent a couple of years at WineShopper before finally getting the CFO job he'd always wanted, at Mozilla. He was there for almost fifteen years.

Steve Kahn didn't stay in that trophy house for long. He's now down in San Diego pursuing his dream of being a professional photographer. I have two of his photos prominently hanging in my house.

Corey Bridges is the only one of us (besides Reed, of course) who stayed in the entertainment business. He spent years doing marketing strategy for James Cameron, before striking out on his own, forming his own consulting company.

Suresh Kumar is *still* at Netflix, twenty-one years later. He's currently an engineering manager, and he still has that silver dollar from predicting the hundredth order.

And Kho Braun? I have no idea where Kho Braun is.

Netflix has gone on to do many things in the years since I left. As I write this, the company has just passed 150 million subscribers, with customers in nearly every country in the world. Netflix makes its own TV shows, produces its own movies, and has changed the way people consume entertainment. It introduced the concept of binge watching, and is a popular euphemism for getting laid.

I know that the stock market is never an indicator of real value — but I can't help but note that as of this writing, the little DVD-by-mail company that Blockbuster could have purchased for $50 million is now worth $150 billion.

And guess where Blockbuster is?

They're down to one last store. It's in Bend, Oregon.

I keep thinking I'll make a trip to pay my respects, but I haven't found the time.

I can't take credit for all of Netflix's successes in the years after I left. But even though many of the company's initiatives took place after my watch, I think it's clear that a lot of them have my fingerprints on them.

So many aspects of the corporate culture spring from the way Reed and I treated each other and the way we treated everyone else. Radical Honesty. Freedom and Responsibility. Those were there from the beginning — in the car on 17, in the Hobee's dining room, in the first days in the bank vault.

So was Netflix's emphasis on analytics. It's what happens when you put a guy with direct marketing experience into a car (and then a conference room, and then a boardroom) with another guy with a brilliant math mind.

Reed brought the drive for scale. I made sure that we never stopped focusing on the individual customer. And both of us came to realize that how we treated individual customers was as important at 150 million subscribers as it was at 150.

Netflix has thousands of employees now. It's been sixteen years since I pulled out of the parking lot for the last time. But whenever I come across a news story about their movie deals, read an interview with Reed, or just fire up an episode of *Ozark* at home, I feel a thrill of pride. That was my company, I think — and it still carries my DNA. The child may not look exactly like me, but it definitely has my nose.

And when I'm not binge-watching Netflix or writing this book? You can't ever stop being a startup guy. After leaving in 2003, I knew I didn't have it in me to immediately start another company — I'd wait until 2012 for that — but I also knew I couldn't walk away entirely. Instead, I realized that I could get my fix by helping other founders of young companies make their dreams come true. Over the past fifteen years, I've helped scores of startups as a CEO coach, invested in dozens of others as an early-stage investor, and mentored hundreds of young entrepreneurs from all over the world. As I did at Netflix, I still get to wade into a crisis and help solve complex problems with smart people — only now, I get to go home at five o'clock, while they stay up all night actually making those things happen.

Sometimes you have to step back from your dream — especially when you think you've made it real. That's when you can really see it. In my case, I left Netflix because I realized that the finished product of Netflix wasn't my dream. My dream was building things. My dream was the *process* of making Netflix.

Leaving allowed me to keep building things, and help others with the process of turning their dreams into reality. And moving on to my next stage has given me the time to pursue the other things in my life that are important. Even though I don't have a W-2 job anymore, I'll never stop being a type-A person. I still make obsessive lists of things to be done. Only now, the only things on my lists are things that *I* put there. I follow my passions: mastering the perfect cappuccino, growing my own grapes and making my own wine. Understanding the evolution of Roman church floor tile.

(I know, I know. Once a dork, always a dork.)

I'm really proud of what we accomplished at Netflix. It's been successful beyond my wildest expectations. But I've come to realize that success is not defined by what a *company* accomplishes. Instead, I have a different definition: Success is what *you* accomplish. It's being in a position to do what you like, do what you do well, and pursue the things that are important to you.

By that definition, I've done okay.

But success could also be defined a bit more broadly: having a dream, and through your time, your talent, and your perseverance, seeing that dream become a reality.

I guess I'm proud to fit that definition as well.

But do you know what I'm proudest of? I've done all those things while staying married to my best friend and having my kids grow up knowing me and (as best I can tell) liking me. I just spent two weeks at the beach with Lorraine, Logan, Morgan, and Hunter. Doing *absolutely nothing*. Just enjoying their company.

I think that's the version of success that Randolph's Rules point toward — that my father always wanted for me. Fulfilling your goals, making your dreams a reality, nourished by the love of your family.

Forget money, forget stock options.

That's success.

Okay, one more time — *the story doesn't end there.*

Because now the story is about you.

Flip your book over. Read the title again.

"That will never work."

That was the first thing out of Lorraine's mouth the night I told her the idea for Netflix. She wasn't the only one. I heard that from dozens of people, dozens of times.

(And to be fair to her, the idea as originally conceived *wouldn't* have worked. It took years of adjustments, changes in strategy, new ideas, and plain old luck for us to land on a version of the idea that worked.)

But everyone with a dream has had that experience, right? You wake up one morning with a great idea that's going to change the world! You can't wait to run downstairs and tell your husband. Explain it to your kids. Run it by your professor. Or burst into your boss's office to lay it all out for him.

What do they all say?

That will never work.

By now, I hope you know what my answer to that line is.

Nobody Knows Anything.

I only get to write this book once. And I'd feel like I missed an opportunity if I ended this story without giving you some advice.

The most powerful step that anyone can take to turn their dreams into reality is a simple one: you just need to start. The only real way to find out if your idea is a good one is to do it. You'll learn more in one hour of doing something than in a lifetime of thinking about it.

So take that step. Build something, make something, test something, sell something. Learn for yourself if your idea is a good one.

What happens if your idea doesn't work? What happens if your test fails, if nobody orders your product or joins your club? What if sales don't go up and customer complaints don't go down? What if you get halfway through writing your novel and get writer's block? What if after dozens of tries — even hundreds of attempts — you still haven't seen your dream become anything close to real?

You have to learn to love the problem, not the solution. That's how you stay engaged when things take longer than you expected.

And trust me, they will. If you've read this far, you've seen that the process of turning a dream into reality has a dramatic arc — it isn't quick and it isn't easy, and there are obstacles and problems along the way.

One of the things I learned from William Goldman's *Adventures in the Screen Trade* — aside, of course, from *Nobody Knows Anything* — is that every movie begins with an inciting event, one that sets the plot in motion. The protagonist of a film has to want something — and for the film to be interesting, there have to be obstacles between the protagonist and what he or she wants.

In my own case, there were quite a few obstacles — or, in screenwriter-speak, complications — between the dream of Netflix and its reality. But the great thing about having a dream is that you get to write your own story. You're both the protagonist and the writer of your movie.

And your idea is your inciting event.

I trust that at least a few things I've said have made you think about an idea that you have. Something that you would like to accomplish. A company you want to start. A product you want to make. A job you want to land. A book you want to write.

Nolan Bushnell, the co-founder of Atari, once said something that has always resonated with me. "Everyone who has taken a shower has had an idea," he said. "But it's the people who get out of the shower, towel off, and do something about it that make the difference."

Maybe you're already thinking about whether you could apply some of the tips I've given you to make that dream come true. Maybe you've gotten the confidence that there is a way to take those difficult first steps toward making your dream a reality. Maybe you're ready to get out of the shower, towel off, and do something about it.

In that case, my job is done.

From here, it's all up to you.

Acknowledgements

When I tell people I wrote a book, their first question is usually "Did you write it yourself?" I guess they expect that I used a ghostwriter, or wrote an "as told to" tale. Or, conversely, that the words simply poured out of me, like water from a pitcher, stimulated by a dream about a late fee on a movie.

But as I hope you've figured out by now, no venture — whether it be book or company — is ever the product of a single person. So did I write this book by myself? Of course not. Like Netflix, this book is the product of scores of people each adding a little bit of themselves to the mixture. I'll never be able to thank them adequately... but if you'll bear with me through a few more pages, I'm going to try.

First, a huge thank-you to Jordan Jacks, who — with his patient coaching and countless supportive cries of "this is pure gold" — reviewed, massaged, rearranged, shaped, and infinitely deepened the manuscript. Jordan, I owe you big time.

Also to my friend Doug Abrams of Idea Architects, who, on one of our hours-long walks in the woods, convinced me that there might be a book inside of me, and then spent countless hours helping me bring it to life. This book wouldn't exist without him.

To my editors: Phil Marino at Little, Brown, who took the how-to book that I initially pitched him and realized that it would be stronger and more powerful as a memoir. He was right. His ongoing edits and suggestions made the book infinitely stronger. And to Claudia Connal, my UK editor at Endeavour, who not only helped me avoid an international incident by misspelling colour (or endeavour), but also provided numerous great suggestions that made the book tighter and clearer in every country.

To Janet Byrne, my copyeditor, who painstakingly found every misplaced comma, misspelled word, and factual inaccuracy. You don't notice these things until someone points them out to you. If not for her, you may have gotten the impression from me that Dr. Evil's testicles were "freshly shorn," not simply (and more accurately) "shorn."

A huge shout-out to all the members of the early Netflix team who spent countless hours with me on the phone and in person: Christina Kish, Te Smith, Jim Cook, Eric Meyer, Suresh Kumar, Mitch Lowe, Patty McCord, and Steve Kahn. They shared their stories, filled in holes in my memory, and reviewed early drafts of the book for tone and content. I'm sorry I couldn't fit in all of your great stories, but I loved hearing them.

I owe a special debt to Gina Keating, author of *Netflixed*, who selflessly shared her original notes and interview transcripts, all of which helped me more accurately capture not just what people said, but how they said it.

To my first advance reader, Sally Rutledge, who, by reading the entire book on a single transcontinental plane flight, first demonstrated that it might be bingeworthy (which is appropriate for a book largely about Netflix).

To the rest of Doug Abrams's team at Idea Architects: Lara Love, Ty Love, Cody Love, Mariah Sanford, and Janelle Julian, who spent two long days patiently listening to my Netflix stories and helping me build them into something approaching a narrative.

To the publishing team at Little, Brown: Craig Young, Ben Allen, Maggie Southard, Elizabeth Gassman, and Ira Boudah; and to the team at Endeavour: Alex Stetter, Shona Abhynakar, Caro Parodi, and Juliette Norsworthy — who all patiently tolerated an insatiably curious newbie trying to understand how the publishing industry works. Oh...and they promoted and published the book, too.

To Caspian Dennis and to Camilla Ferrier, who helped bring this book to other international audiences.

And a quick call-out (literally) to Anthony Goff and Chrissy Farrell, the people responsible for the audiobook. Thanks for letting me know that I've been pronouncing *timbre* and *inchoate* incorrectly for all these years.

There was a big group of people involved in letting the outside world know about this book. I'm particularly grateful to Heidi Krupp, Mariah Terry, Jenn Garbowski, Alana Jacobs, Lindsey Winkler, Colleen McCarthy, and Callie Rome at K2 communications; to Barrett Cordero, Ken Sterling, Blair Nichols, Daria Wagganer, and Aggie Arvizu at BigSpeak; to Rob Noble, Jinal Shah, Simon Waterfall, Kyle Duncan, and Paul Bean at Group of Humans; to Kristen Taylor at KThread; to Colby Devitt at Catch the Sun Media; and to TJ Widner, who — as far as I can tell — doesn't have a name for his business.

Does that last paragraph strike you as a big group of people? Do you wonder how one could possibly keep that crew coordinated and marching in the same direction? Me too. And that's why my friend Auny Abegglen gets a special thank-you for taking on the thankless task of herding all those cats. Thanks, Auny. I hope this was more fun than doing dog food commercials.

We're getting to the end here, but not before mentioning the students at High Point University and Middlebury College, who over the years have shared all their great ideas for new ventures with me — and helped me realize that the lessons I learned as an entrepreneur can be used by anyone with a dream they want to make real. Thanks, in particular, to Jessica Holmes, past director of the Middlebury College MiddCORE program. It was with her support and patience that I figured out how to more clearly articulate these hard-won truths in ways that other people could understand.

Acknowledgements

None of this would have been possible without all of my friends and colleagues — past and present — at Netflix. Stay tuned for the companion volume to these acknowledgements in which I thank all 7,137 Netflix employees. But while you're waiting for that, let me at least thank the much smaller group who — in addition to those named earlier — were the other full-time pre-launch employees: Corey Bridges, Bill Kunz, Heidi Nyburg, Carrie Kelley, Merry Law, Boris Droutman, Vita Droutman, Greg Julien, and Dan Jepson. OK, folks, who am I forgetting?

There really aren't enough words for me to properly thank Reed Hastings. Without him in the picture, I wouldn't be writing this book. Or at the very least, it's doubtful you would be reading it. Revisiting the events that took place so many years ago gave me an even better appreciation for how amazing his contributions were, and how much I learned from him. Honoring our friendship and what we created together was one of my highest goals. Hope I pulled it off. Reed, when you're done with Netflix and ready for the next one, I'm in!

And lastly, to my family. Thanks so much for your love and support. And your tolerance. Even now, we are on vacation, my wife and daughter are at the pool, and I'm holed up in our hotel room writing. Sorry again.

Thanks to my kids, Logan, Morgan, and Hunter. In addition to your continual support, all three of you read multiple versions of the book as it took shape and provided valuable feedback. The first glimpse I had that I might be on to something came as the three of you took turns reading chapters out loud while we were on vacation last Christmas. And doing so willingly.

Lorraine, I can't ever thank you enough. For your support, for your advice, and for your love. Thanks for seeing that writing this book was important to me and for being with me through every minute of it. I love you.

And Kho? Thanks, wherever you are.

Index

Index

business model
  for DVD world, 58
  subscription model, 206–17, 233
business ownership, 13–14
business plan, 36

C-Cube Microsystems, 55, 58
CAC (cost of acquiring a customer), 157
Cadabra, 95, 151
Canada Principle, 215–17, 231, 255, 302
Candescent, 203
CES (Consumer Electronics Show),
  127–32
Chesky, Brian, 7
Cinematch, 226, 229, 254
Clinton DVD, 167–74
Coins in the Fountain, 199–200, 259
collaborative filtering, 224–25
confirmation emails, 111, 117
consumer electronics companies
  cultures of, 128
  and DVD technology standardization,
    128–29
  negotiating with, 214
  product development timelines for, 132
Consumer Electronics Show (CES),
  127–32
Cook, Jim, 40–41
  and Clinton DVD, 171, 173–74
  on costs of mailings and packaging,
    142–43
  and culture of Netflix, 79
  departure of, 202
  drive and creativity of, 165
  handling of DVDs by, 144
  on launch day, 107, 109, 112, 113,
    117–18
  and name for company, 97, 98
  post-Netflix work of, 306
  on startup team, 40, 72
  and storage for inventory, 75, 85
  at WineShopper, 269–70
cost of acquiring a customer (CAC), 157
costs
  lowering, through layoffs, 258
  of mailings and packaging, 142–43
  of subscription service, 233, 254–55
Covey, Joy, 147, 148, 151, 152
crowdsourcing, for recommendations,
  224–26
culture (in general)
  of consumer electronics companies, 128
  and hiring/keeping of star players, 267
  of startups, 33, 74

culture (of Netflix), 307
  codifying, 197–99
  corporate retreat for building, 236–37
  and growth of team, 165
  and lunch ritual with new employees,
    134–35
  Randolph's love of, 291
  at startup, 79–83
  as team grew, 193–201
customer acquisition, 73, 157

data warehouse, 123
database, initial, 85–91, 110
Deutsche Bank, 229, 230
Digital Bits, 134
digital delivery, 270–73
Dillon, Tom, 203, 219, 220, 229,
  268–69
dilution, 34
distributors, 75, 84
Doc Hollywood, 220–21
dot-com bubble, 229–33
dreams
  ownership of, 186
  pursuing, 175–76, 273–74
  stepping back from, 308
  and success of company, 185, 186
  turned into reality, 309, 310
Drkoop.com, 232
Droutman, Boris
  and Clinton DVD, 169
  commute for, 164
  at corporate retreat, 238
  drive and creativity of, 165
  and kitchen snacks game, 201
  on launch day, 109, 111, 114–16
  and name for company, 97
  post-Netflix positions for, 305
  on startup team, 39, 72
Droutman, Vita
  commute for, 164
  on launch day, 109, 111, 114
  layoff of, 265, 270
  and name for company, 97
  post-Netflix work of, 305
  on startup team, 39, 72
Dubelko, Michale, 133–34
DVD Daily, 134
DVD Express, 133–34
DVD players
  diminishing cost of, 157
  ownership of, 127
  rental promotion with, 130–34, 138–39,
    156–57, 161–62, 213

317

Index

Index

Index

startups helped by, 307–8
stock options re-split, 188, 202
valuation of idea for DVD by mail, 33
value of shares belonging to, 229
Wilderness School experience of, 50–55
Randolph, Morgan, 20, 21, 100, 124, 136, 137, 141, 142, 303, 308
Randolph's Rules for Success, 293–94
rating movies, 225–26
recommendation engine, 222–26, 229, 254
recruiting engineers, 135–36, 164
Redbox, 303
reflection-point method, 268–69
rentals
  à la carte service, 213–17
  algorithmic matching service for, 223–26
  cost of mailings/packaging, 142–43
  decision to focus on, 154–55
  and DVD player ownership, 127
  DVD player promotion, 130–34, 138–39, 156–57, 161–62, 213
  in first month after launch, 124
  focus on, 154
  free trial users for, 157
  new business model for, 205–17
  revenue potential with, 140
  sales/rentals partnership with Amazon, 177–78, 204–5
  of soft-core pornography, 238
  at two months after launch, 140–41
reputation, 85
responsibility toward employees, 16
retreat at Alisal Ranch, 228, 235–41
"road show" for IPO, 281–82
Rossmann, Alain, 55
rules, 196–97

S-1 registration statement, 229, 230, 276
salaries, during startup phase, 74
sales
  as commodities business for DVDs, 140
  cost of mailings/packaging, 142–43
  in first month after launch, 124
  getting out of, 154, 177–78
  measuring difficulty of assignments, 53
  price needed for, 169
  sales/rentals partnership with Amazon, 177–78, 204–5
  at second month after launch, 140–41
  as theater, 62
San Francisco Chronicle, 108, 114
Sand Hill Road motorless car race, 46
Santa Barbara Airport, 242–43

Santa Cruz, 41, 163
Santa Cruz post office, 28–30
Santa Cruz Sentinel, 108, 113
Sarandos, Ted, 229, 237
Schell, Rick, 155
Scotts Valley office space, 65–67, 163, 176
scraping barnacles off the hull, 255–57
Seagate, 203
"seed round," 61
seeking strategic alternatives, 233–34
serialized delivery, 206–9, 217, 268
shared values, 79
shipping
  "hubs" for, 268–69
  mailers, 76–77, 142–44
  overnight delivery, 218–20, 268–69
  for subscription service, 217–18
shit sandwich, 180–81, 249–50
Sickles, Steve, 134
Silicon Valley
  casual atmosphere in, 235
  exuberance in, 37
  Indian engineers in, 136
  meritocracy in, 235
  and Nobody Knows Anything, 211, 212
  nonsense phrases in, 234
  prices in, 27
  response to pitches in, 58
  speed of change in, 36–37
  tech talent scarcity in, 35
Simpson, Jessica, 166
Smith, Te, 16–17
  and Clinton DVD, 168–70
  and culture of Netflix, 79
  and ideas for a new company, 17
  and kitchen snacks game, 201
  on launch day, 107–8, 112, 113, 116
  and name for company, 98
  new hires' dress-up tradition, 165
  post-Netflix marketing positions for, 305
  in refining original Netflix idea, 19–24
  and size of DVD library, 31
  and Sony promotion, 137–39
  on startup team, 39, 72
  at Zone Labs, 270
Society for the Preservation and Encouragement of Barber Shop Singing in America (SPEBSQSA), 190–92
Sony, 130, 132
  at CES conference, 129
  credibility provided by, 178
  culture of, 128

Index

Index

About the Author

Marc Randolph is the co-founder of Netflix, serving as their first CEO, the executive producer of their website, and a member of their board of directors. Additionally, he's founded or co-founded more than half a dozen other successful startups, mentored rising entrepreneurs, and invested in numerous successful tech ventures.